'TIL
DEATH OR
DISTANCE
DO US PART

'TIL DEATH OR DISTANCE DO US PART

Love and Marriage in African America

Frances Smith Foster

OXFORD
UNIVERSITY PRESS
2010

OXFORD
UNIVERSITY PRESS

Oxford University Press, Inc., publishes works that further
Oxford University's objective of excellence
in research, scholarship, and education.

Oxford   New York
Auckland   Cape Town   Dar es Salaam   Hong Kong   Karachi
Kuala Lumpur   Madrid   Melbourne   Mexico City   Nairobi
New Delhi   Shanghai   Taipei   Toronto

With offices in
Argentina   Austria   Brazil   Chile   Czech Republic   France   Greece
Guatemala   Hungary   Italy   Japan   Poland   Portugal   Singapore
South Korea   Switzerland   Thailand   Turkey   Ukraine   Vietnam

Copyright © 2010 by Oxford University Press, Inc.

Published by Oxford University Press, Inc.
198 Madison Avenue, New York, New York 10016

www.oup.com

Oxford is a registered trademark of Oxford University Press

Library of Congress Cataloging-in-Publication Data
Foster, Frances Smith.
'Til death or distance do us part : love and marriage in African America /
Frances Smith Foster.
p.   cm.
Includes bibliographical references.
ISBN 978-0-19-532852-3
1. African Americans—Marriage—History.   2. African Americans—
Marriage customs and rites—History.   3. Slaves—Family relationships—
United States—History.   4. Marriage customs and rites—United States.   5. Marriage—
Moral and ethical aspects—United States. 6. United States—Social conditions—
To 1865.   I. Title.
E185.86.F673 2009
305.896'073—dc22   2009023899

1 3 5 7 9 8 6 4 2

Printed in the United States of America
on acid-free paper

For Mr. and Mrs. Quinton T. Smith,

For Ruby Dee and Ossie Davis,

For all those whose love and marriages

neither death nor distance could put asunder.

CONTENTS

SEVEN
Alchemy of Personal Politics
[143]

EIGHT
Me, Mende, and Sankofa: An Epilogue
[159]

PREFACE

First comes love, then comes marriage,
Then comes Mama with the baby carriage!
—U.S. American folk rhyme

AS CHILDREN WE LEARN THE SEQUENCE OF STEPS TO take if we want to live happily ever after. In the United States, especially, our personal evolution should move from love to marriage, and then parenthood. Adults may know more than children about the missteps that might come along the way. Nonetheless, whether they are in love, have ever been in love, or are looking for love, most of them affirm the sequence: love should beget marriage, marriages should make families, and families should and do form the bedrock of civilization. According to our shared sense of American rightness, here abides love, marriage, and family, but the greatest of these, what we simply can't do without, is marriage.

Marriage means a lot. But what it means and how it should be experienced is not all that clear. Social scientists assert that a civilized society cannot emerge from unregulated love, nontraditional marriage, or eccentric family arrangements. Romantic love may be the proper prelude to marriage, but more important is the social foundation it establishes. A correct union is between one man and one woman, preferably of the same religion, nationality, and culture. Though variants such as blended, adopted, or extended families may be permitted, to qualify as an *all-American* family, one needs a husband, a wife, and the offspring of their union—all residing together in tranquility. In the United States, we never seem to tire of talking about marriage. What it is and what it should become. Who should and who may not marry. How married couples are to live and work. Some of us may disagree vehemently and sometimes violently about these questions, but almost everyone agrees to at least one thing: the practice of marriage has changed. Wedlock is not as durable as it once was. It does not hold as fast or as firm as it used to. Statistics show that fewer people marry and about half of all marriages do not last. Stephanie Coontz and other historians of marriage demonstrate that marriage has always been a changing institution and that the lived experiences of married people rarely follow the sequence of events we collectively envision. While the work of social historians like Coontz has gained media attention, Middle America (as well as Americans in the East, West, North, and South) tends to view such pronouncements with anxiety and suspicion. Even when we recite the familiar refrain "Marriage takes work, each partner must contribute at least 60 percent," everyone harbors hopes that after saying "I do," a couple will live happily ever after. No matter what we know about the relationships of our parents, grandparents, and great-grandparents, we cling to the myth of a golden age of marriage.[1]

There are exceptions. When people refer to domestic arrangements in African America, present and past, North and South, they shake their heads, or hang them, and sigh over the sorry state of the world. Here a different story takes hold. That well-rehearsed narrative proclaims that marriage among African Americans is now, and always has been, fragile and fraught. We do not allow facts or statistics to change our belief that marriage was once a strong and lasting institution for Euro-Americans. But despite evidence to the contrary, we assume that for African Americans, such a matrimonial golden age never existed. Teachers and preachers, welfare workers and mental health professionals, journalists and front porch philosophers may tell different stories, but they all share the same refrain: marriage among African Americans was and is a rare, often doomed endeavor. Some cast drugs, crime, or homosexuality as the culprit. We hear that men who should be protecting and providing for their wives and children are in prison—or they have AIDS. Women are demanding, emasculating, or traumatized, we're told, and so fail to function as good mothers and wives. Sometimes poverty, illiteracy, sickness, or other social disadvantages play significant roles. Some commentators admit that a social structure pervaded with racism and discrimination makes things hard and heroes rare. Some see African Americans themselves as the problem, a viewpoint influenced by antebellum science that declared that unrestrained sexuality and irresponsible parenting were inevitable as part of the genetic imprint of Africans. Others don't buy the idea that it's "in their blood," but they do regard dysfunctional domestic lives as a legacy of enslavement. During slavery, we're reminded, family members were torn apart and sold. Legal marriages were impossible. Though they may differ on the origins of the problem, a plethora of stories about promiscuous coupling and fatherless families, instability, and group dysfunction provide the drama that explains the difficult domestic lives of African Americans.

The core story goes something like this. Most, if not all, African Americans were enslaved. Rampant rape and concubinage destroyed their self-esteem and sowed seeds of distrust between African American women and men. Even if they wanted to marry, by law they were chattel, not humans, property that couldn't hold property. Even if they did manage to marry, husbands could not be the heads of their households. They couldn't provide for, nor protect, their wives. Men could not expect sexual fidelity from their wives or prevent themselves from being used as studs. A child was "Mama's baby, Papa's maybe." Individual stories vary, but the messages are variations upon a theme. The chickens have come home to roost. The legacy of slavery has moved perilous relationships from bad to worse. Yesterday's bad seeds have blossomed into full-blown disaster.

The oft-told story is not pure fantasy. Fiction and poetry, court cases and legal histories, statistics, sermons, essays, articles, and personal narratives buttress such accounts. Nearly 90 percent of the women and men in antebellum African America *were* enslaved. Their owners had legal authority to do with them anything they wished. Enslavers subjected the enslaved to the most degrading and soul-killing circumstances imaginable. But the system could not flourish unless people believed that slaves were not human. And so in this world, too, a set of stories were circulated to support the structure of abuse. By word of mouth and word of print, stories were spread that *proved* that people of African descent were sub-human, or even an entirely different species. Scientists supplied theories and evidence to buttress myths of racial inferiority. Theology, law, economics, and eventually tradition strengthened the power of the myths.

Nonetheless, wishes and words have their limits as truth. And a lot of enslaved people had other wishes, different words. They knew themselves to be people, not chattel. They had stories, ideas, and myths of their own.

Most of what we know today about antebellum America does not include the stories that antebellum African Americans told among themselves. In fact, the historical narratives about them come primarily from stories told by people who were not enslaved themselves. Much of what we are taught and most of what we read are spectator reports: the writings of white journalists and privileged letter-writers, the record books and depositions of court witnesses and slave owners; the poems, songs, stories, and reports of abolitionists, evangelists, and southern tourists. Antebellum slave narratives, which are testimonies of slaves and ex-slaves about their lives in bondage and their pursuit of freedom, do also exist, and there is evidence that these documents were popular reading among whites and blacks alike. But those who have created the picture of African American love and marriage that dominates the contemporary imagination have tended to misinterpret this more immediate evidence. The slave narratives have been cast as documents that were essentially rewritten by whites or as the handiwork of blacks whose political motivations encouraged them to suppress objectivity. Many analysts, especially the supposedly scientifically minded, have ignored them altogether.

It's time they got a proper hearing. Slave narratives represent a wide range of different regions and roles, a diverse spread of writers and readers. They began to appear as early as 1734. What's especially important in this telling, however, is the line that can be drawn between those that came more or less directly from slaves and those produced by others. Although the plots, settings, and characterizations of both types share many similarities, thee immediate and unmediated tellings that have come directly from slaves do deviate in ways that complicate and even contradict the stories told by those who had not themselves been enslaved.

Incidents in the Life of a Slave Girl, also known as the autobiography of Harriet Jacobs, was published in 1861 by Jacobs herself. It is in many ways a classic slave narrative. For starters, it confirms many stereotypes of its time. For example, she writes: "My master was, to my knowledge, the father of eleven slaves. But did the mother dare to tell who was the father of her children? Did the other slaves dare to allude to it, except among whispers to themselves? No, indeed! They knew too well the terrible consequences."[2] Jacobs's narrative, in fact, focuses on her own struggle to avoid her owner's sexual assaults. But in her account, she was not raped, nor was rape her owner's goal. He wanted her to believe that as his "property," she "must be subject to his will in all things." Jacobs describes their conflict as psychological assault, an example of the spiritual damage wrought by slavery. Their struggle was a struggle of will symbolized by the idea and ideal of consensual sex. Her owner, Jacobs asserts, "had power and law on his side; I had a determined will. There is might in each" (70).

"Power and law" were formidable adversaries, and Jacobs did not win every battle. For example, she lost her first love.

> I loved him with all the ardor of a young girl's first love. But when I reflected that I was a slave, and that the laws gave no sanction to the marriage of such, my heart sank within me....If I was married near home I should be just as much in [the master's] power as I had previously been, for the husband of slaves has no power to protect [his wife]. Moreover, my mistress, like many others, seemed to think that slaves had no right to any family ties of their own; that they were created merely to wait upon the family of the mistress. (33–34)

Harriet Jacobs, like other enslaved people, faced formidable odds against being able to marry a person of her own choosing. However, her story could have had a happy ending. Jacobs's lover was free, he wanted to marry her, and he was able to buy her freedom. In antebellum America, the percentage of such happily-ever-after love stories was low, but the number of lovers whose partners did buy their freedom was substantial enough that this couple could hope their petition would be accepted. It was not. Jacobs's owner refused permission. He did, however, offer Jacobs her choice of any husband from among a group of men he owned. She refused. "Don't you suppose, sir, that a slave can have some preference about marrying? Do you suppose that all men are alike to her?" This was not an unusual confrontation. African American literature contains many scenes in which an owner assumes the right to choose a mate for an enslaved person. However, Jacobs neither acquiesced nor passively resisted. Her response to her owner astonishes most readers. "How I despise you!" she retorts; "you have no right to do as you like with me" (35).

While this narrative employs a number of novelistic techniques of the day, it is not fiction but an autobiographical account whose authenticity has been amply proven. Jacobs's life story stresses many elements common to stories of enslaved Americans. In her preface, she acknowledges that the focus on her sex life could be considered a breach of decorum and that her behavior was unbecoming for a lady. Though she is heroic and ultimately triumphant over the slave master who abused her, she is wound up in history all the same. She is an unmarried mother of two children. She is poor, works as a domestic, and has no home of her own. She concludes her narrative:

> Reader, my story ends with freedom; not in the usual way, with marriage....The dream of my life is not yet realized. I do not sit with my children in a home of my own. I still long for a hearthstone of my own, however humble. I wish it for my children's sake far more than for my own. (156)

Incidents is not a stereotypical account of a helpless victim or a motherless child. Jacobs is neither Wonder Woman or Wanton Woman. And, most important for this discussion, Harriet Jacobs does not fit stereotypes of antebellum African Americans...Jacobs and her testament in this book are one example of a much less well—known African American figure. Her account offers a history that runs counter to the narratives of fractured families and loveless lives that are so familiar. Hers is a story of love and marriage, and is one of many such stories that antebellum African Americans told to and for themselves. These stories run contrary to more familiar accounts about African American love and marriage, but they are not rare. Their voices, which have been absent from the chorus of public opinion, provide a crucial perspective that has been missing. It needs to be heard.

SPEAKING FOR (AND TO) OURSELVES

We wish to plead our own cause. Too long have others spoken for us. Too long has the publick been deceived by misrepresentations, in things which concern us dearly...

—*Freedom's Journal* (March 16, 1827)

The front page of the first edition of *Freedom's Journal* contains a description of the paper's purpose. It says that African Americans have no formal medium in which they can counter the stories coming from other quarters with the stories they tell and know themselves. *Freedom's Journal* proposes to fill this void. Organized by a committee of African Americans from several cities and states, the paper will be "devoted to the dissemination of useful knowledge" and to facilitating the "moral and religious improvement" of African Americans. The editors invite African Americans to subscribe and to contribute. They vow the paper will not advocate any particular religious or political views but will communicate "whatever concerns us as a people." The first issue contains many different elements, including the first installment of the serialized "Memoirs of Capt. Paul Cuffee"; a poem—"The African Chief"; and a variety of news, fiction, and essays. Later editions display a similar variety of forms. Virtually every issue discusses love, marriage, sexual morality, gender roles, family, and community ethics. Produced for African Americans by African Americans about African Americans, *Freedom's Journal* served them as a medium for telling their own stories as they were—or as they wanted them to be known. And clearly, family relationships were a central concern.

Like Jacobs's narrative, *Freedom's Journal* and the magazines and newspapers that followed it are treasure troves of ideas, experiences, and ideals that can have a great impact on twenty-first-century readers' understanding of the history of marriage in African America. Much of the earliest writing by African Americans for themselves portrays marriage as natural, necessary, and of "God's design." The pages of black newspapers and magazines illustrate that contrary to popular belief, African American marriage, even during antebellum times, was frequent, that family ties were strong, and that love was both an adolescent fantasy and a fulfilling adult reality.

The details sketch the whole. An 1828 article in *Freedom's Journal* argues that love can compensate for many deprivations and much oppression. The writer suggests that a loving marriage may be more important than financial gain or possibly even "freedom":

> And without domestic peace and harmony, what are any, or all of the blessings of this life?...When love unites hearts and gracious principle is the guardian of conjugal love, how many of the comforts of life may be wanting, without being much missed; and how many of the trials of life borne without being much felt?

In spite of slavery and legal restrictions, and in spite of the stories we've been told, in African America mature men and women were expected to marry, and marriage was understood as the prerequisite to parenthood. The February 9, 1861, issue of the *Christian Recorder,* a weekly newspaper published by the African Methodist Episcopal (AME) Church and circulated internationally among people of African descent, carries W. D. W. Shureman's declaration that "marriage is the union of sexes, under matrimonial obligations. It is the proper mode to carry out a

Divine mandate." Numerous other African American writers make it clear that this Divine mandate is to "replenish the earth" with "doers" of "God's word." Antebellum African American writings praise beautiful women and urge them to judge men by their character and not their appearance. Newspapers and magazines offer tips for courting and keeping the object of one's affections. They tout love as desirable and matrimony as the enabler of emotional, spiritual, and physical endurance and transcendence, even as they imply that economic sufficiency and social respectability are perhaps more important benefits. These writers repeatedly declare that love and marriage are especially important for enslaved African Americans. For example, Frances E. W. Harper's poem "The Fugitive's Wife" begins:

> It was my sad and weary lot
> To toil in slavery;
> But one thing cheered my lowly cot—
> My husband was with me.

This book shows that slaves could and did marry, that slave marriages were valued, that strong self-esteem was possible, and that love among slaves could and often did last despite distance and beyond death. It reveals that men were not inevitably emasculated nor women routinely raped. At the very least, it shows that these familiar notions are not the full picture of African Americans' antebellum past. Although the familiar stories contain some truth, the testimonies of African Americans often contradict them. There is ample evidence that slavery and laws wounded people of African descent and that these experiences inform the self-definitions of their descendants. However, such evidence is just one part of a much bigger and more complex narrative. Antebellum African Americans, whether enslaved or free, created a culture for themselves and of themselves, a culture influenced, but not determined, by others.

SANKOFA

Without retracting what I've just said, I'd like to situate these ideas. I know that for some people, their life experiences make these ideas plausible even when they have heard otherwise. I dedicated this book to my parents who were married for over fifty years. After Daddy died, Mama refused to remove her rings, steadfastly believing that they would be reunited in heaven. In their memoir, *With Ossie & Ruby: In this Life Together* published just months before their fiftieth wedding anniversary, Ruby Dee writes: "We are not a fairly tale couple—far from it; rather we have clawed our way to some clarities and satisfaction by dint of trial and error…we have achieved some sense of our worth as married people, lovers, and friends." In African America, to this day, silver, gold, and even diamond anniversaries are celebrated with great pomp and feasting. It is not unusual for the couple to have the wedding ceremony, complete with gowns, flowers, and vows that they might not have been able to afford when they first married.

But, given the cultural barrage that directly contradict them, even as they participate and celebrate wedding anniversaries, many do not know these are rituals that began in antebellum times. Others, especially those who are not African American, can be astonished at what this book reveals. Beginning with the origin stories of Africans arriving in the Americas allows me to make an honest declaration of my hopes for this book. The cultural history recorded by antebellum African Americans is not necessarily—and in the great scheme of things actually may not be—any more accurate or more factual than the perspective we currently hold to be true. At the same time, a too-simple truth always carries within it the seeds of falsehood. The actual world is never as tidy as the choice between two possibilities would suggest: forward or back, North or South, black or white. Incorporating into U.S. history the testimonies African Americans spoke just to and for each other, however widely these stories vary, brings that history closer to a more complete, if more complicated or even more contradictory, idea of what really happened, back then. What was it like? Who said what? How could it have happened? For a people to know more of who they are and where they come from can help them live their lives today. Seeing more allows them to work toward a better future, one that is more free and democratic, with more personal satisfaction and social responsibility.

To get there, Sankofa—an ancient Akan concept with direct bearing on the question of what's fiction, what's real, what's important–can help. Sankofa translates, more or less, as the following imperative: "We must go back and reclaim our past so we can move forward; so we can understand why and how we came to be who we are today."[3] The word and the symbol may seem new, but Westerners already know the idea in a different form. January is the recognition of Janus, the two-faced Roman god of beginnings and endings. Every possibility is formed in part by the rejection of all the other possibilities. The sun must set if it is to rise. The study of history rests on the belief that the past may be applicable to the present. If Sankofa cannot give back some measure of pride and self-respect to those from whom it has been taken, it can at least remind them to consider the source of the ideas they encounter and to be careful of the stories they repeat—for we human beings do become the stories we tell ourselves.

In the chapters that follow, the stories of love and marriage in antebellum African America that are told by those who lived them are brought to the fore. This book could be called "Antebellum African Americans Speak for Themselves about Love and Marriage And What They Say Has Relevance for All of Us Living and Trying to Love in the Twenty-First Century," for its message and its usefulness is both particular and general. In essays, memoirs, sermons, and songs, antebellum African Americans reveal their philosophies and theologies, hearts' desires, and souls' aspirations. Personal narratives, letters, folklore, and aphorisms, provide glimpses, beyond the veils of privacy and dissemblance, of their intimate and often inspiring stories of struggles to make marriages work and attainments that made families strong. In the process, perhaps some popular diagnoses that claim to explain familial dysfunction and despair in the contemporary African American community will be drastically altered. In the process, hopefully, stories about other things and other people will be reviewed, reconstructed, and expanded.

Offered here, for the first time, are documents written by African Americans, for African Americans, about African Americans that can serve as the basis for a discussion that for too long has taken place without the voices of those who have the most to contribute. The ways antebellum African Americans viewed and reported love and marriage are directly relevant to everyone's lives today. They offer insights, they record experiences, and they suggest alternatives that can be applied to our lives today and to the lives we envision in the future. Some of these ideas or a given genre may be "old news" to some readers; nonetheless, consideration of these materials at the same time and woven together—a rich and distinct archive of self-definition—is bound to give rise to something new. By looking back, we can see where we have been and where we might go. William Faulkner, one of our Euro-American ancestors, mused a great deal on what came before him. As he saw it: "The past is not dead, it isn't even past." Sankofa, part of our African inheritance, tells us what to do with this insight. Go back, it says, and then see who you are when you come back to here.

This book, then, is a Sankofa text.

'TIL
DEATH OR
DISTANCE
DO US PART

ADAM AND EVE,
ANTONEY AND ISABELLA

THE AMERICAN DREAM OF ASPIRING ADULTS, LIKE THE "First comes love," chant of children, assumes a nuclear, heterosexual, monogamous family. Dad, Mom, Dick, Jane, and Spot may have given up their white picket fenced home, bought an SUV, and moved to the suburbs. John and Mary may have chosen to have 2.3 children, home school them, and arrange play dates with others who live in their condo or gated community complex. But, even when knowing what they have learned about difficulties of love and the chances of a long, happy marriage, postmodern people still assert, that as much as possible, first comes love, then marriage, and then parenthood. They speak and dream of one love, one life, lived happily ever after. Such beliefs derive, in part, from the story of Adam and Eve whose relationship Jews, Christians, and some others believe to be marriage's prototype. Whether we believe literally or metaphorically, we tend to accept John Milton's affirmation of them as "our Grand Parents."

The origin stories in Genesis upon which we based these beliefs are vague on the details, but we readily fill them in. Genesis 1:27–28 says that God created humans, "male and female he created them." Then "God blessed them, and God said to them 'Be fruitful and multiply, and fill the earth.'"[1] Obviously, God's blessing was the first marriage ceremony. Clearly, the couple was supposed to and did have children. Indeed, quoting Milton again, Eve is "The Mother of Mankind" for most Christians and Jews. Islam and other religions may not use the names "Adam" and

"Eve" but they have similar stories, if not similar interpretations of their potent. Genesis does not say that Adam and Eve loved one another, but we assume at least Adam loved Eve. Otherwise, why would the biblical narrator say "Therefore a man leaves his father and his mother and clings to his wife, and they become one flesh"? (Gen.1:24),

In African American history, Antoney and Isabella were the first known Africans to marry and have a child in the North American colonies. They, then, can be considered the Grand Parents of African America. Again, the original sources do not mention love, but the assumption that love had something to do with it persists. For example, Lerone Bennett, arguably the best known historian in African America, writes that African America "began with a love story." He explains: "Antoney, who had no surname, fell in love with Isabella and married her. In 1623 or 1624 Isabella gave birth to the first black child born in English America. The child, a boy named William, was baptized in the Church of England." He continues: "There were other ships, other Williams, Antoneys and other Isabellas—millions after millions."[2]

Most historians of the United States limit their narratives to the stories of British settlements. They date the arrival of African settlers from John Rolfe's brief mention of the 20 or so Negars who arrived at Jamestown in 1619. They equivocate as to whether these first Africans were "slaves" or "indentured servants," but they agree that the group social status was more important than individual activities, attitudes, and attributes. The bulk of our documentation for early African Americans is numbers, not names, business ledgers and legislative records rather than personal testimonies. Lerone Bennett is one of a relatively few historians who actually write about the earliest Africans in America as individuals, as human beings who lived, loved, dreamed, and generally made the most they could with what they had or could get. The available historical narratives offer very few details about these first traceable African Americans. It's not certain who all these Africans were, what tribes they represented, or the status of their relationships to the British settlers and indigenous people among whom they lived. But then, not a whole lot is known about the details of life in Jamestown generally.

Early census data indicate that there were seven European males for every one European woman in the colony but those Bennett calls "these seminal African Americans" were fairly evenly divided by sex. What the domestic relationships were like, whether one-seventh of the male population formed heterosexual unions and began families or what other kinds of unions occurred and how long they lasted is open to conjecture. What is known is that the 1620 census lists 222 "habitable houses," so some kind of family groupings must have existed by then. Census data for 1624 list 23 people of African ancestry, 10 women, 11 men, and 2 children, living in six different communities.[3] Since the sex ratio among the Africans was practically one to one, they more than the Europeans could have formed heterosexual unions and created families—if they wanted to. We can speculate also that intercultural marriages did occur. Otherwise, there would have been no practical reason for a fairly rapid rise of laws against marriages between blacks and whites.

Neither Lerone Bennett nor other historians tell much about the relationship between Antoney and Isabella other than that they "married" and had a child. They are silent about when, why, or how they married. We can only speculate on whether they stayed together as husband and wife until death. But even with few details, some telling information exists. Antoney and Isabella are noted in records as Antoney and Isabella Negro. Their son William was baptized in the Church of England with the surname William Tucker, the man for whom Antoney and Isabella worked. In addition to Antoney and Isabella, the records note at least one other early African American couple: "Antonio, a Negro," married "Mary, a Negro woman," and that couple had four children. These are tantalizing details but hardly the full story. They are fulsome enough, however, to enable the recognition that the extant stories of marriage and family in early African America follow the same plot: a man and a woman of African descent marry, then have children.

History is unclear about whether "Antoney Negro" or "Antonio, a Negro" changed his name to "Anthony Johnson" or whether Anthony Johnson was a different person altogether. But history does relate that in 1641, Anthony Johnson "was master to a black servant, John Casor."[4] And in 1645 "Anthony, the Negro," stated: "now I know myne owne ground and I will worke when I please and play when I please" (Johnson 38). It is unclear but documented that whether African Americans were legally enslaved for life or whether their servitude was for a specified period of time, some were free to own homes, servants, and other pieces of the American Dream.

Whether as a life sentence, indenture, or apprenticeship, from 1619 until the Civil War ended in 1865, most African Americans were in servitude. The common interpretation of this fact is that before the Civil War, that is, in antebellum times, African Americans were slaves. They rarely married because marriage between enslaved people was illegal. For those who did, the story goes, marriage was conditional. They vowed to be married until death or distance parted them. The interesting thing is that documentation by antebellum African Americans does not generally support this story. There is a great deal of evidence that contradicts or complicates the master narrative that informs much of today's personal and public politics. At the same time, the counter—narratives told by antebellum African Americans can still affect everyone's lives today. Adding stories about individual lives to the generalized histories can alter our preconceptions; it may help envision more appropriate laws and engender better lives today. This book explores the possibilities Sankofa offers for our ideas about love and marriage in early African America. It begins with the myth about such marriages that the vows, at best, could only be "'Til death or distance do us part."

ROOTS

... when a griot dies, it is as if a library has burned to the ground. The griots symbolize how all human ancestry goes back to some place, and some time, where there was no writing. Then the memories and the mouths of ancient elders was the only way that early histories of mankind got passed along...for all of us today to know who we are.

—Alex Haley, *Roots* (1976)

Griots were to Africa what bards were to Europe; they composed, sang or recited the histories, legends and myths that defined the culture.[5] Once upon a time, such storytellers were the most authoritative sources for people knowing who they were, where they came from, and how they should behave in this world. Then, as is often the case with immigrants, they forgot their stories or they forgot to pass them on to the next generations.

Nowadays, historians, journalists, and docudramatists have largely displaced griots and bards. We have been socialized to favor the written over the oral, textbooks and biographies over novels and folklore, mainstream publishers, official documents, museums, and public media over family records, diaries, and letters. Internet resources such as blogs and Wikipedia have strong impacts because they deliver written information via a new technology that strengthens our acquired respect for published writing with the implied imprimatur of science. When master narratives, that is, the stories told and taught by the official and mass media, contradict our remembered or inherited stories, we tend to choose the master narratives. We deny or suspend our own disbelief in favor of common knowledge. Too often, even if we do not disregard family stories, cultural wisdom, and common sense entirely, we harbor skepticism toward counter—narratives.

Sankofa invites us to go back and to reconcile this breach, to listen to the stories of our past, to select what is good, and to use that good for positive growth. Sankofa is "the benevolent use of knowledge." For it to work right, we have to employ a hermeneutic of suspicion; or, as my grandmother would say, we have to "consider the source." The dominant view maintains that if African Americans married, they had little or nothing to do with choosing their mates. It tells us that their marriages were ad hoc and their wedding rituals as simple as jumping over a broom. If a couple exchanged vows, such stories go, their pledges were conditional; hence the promise to be married "'til death or distance" parted them.

Such stories are not necessarily false, but they are incomplete, oversimplified, and misleading. First of all, marriage was not illegal for all Americans of African descent because not all antebellum African Americans were enslaved. For enslaved African Americans, marriage was legally impossible because marriage was then as now a legal contract between human beings and by law, slaves were chattel or property that, for particular legal purposes were defined as three-fifths human. Legally defined as partial people, they could not enter into legal contracts. But not all religions, not all slaveholders, and certainly not all enslaved African Americans agreed entirely with the law. And many slaves married.

Numerous stories and documents, including freedom papers, military records, and the United States census make it clear that free African Americans made up a sizeable and significant portion of antebellum America from the days of the early colony in Jamestown to the fall of the Confederate capital in Richmond. These citizens were free to contract legal marriages. Their testimonies and the records of their community organizations show that marriage was an expected and a respected way of life. The records also describe many forms of weddings and of marriage vows. And documents written by African Americans rarely confirm the notion that they married merely "'til death or distance." Rather, African American literature generally extols marriage as an unconditional lifetime commitment that does not require the continual presence of a spouse, that withstands temporary, though long-term separations, and that can continue after death.

While this chapter focuses on the narratives about love and marriage authored by antebellum African American griots of the quill and of the printing press, it begins with a twentieth-century narrative about antebellum African America that has reached mythic proportions. Alex Haley's *Roots: The Saga of an American Family* is a unique example of how one person's Sankofa can influence the lives and imaginations of millions of people. It proves that master narratives can and sometimes do change in response to counter—narratives. And it warns all of us of how counter-narratives can be misinterpreted, misconstrued, and absorbed into master narratives.

Roots began with stories Haley heard from his grandmother about her grandparents and their grandparents. She also taught him words, such as *Kamby Bolongo*, passed down through their family even after they had forgotten their meanings. As an adult, Haley began a quest to define the words and to document the stories he had been told. Twelve years, three continents, and a half million miles later, he declared that he had found what he sought. The story he wrote was deliberately framed as the story of "an American family." *Roots*, Haley's story of his quest for his ancestry, generated an incredible amount of publicity and changed both his life and the lives of millions. It was adopted and adapted into master narratives, including those about marriage during the period of slavery in the United States.

Part of its impact was its timing. In 1976, when *Roots* was published, traditional narratives of the United States and its history were being reconstructed to accommodate the experiences of various groups that until then had been ignored or misrepresented. At the same time, exploration of family genealogy was fast becoming a national pastime. *Roots* replaced Booker T. Washington's *Up from Slavery* as the ideal African American subplot in U.S. mythology. Public Broadcasting Station fans may vote for Toni Morrison's *Beloved* as the most influential African American historical novel of the twentieth century, but in terms of actual audience and effect on the politics and policies in this country, *Roots* has been the most influential such story told in the modern era. In its first year, according to *Publisher's Weekly*, the book sold over a six million copies. In 1992, another source gave a sales figure of 12 million in 37 languages. *Roots* won a Pulitzer Prize and the National Book Award. It was serialized in *Reader's Digest* and made into a television miniseries that claimed an initial audience of 130 million viewers, or approximately three out of every four families in the United States. The television series garnered awards that included a Peabody and nine Emmys. *Roots: The Saga of an American Family* begat sequels: the 14-hour special *Roots: The Next Generation; Roots: The Gift;* and *Alex Haley's Queen.* In 2007, a consortium of businesses marked the thirtieth anniversary of the phenomenon by simultaneously releasing a new paperback edition, an audio book read by Avery Brooks, and a thirtieth-anniversary DVD boxed set.

But *Roots* and the variations it begat are more than popular entertainment and profitable business ventures. They instigated a series of cultural changes that continue to this day. Haley's stories fueled an intense interest in African American family genealogy and cultural history, and inspired several civic organizations to devote themselves to perpetuating the work Haley began. The Kunta Kinte–Alex Haley Foundation, for example, is part of a coalition that set up a memorial at the place in Annapolis, Maryland, where Kunta Kinte, the ancestor to which Haley traced his roots, landed in the mid-1700s. The centerpiece is a sculpture installation that shows a group of raptly attentive children listening to Haley. Haley's farm is now owned by the Children's Defense Fund and used as a national training center and conference site. And, of course, *Roots,* the historical novel, is taught in colleges and schools. The television series is rebroadcast almost every Black History Month and is used as a teaching aid for history classes everywhere.

Roots shows that our own experiences, our family tales and memories, and even the story fragments, the phrases and words that have survived through time, can be useful in recovering who we are, where we come from, and what we can expect of ourselves. Like many African Americans, Haley did not find enough of his past in the history books of his present. But he had stories about "the African," he had words such as *Kamby Bolongo,* and he had the will to research not just the standard documents of history but the less-used and the ignored—the previously unknown sources. His quest led him to a griot, and the sum total of his work impacted the written history of the United States.

Alex Haley's story is a good place to begin our Sankofa journey toward a better understanding of the possibilities of the past for strengthening our present and future understandings of love, marriage, and family. First of all, *Roots* directly refutes several convoluted, contradictory but pervasive narratives about antebellum African America, for example the allegations that before the Civil War, African Americans did not marry; or if they did, they did not live together as families; or if they did marry and live together, they lost knowledge of their family histories. *Roots* refutes the commonplace that African American families today, as a result of such a past, have no coherent and consistent traditions that support strong values, faithful and respectable sexual relationships, and lifelong marriages. From such success also comes failure. The book and the movie are taught so frequently that numerous websites and teaching aids abound. Gale Publishing devotes a chapter to *Roots* in its *Novels for Students* series. *Book Rags,* a website for ready-made bibliographies, term papers, and other resources, offers a 467-page "Study Pak" for *Roots.*[6]

Such popularity can make a book a legend, and legends, inevitably, morph from reportages to creative summation and reconstruction. Such is the fate of *Roots.* Haley's historical fiction becomes fiction to support the kinds of histories it intended to undermine. Teachwithmovies.com is a website that sells subscriptions to "more than 270 *Learning Guides* and seven *Movie Lesson Plans*" for those who want "to supplement what their children learn in school."[7] The ad for a *Learning Guide* for "ROOTS VOL. IV" says this segment is useful for teaching U.S. history from 1812 to 1860 as well as particular values such as diversity, character development ("rebellion"), and morality and ethics ("respect"). It says, too, that "slave families were often disrupted and family members sold to distant plantations. This practice was so common that the marriage vows of slaves were modified. The traditional words 'til death do us part' were changes [*sic*] to the words til death or distance do us part.' "

The positive aspect to declarations such as this is that they counter the common wisdom that since marriage was against the law for slaves, marriage did not exist in antebellum African America. The *Learning Guide* ad also acknowledges that enslaved people did have families and that some were not sold away and thus "disrupted." A major problem with this ad, however, is that it says "the marriage vows of slaves were modified"—that enslaved people married conditionally, "'til death or distance" parted them. Haley's story has been augmented, rearranged, and reinterpreted so much that what we now believe is hard to reconcile with the original. On marriage, for example: when Kunta Kinte and Bell marry, Aunt Sukey begins the ceremony with the following words.

Now, I ax everybody here to pray for dis union dat God 'bout to make. I wants y'all to pray dat dis here couple is gwine a stay togedder....An' dat nothin' don't happen to cause 'em to git sol' away from one 'nother. And pray dat dey has good, healthy young'uns. (Haley 275)

She then asks Bell and Kunte if they are sure they want to marry. They say "I do," and they jump over a broom. The ceremony concludes with Aunt Sukey's admonition that "What God done 'jined, let no man pull asunder. Now y'all be faithful to one 'nother, and be good Christians." In the novel, all pray that the marriage will be long lasting and the children healthy. The shadow of separation hovers over the wedding, but the vows and the prayers defy its power: "What God done 'jined, let no man pull asunder." The similarity to the traditional vows of Christian weddings in the United States is clear, though in context Aunt Sukey's pronouncement has more serious, perhaps subversive, implications. In the United States' version of slavery, those who claimed ownership of others did believe they had the right to bring couples together or set them asunder. Aunt Sukey says otherwise. The other significant wedding in the novel, that of George and Matilda, offers similar dialogue. Theirs combines "jumping the broom" with rituals generally enacted by Euro-American Christians also. The "hired white preacher" asks, "Matilda and George, do you solemnly swear to take each other, for better or for worse, the rest of your lives?" When they answer affirmatively, he pronounces them "man and wife" (Haley 428).

It may be that the actors in the movie version of *Roots* vowed to be together until one died or moved away. But no matter how convincingly actors speak their wedding vows and no matter how logical these words might seem, unless we can prove they are quoting from actual ceremonies, we must regard "'til death or distance" as poetic license, as fiction, not fact. Haley's story and the stories of Haley's story demonstrate both the strengths and weaknesses of reconstructed histories. They help explain why we must continually take stories seriously but always consider their sources and continue to consider other stories, told less often.

Before turning to a story less told that is useful to balance what has become the dominant version of *Roots* and a persistent but inaccurate representation of marriage in antebellum African America, I want to be clear about narratives and variations on narratives. I do not advocate substituting one story for another uncritically or even completely. Truth is not simple. History is conjecture at its best. We never have all the pieces, and all the pieces we have don't fit easily into any one narrative line. The past is a conundrum. No one story fits all. Thus, I do not offer Teachwithmovies.com as the first or only source for believing enslaved marriages were illegal, imitative, and impermanent. "'Til death or distance do us part" or similar phrases appear in many accounts. But the evidence we would expect to back up such a pervasive idea is remarkably scant. Still, some history textbooks do report these words as the standard in wedding ceremonies between African Americans.[8]

Under the laws of slavery, the owners could and did separate enslaved couples whenever or however they liked. Sometimes they forced enslaved persons to marry. Moreover, as has been true throughout the history of marriage, not every person entered into wedlock with the assumption that they could never escape their marital bonds. African Americans are no exception. Numerous examples appear in the oral histories recorded by the Works Progress Administration (WPA), Charles S. Johnson and researchers at Fisk University, and others. The most accessible collection is that edited by George P. Rawick, *The American Slave: A Composite Autobiography*, which includes this testimony by Turner Cancer, a formerly enslaved woman from Tennessee:

> I'se bin' married three times; de firs' time wuz in slavery time an' me and dat nigger jus' jumped de broom stick; dey called him Calhoun, but he wuzn't no regular husban'; he lef' me an' had three or four udder wives....I used to cuss an' swar dat I wudn't never marry no mo' but I did; de nex' time I wuz married we wuz free....I lived wid him 'til death tuk him 'bout 30 years ago.

A report on Ellen Crowley, of Jefferson County, Arkansas, in that collection declares: "When asked about her marriage she would say: I been married seven times but Jones, Brown and Crowley were the only husbands she could remember by name. She said the other 'four no count Negroes wasn't worth remembering.'"

The WPA narratives collected in *The American Slave* were obtained by a motley group of interviewers, few of whom were trained professionals. They vary greatly in form and accuracy; especially suspect are their recordings in dialect. But overall, these accounts are as authoritative as any collected about incidents that occurred more than a half century earlier can be. Still, after more than a decade of researching newspapers, magazines, letters, and organizational records by antebellum African Americans, I have found no evidence that such conditional marriage vows were common. In fact, I have found just the opposite. I have read an abundance of printed sources that portray African Americans, even those who were enslaved, making vows to last for as long as they lived. These stories show that some spouses were willing to die before letting distance destroy their marriages. Some show that wives and husbands did die trying to live up to their marriage vows. Some stories tell how spouses overcame distance and maintained their marriages without sacrificing their lives. Some show that despite the best efforts of a couple, marriages simply could not survive. But accounts of remarriages suggest that the first failure did not necessarily change ideals and aspirations. The next marriage brought the same intentions and vows to live as husband and wife for better or for worse, for richer or for poorer, until death did them part—and maybe even afterward.

THE TRIALS OF HENRY BIBB: HUSBAND, FATHER, AND FUGITIVE

Alex Haley did years of research, and he based his book on the material he found. Among his sources were fugitive slave narratives, personal accounts by African Americans of their lives in bondage and their attempts to become free. *The Life and Adventures of Henry Bibb, An American Slave,* is one such narrative, and the similarities between Haley's George and Matilda and Henry and Malinda Bibb are striking. *The Life and Adventures of Henry Bibb, An American Slave,* published in 1849, helps us understand *Roots: The Saga of an American Family* within an African American literary tradition.[9] But *Roots* is historical fiction, a novel. Haley could not write about the nineteenth century as one who lived it. Henry Bibb wrote in the nineteenth century about his own life. Bibb's autobiographical account offers a counter—narrative to Haley's fiction.

In *Roots,* Chicken George flees to Canada but returns to rescue his wife, Matilda, and their family. Haley's George has actually obtained a set of "free papers," the antebellum documents that served as passports for African Americans who were not legally enslaved. He returns to his family only to discover as was often the case in real life—that according to state law, a free African American who stayed in the state for 60 days would be enslaved. George leaves, vowing to return. During the Civil War, George's wife and family could run away, but they stay where they are because they don't want him to come back and not be able to find them. Their story ends happily. George does return, and the entire family moves to Henning, Tennessee, where they settle and prosper.

Bibb's narrative also ends with him happily married and in the process of becoming a prosperous land owner. In fact, Henry Bibb and his wife were leaders in their community, edited an abolitionist newspaper, established schools, and generally modeled the public behavior of an ideal marriage. However, this was Bibb's second marriage. Despite their best efforts, his first had been disastrous. Bibb's narrative offers a trove of helpful information about antebellum married life, especially as experienced by enslaved couples. The failure of the first marriage shows how even a most privileged and faithful couple does not necessarily survive, while witnessing to the depth of this couple's love and the persistence of their hope for a lifelong relationship.

The first part of Bibb's narrative is fairly standard for fugitive slave narratives. It begins by describing the horrors of enslavement, inadequate food, extreme working conditions, capricious and violent punishments. Like other stories about slavery, Bibb's account includes a lot of whips, lashes, and chains. He writes:

> I was born May 1815, of a slave mother in Shelby County, Kentucky, and was claimed as the property of David White Esq....I was brought up....Or, more correctly speaking...I may safely say, I was *flogged up*; for where I should have received moral, mental, and religious instruction, I received stripes without number, the object of which was to degrade and keep me in subordination. (Bibb 13)

Bibb's descriptions of beatings and of sexual harassment are more graphic than those of narrators such as Harriet Jacobs or William Wells Brown. Bibb also describes, in greater detail than most, the everyday or routine pleasures and pains of domestic life for enslaved people.

Bibb tells how he courted Malinda despite the disapproval of his mother, her mother, and several rival suitors. His mother thought he was too young and too impulsive to marry. Malinda's mother thought another suitor would provide for her better than Henry could. In some ways, Bibb's story shows both mothers were right. Though the couple resisted their parents' disapproval, Bibb's account also reveals that he and Malinda did not jump into marriage. They gave a good deal of thought to it and achieved consensus on their values and feelings. For example, they agreed that "Religion and Liberty" would be their goal. They would "comply with the requisitions of the gospel, both theoretically and practically," and work to "be free, either by purchase or running away" (Bibb 36–37). They agreed they would be engaged for one year and then if their feelings had not changed they would marry.

Like many enslaved couples, Henry and Malinda Bibb had an "abroad marriage": they lived separately and visited on weekends and holidays. That period, Bibb says, "was one of the most happy seasons of my life....Malinda was to me an affectionate wife. She was with me in the darkest hours of adversity. She was with me in sorrow and joy, in fasting and feasting, in trial and persecution, in sickness and health, in sunshine and in shade" (Bibb 41).

Their love and devotion was so profound and evident that when Henry Bibb's "owner" decided to relocate, he agreed to Bibb's proposal "to sell me to his brother, who lived within seven miles of Wm. Gatewood, who then held Malinda as his property" (Bibb 41). The slave owner may have been a bit tender hearted, but Henry Bibb lets us know the owner knew he had little or no choice. Bibb writes that the man knew that if he made Bibb leave, Bibb would simply run away. Bibb describes the man who bought him as "oppressive and unreasonable," but Bibb was able to convince this second owner to sell him to William Gatewood.

The couple now lived together. But all was not well. Bibb's reasons are those common to other enslaved couples who lived together. "I was much dissatisfied," Bibb writes:

> Not that Gatewood was a more cruel master than my former owner, not that I was opposed to living with Malinda, who was then the centre and object of my affections but to live where I must be eye witness to her insults, scourgings and abuses, such as are common to be inflicted upon slaves, was more than I could bear. If my wife must be exposed to the insults and licentious passions of wicked slave-drivers and overseers; if she must bear the stripes of the lash laid on by an unmerciful tyrant; if this is to be done with impunity, which is frequently done by slaveholders and their abettors, Heaven forbid that I should be compelled to witness the sight. (Bibb 42)

When their child, Mary Frances, was born, Henry's distress increased. Now he witnessed not only his wife's abuse but that of their child. The "unmerciful old mistress" would slap the baby "until her little face was left black and blue....Who can imagine what could be the feelings of a father and mother, when looking upon their infant child whipped and tortured with impunity.... My happiness or pleasure was then all blasted" (Bibb 42–43). For Henry Bibb, living daily with his family, instead of visiting on weekends and holidays, did what separation did not. It made their enslavement so intolerable that on Christmas Day of 1837, without telling his wife, Henry Bibb ran away.

Five months later, he returned to rescue his family. He went first to his mother's home, where he discovered Malinda and Mary Frances, there on a weekend visit. Bibb writes that Malinda was overwhelmed with joy and that she had believed he was dead. Still, she had continued to live as his wife. With Malinda's father's help, the couple planned their escape. The plan failed; Henry was captured and taken to Louisville, Kentucky, as a slave. The intrepid husband escaped and went, again, to find his wife and daughter. This time they left, but they were captured and sent to Louisiana. Bibb escaped again, and, again, he returned for his wife and daughter. All in all, he ran away six times, and he returned five times to rescue his wife.

The last time Malinda and Henry actually saw one another was in Louisiana in 1840. Henry had convinced his latest "owners" to buy his family. But Malinda's owner, Bibb wrote, "would sooner see me to the devil than indulge or gratify me after my having run away from him." Bibb describes their highly traumatic separation. Desperate to convince Malinda's owner, who was a church deacon, to sell her, Henry and Malinda fell to their knees and began to pray loudly, whereupon the deacon began to whip Malinda. Bibb says:

> The louder we prayed the harder he whipped, amid the most heart-rending shrieks from the poor slave mother and child, as little Frances stood by, sobbing at the abuse inflicted on her mother....
>
> As we left the plantation, as far as we could see and hear, the Deacon was still laying on the gory lash, trying to prevent poor Malinda from weeping over the loss of her departed husband, who was then, by the hellish laws of slavery, to her, theoretically and practically dead. (Bibb 148–49)

Bibb wrote that realistically, from that point he and the marriage were "theoretically and practically dead." But he persisted. Five years later, in 1845, Henry Bibb tried once more. This time when he stopped at his mother's home in Kentucky, his mother had devastating news. Malinda had written to her mother and friends that she had given up hope of ever seeing her husband again and that she had been sold to a man "at a high price, and she was better used than ordinary slaves." They knew these words meant that she no longer considered herself Henry Bibb's wife and was now her master's concubine. Bibb writes:

> my mother thought it was no use for me to run any more risks, or to grieve myself any more about her.
>
> From that time I gave her up into the hands of an all-wise Providence. As she was then living with another man, I could no longer regard her as my wife. After all the sacrifices, sufferings, and risks which I had run, striving to rescue her from the grasp of slavery; every prospect and hope was cut off. She has ever since been regarded as theoretically and practically dead to me as a wife, for she was living in a state of adultery, according to the law of God and man. (Bibb 189)

The law of man could not prevent the Bibbs from being married in the eyes of themselves and their community. Distance did not divorce them. But when Malinda gave up "hope," when she consented to a marriage-like relationship with another person, Henry considered her an adulterer. "Poor unfortunate woman," Bibb writes; "I bring no charge of guilt against her, for I know not all the circumstances connected with the case." But he felt it "reasonable to suppose that there might have been some kind of attachment...and...quite probable that they have other children according to the law of nature, which would have a tendency to unite them stronger together" (Bibb 189–90). His marriage to her was over.

"'Til death or distance do us part" is an oft-told story, but it may be one that has grown more believable the farther away the slave era becomes. Whether these were actual vows made by antebellum African Americans might one day be proven. But it is highly improbable that such conditional vows were routinely exchanged. The extent to which antebellum African American couples actually believed their marriages would last until or even after death will also probably remain a mystery. But counter—narratives such as *The Life and Adventures of Henry Bibb, an American Slave* make clear that marriage vows were sincere and lasting testaments of desire even when such desires were not realized.

Henry Bibb was not unique in risking his freedom to preserve his marriage and his family. His story is unusual, however, because of the number of times he escaped and returned, trying always to rescue his wife and daughter, and because of how often he was captured, imprisoned, beaten, sold farther south, and otherwise subjected to extreme emotional and physical abuse. Maybe if Harriet Tubman had actually written her own narrative instead of being interviewed and written about, hers would be markedly similar. Tubman is still known as the "Moses of her People" because she reportedly made 19 successful trips into slave territory and rescued her loved ones and hundreds of other people. Beyond Tubman and Bibb, there are few who went so often, risked so much, for family and for love. On the other hand, less spectacular accounts by individuals, including Josiah Henson, Samuel Ringgold Ward, and Henry Highland Garnet, do demonstrate that bonds of love were so strong, even among the enslaved in the deep South, that heroic efforts to rescue or redeem husbands, wives, children, and other loved ones were not unusual.

"BOUND AS FAST IN WEDLOCK AS A SLAVE CAN BE"

Stories such as *Roots* and *The Life and Adventures of Henry Bibb* have a particular importance because they deal with love and marriage among enslaved African Americans, a status that likely represented 90 percent of antebellum African Americans at some time in their lives. Slavery was not the same for everyone, everywhere, all the time. But some generalizations even about individual lives can be appropriate. In the antebellum United States, as in postbellum times and now in this bellicose twenty-first century, not every married couple have been able to live together for all their lives. Reasons beyond their control—serving in the military, going to school, searching for work, traveling to employment and a myriad more—have allowed distance to part them. Enslaved people had about as much power to prevent their lives from being disrupted by distance as they had to prevent death. But they hoped, dreamed, schemed, and worked to fulfill their promises. *The Life and Adventures of Henry Bibb, an American Slave* is both instructive and provocative on this topic. It is especially significant in its subtle definitions of what was understood as sexual morality, matrimonial expectation, and unforgivable behavior.

Bibb's narrative shows that distance created by involuntary separation and intolerable circumstances could not dissolve a marriage but that giving up the struggle could. In its conclusion, Bibb's narrative appears to espouse a strange and impossibly high standard of behavior, one that deserves more careful examination. The explanation Bibb gives for his actions may reflect the expectations and standards of a very small minority—maybe a minority of one. But Bibb appears to believe that his readers will understand and agree with his decision to terminate his marriage. He expects readers not only to condone but to endorse his subsequent marriage, a marriage he may well expect to last until one partner dies, if not beyond. Because it illuminates something about the acceptable reasons for dissolution and remarriage, we shall linger with this narrative a bit longer.

When he heard that Malinda had been sold to a man to be his concubine, Bibb states, "my wife was living in a state of adultery with her master, and had been for the last three years.... This was a death blow to all my hopes and pleasant plans...I could no longer regard her as my wife" (Bibb 189–90). Since he acknowledges that he doesn't know the full story, as twenty-first century readers, we wonder why, after all these years and sufferings, he does not at least talk with Malinda. To understand this better, we need to think about earlier episodes in his story. Bibb has written that marriage offered no protection from sexual abuse and that at one time when they were on the slave coffle, the trader tried to seduce Malinda. After two days of trying to persuade her to have sex with him, the trader took Malinda away. Several days later, she returned bleeding and bruised. Bibb wrote that Malinda had been told she must "submit or die," but still she had resisted. She had refused to submit when their daughter was taken as hostage. About that incident, Bibb wrote that the man had tied Malinda "and flogged her until her garments were stained with blood" and then returned her to the jail. As did Harriet Jacobs in *Incidents in the Life of a Slave Girl,* Bibb suggests that the contest was not merely about sex. She could have been raped as readily as she had been beaten. This was a contest of will, a matter of psychological submission. And, again, the enslaved woman refused to consent.

A few days after Malinda returned, she was taken away again. Bibb reported, "it was several weeks before I saw her again, and learned that he had not sold her or the child" (Bibb 98). This time Bibb does not describe how Malinda appeared when she returned or what had happened in those several weeks. He simply resumes the narrative by describing the slave coffle's journey to Louisiana. His silence invites the idea that this time, Malinda had not been able to resist. She had been raped or, to save her child, she had submitted. Bibb continues to profess his love for her. He reported their further experiences as if that episode had not occurred. And he continued trying to find someone who would buy the entire family.

The scene I related earlier of their final parting in Louisiana demonstrates both their great love and their sense of finality. He writes, "I can never describe to the reader the awful reality of that separation" (Bibb 147). Still, he defied that "reality" until he learned "upon inquiry, and from good authority," that Malinda had been sold for her sexual services. How was this different from the slave coffle episode, and probably others, during the years of their separation? Malinda had been sold. Why would he blame her? That Malinda was now being treated better than most enslaved people would seem to be good news. Why, then, did *this* news warrant divorce? Henry well knew the lengths to which Malinda would go to avoid sexual relations outside their marriage. He had witnessed her withstanding the threat of losing her child and of being killed; he had seen her being repeatedly beaten but not submitting. It seems that even if Henry did not know "all the circumstances connected with the case," he would have known that the "poor unfortunate woman," as he called her, would not have endured willingly her new situation. Surely there were extenuating circumstances. And yet, on his sixth attempt in eight years to rescue Malinda Bibb, this time Henry Bibb decided he should not "run any more risks," not "grieve myself anymore about her" (Bibb 189).

His decision makes more sense if we think of marriage as an emotional commitment and fidelity as something made manifest by intentions and motivation as much—maybe more so—as through actions. From this perspective, sexual exclusivity is not intrinsic to the sacredness of marital vows. A significant difference between earlier incidents and the final episode that ended their marriage was what Malinda had reportedly said. This time, she had written to her mother and friends informing them "of the time and manner" of her separation from Henry, that he had been taken "to where she knew not; and that *she had finally given me up*" (Bibb 189, my emphasis). She informed them that she had been sold at a high price as a concubine, or, as Bibb tells us, to live "in adultery." Telling their community that she was treated better than most enslaved people was part of Malinda's affirmation that she was compliant with that arrangement. "It was consistent with slavery," Bibb says, "to suppose that she had become reconciled to it, from the fact of her sending word back to her friends and relatives." Bibb and Malinda's other family would then find it "reasonable to suppose" that the couple had formed an "attachment." Their attachment may have been strengthened by their children. Thus, Bibb says "my wife was living in a state of adultery with her master, and had been for the last three years."

The key here is choice and consent. If Malinda were assaulted or coerced into sexual intercourse, the act would be one of violence. It is regrettable, an outrage, but it is not a violation of marital vows. If she were forced to live intimately with someone else, but did not acknowledge it, or if she explicitly failed to acknowledge benefits accruing from that relationship, it would be yet another cross to bear. But it appears that Malinda Bibb was doing otherwise when she had informed their community that she had "finally given [her husband] up." She was telling them that she had effectively dissolved her marriage. Henry Bibb had been living separately from the woman he considered his wife. Now, he discovered that she had now abandoned this emotional commitment. That he considered Malinda to be "living in a state of adultery," implies that their marriage had remained in effect until both of them accepted its dissolution.

African Americans in the antebellum period and long afterward were accustomed to women, especially those who worked as domestic servants or house slaves, being forced into intimate relationships or being raped. They were not reconciled to it. They did not approve or desire it. But they knew it happened, and it was not usually a matter that would destroy or even appreciably damage a marriage. If a woman initiated or seemed unperturbed by sexual relations with someone other than her spouse, this was a different story. Henry Bibb's statement also implies that an intimate relationship between an enslaved person and a slaveholder could, under certain circumstances, become cemented by reciprocal emotional bonds. If it was not a "marriage," it was at least an "attachment." Bibb writes that it is "reasonable to suppose" that living together, having children together, and receiving preferential treatments could result in a strong union, despite the disparate race and caste status of the couple. Other writers, for example William Wells Brown in *Clotel* and Frank Webb in *The Garies and Their Friends,* similarly show that love could and did exist between consenting adults over and across the lines of color and caste.

From this perspective, Bibb's dissolution of his marital bonds makes more sense. When Henry Bibb wrote about their marriage, he stated: "notwithstanding our marriage was without license or sanction of law, we believed it to be honorable before God, and the bed undefiled" (Bibb 40–41). For the Bibbs, for enslaved African Americans generally, and, I suspect, for the thousands of antebellum African Americans who were legally free even if not exactly full citizens, marriage was a commitment between individuals and their God.

But, I must add, even if it makes sense, Bibb's attitudes and expectations about marriage were complicated and contradictory. Two paragraphs after his "divorce," Bibb briefly describes how he met "Miss Mary E. Miles, of Boston," and after another one-year engagement, they married. Bibb writes, "We had the happiness to be joined in holy wedlock. Not in slaveholding style, which is a mere farce, without the sanction of law or gospel; but in accordance with the laws of God and our country" (Bibb 191). But by the laws of his country, Henry Bibb was still a slave. His union with Mary E. Miles was no more legitimate than that with Malinda. We can explain this apparent fallacy by making the same distinction between civil law and divine law that was used for marriage between enslaved persons. When Bibb goes on to belittle such marriages and to denounce Malinda for giving up hope in his ability "to secure her restoration" without telling him so, we can understand that he despaired less of her actions than of her attitude. Were Henry Bibb's autobiography the only counternarrative about marriage among enslaved people of African descent, we might be left confused. We might even prefer the dominant narrative that slavery made marriage illegal and that the commitments made by those enslaved people were conditional. Fortunately, there are many other stories.

In *The Life and Adventures of Henry Bibb, an American Slave*, it is the woman who weakens first. In *Father Henson's Story of His Own Life*, published in 1858, Josiah Henson relates the great sacrifices his mother made to live with her husband.[10] Henson does not provide the names of his parents but refers to them as his "mother" and his "father." Henson tells us that his mother's master "was far kinder to his slaves than the planters generally were." But Henson's mother, in order to be with her husband, was willing to be hired out to his owner. She undoubtedly knew that she was relinquishing better housing, food, and working conditions. We don't know if she knew she was also jeopardizing her safety; but one day the overseer tried to rape her. She fought back, screaming. Her husband came to her rescue. Henson describes the result this way: "Furious at the sight, he sprung upon him like a tiger. In a moment, the overseer was down, and mastered by rage, my father would have killed him but for the entreaties of my mother, and the overseer's own promise that nothing should ever be said of the matter" (Henson 3). But something was not only said, but done. For the crime of striking a white man, Henson's father was publicly beaten with 100 lashes and had his right ear nailed to a post and then cut off. His father survived the physical brutality, but "from that hour," Henson writes, "he became utterly changed. Sullen, morose, and dogged, nothing could be done about him. The milk of human kindness in his heart was turned to gall. Finally, he was sold to Alabama." The Hensons had tried to stay together. They had literally fought to keep their vows. In the end, however, the sanctity of their marriage had meant nothing to the man who attacked the wife. The "good-humored and light-hearted" husband whose banjo playing had been "the life of the farm" survived physically but not emotionally. Technically, that marriage was dissolved by his being sold away. I believe it was dissolved by death—the husband's soul was murdered.

When it was published in 1960, *Running a Thousand Miles for Freedom; or, The Escape of William and Ellen Craft from Slavery* created quite a sensation for the ingenious way this couple escaped, but it is also significant for what it reveals about family and marriage, death and distance.[11] William says: "my old master had the reputation of being a very humane and Christian man, but he thought nothing of selling my poor old father, and dear aged mother, at separate times, to different persons" (Craft 685). The reason the man gave for selling the Crafts and other elderly people, William writes, was that "they were getting old, and would soon become valueless in the market" (Craft 686). Moreover, this reputedly "very humane and Christian man" sold William's sister and his brother. Though sold away, some of the family managed to stay in touch. Eventually William's mother "became free...by purchase...and after a great deal of difficulty" discovered that her daughter was enslaved in Mississippi. She wrote to William; and in the book, he reports that he has almost raised enough money to buy his sister (Craft 687). This brings up another reason to suspect the idea of "'til death or distance do us part." If distance did not dissolve kinship, why assume that distance would automatically dissolve a marriage?

Like most enslaved lovers, William and Ellen decided to marry anyway. Unlike most, they also decided that it was better to die trying to increase the odds of being together than to live apart. They concocted an ingenious escape plan. Ellen's European ancestry eclipsed her African heritage. She looked "white." William's African ancestry was quite apparent. So Ellen dressed as a man, and William posed as her slave. They purchased tickets and traveled by train, bus, and boat from Macon, Georgia, to Philadelphia. Pennsylvania was a free state, but it was not a safe place for fugitive slaves. With the help of abolitionists, the Crafts continued on to Boston, where they lived and worked for two years. Then in 1850, when the Fugitive Slave Law superseded state laws and required that fugitives from slavery be returned to their legal owners, the Crafts were among the thousands of African Americans who had to flee the United States. William and Ellen Craft went to England, where they juggled the requirements of their lives as immigrants, students, parents, and professional abolitionists. They published the story of their escape as part of their antislavery work. When Ellen Craft died in 1891, the Crafts had been married about 50 years.

Lunsford Lane and Martha Curtis were also owned by different people when they married in Raleigh, North Carolina. Lane writes, "So in May, 1828, I was bound as fast in wedlock as a slave can be. God may at anytime sunder that band in a freeman; either master may do the same at pleasure in a slave."[12] Lane's narrative shows, however, that they were among the more fortunate enslaved couples. Lunsford Lane was able to purchase himself, his wife, and his children. Writing his narrative in 1845 as a free man married to a free woman, Lane assumes that the danger of involuntary separation is over, and, he believes they are now married for life. He says their marital bond "has never been broken; and now it cannot be, except by a higher power" (Lane 104). Lunsford Lane's words are as close as we ever get to finding a confirmation of "'til death or distance" in the writings by African Americans for African Americans.

Clearly, when couples married they knew the danger of separation. But how great the distance might be was another unknown. In any case, unless they lived on a large plantation, married couples were most likely not to live together. (And the number of large plantations was much smaller than popular conceptions have it.) Husbands and wives were regularly separated for periods of time as the men, generally, migrated to seek out better economic possibilities. African Americans called the arrangements wherein the wife and the husband lived apart "abroad marriages." Another example of enduring marriages that were not always coresidential comes from the *Life of William Grimes, The Runaway Slave* (1855).[13] William Grimes was born enslaved in Virginia in 1784. In Connecticut, he met and married Clarissa Caesar. The couple had "eighteen lovely and beautiful children" (Grimes 121). When he wrote his narrative, William Grimes was about 70 years old. All but one of the children were living "scattered all over the world, one son being...in Australia, digging for gold" (Grimes 122). As for his wife, Clarissa, William Grimes wrote, "she is yet very smart, for so fruitful a vine, and I don't think there are many to be compared with her. Like her noble son, she too is seeking for gold, having been for some time in California" (Grimes 122).

Back then, couples often married without intending to live together. These "abroad marriages" were at least as common as commuter marriages are today—probably more so. As the preceding examples illustrate, not all abroad marriages were between enslaved couples, nor were all of them forced. Customarily, the majority who married abroad were enslaved people who lived fairly close to one another. They lived and worked at one place during the week, and on Saturday after their chores were done, or on Sunday during the traditional "day of rest," if all went well, they were allowed to visit their spouses or lovers, until Monday when work began again.

This was not an ideal situation. The privilege could be revoked by either partner's owner at any time and for any reason. It made coparenting especially difficult, though not impossible. Lunsford Lane's parents did not live together, but his narrative shows that both were active parents. Abroad marriages were difficult also because travel was physically demanding. A spouse might have to walk several miles, in snow, rain, hail, sleet, or darkness of night. Unarmed travelers were vulnerable to wild animals or guard dogs. Marauding whites could detain any black person for any reason if they so desired. Travel was so dangerous that generally men visited women and not vice versa. However, we need only recall the example of Aunt Hester in Frederick Douglass's *Narrative* to know that some women took the risk. Like commuter marriages, abroad marriages also had certain advantages. Some couples preferred to live separately. When Henry Thomas and Catherine Craig married, Henry did not move his "goods" from his master's home, even though it was directly across the street from his new wife's home. However, when Catherine Craig's owner complained that her neighbors would think she would not let the couple live together, then Henry moved across the street.

Some African Americans, like some other Americans, especially those from cultures of color and religions beyond Christianity, believed they were married beyond death, and that in their next lives, they would be reunited with their spouses and loved ones. George Pleasant was taken to Shelbyville, Tennessee, when his owner moved. George's wife, Agnes Hobbs, and their daughter, Elizabeth, belonged to another family and remained in Prince Edward County, Virginia. A letter from Pleasant to his wife dated September 6, 1833, includes these words:

Dear Wife:

My dear biloved wife I am more than glad to meet with opportunity writee thes few lines....I feele Determid to see you If life last again....I have wrote a greate many letters since I've beene here...my dear wife, I don't feeld no whys like giving out writing to you as yet and I hope when you get this letter that you be Inncougege to write me a letter....I hope with gods helpe that I may be abble to rejoys with you on the earth and In heaven....I hope to praise god In glory there weel meet to part no more forever. So my dear wife I hope to meet you In paradase to prase god forever....[14]

John and Elizabeth Boston are another example. When the Civil War started, John Boston seized an opportunity to run away, leaving his wife and family behind. He found refuge with a Union regiment from New York. He wrote his wife this letter:

My Dear Wife

...it is with grate joy I take this time to let you know Whare I am I am now in Safety in the 14th Regiment of Brooklyn this Day I can Address you thank god as a free man....I am With a very nice man and have All that hart Can Wish But My Dear I Cant express my grate desire that I Have to See you I trust the time Will Come When We Shal meet again And *if We don't met on earth We Will Meet in heven* Whare Jesas ranes Dear Elizabeth tell Mrs Own[ees] That I trust that She Will Continue Her kindness to you and that god Will Bless her on earth and Save her In grate eternity....Dear Wife I must Close rest yourself Contented I am free I Want you to rite To me Soon as you Can Without Delay....Write my Dear Soon As you C Your Affectionate Husban Kiss Daniel For me.[15]

I cannot say for certain that Lucy Terry believed she would be reunited with her husband after death. But the story I can reconstruct of the marriage of Lucy Terry and Abijah Prince does demonstrate that neither his death nor the distance from her home to his grave made Lucy Terry forget her husband. Terry is famous as the author of the earliest known poem by an African living in the American colonies. The poem, "Bar's Fight," tells the story of an altercation between Native Americans and New England colonists in Deerfield, Massachusetts, in 1746. Historians of colonial New England have regularly acknowledged Terry's poem as an important source for understanding what happened on that fateful day when several colonists were slain.

Lucy Terry had a reputation as a storyteller and poet, and scholars such as Sidney and Emma Nogrady Kaplan tell us that her stories made her house a popular gathering place for young people. Sadly, they don't tell us how Lucy and Abijah met, what their courtship was like, or how and when Lucy became free. The town records of Deerfield include the notation "Abijah Prince and Lucy Terry Servant to Ens. Ebenr Wells were married May ye 17, 1756 by Elijah Williams, the Justo Pace." Records show that Abijah was a free man, about 55 years old, who owned land and paid taxes in a neighboring town. "Servant" was another word for slave, and it appears that when she married, Lucy Terry was still legally the property of the Reverend and Mrs. Ebenezer Wells. But apparently not long after their marriage, Lucy Terry Prince was a free woman who lived with her husband in a house in Deerfield near a brook that in 1989 was still known as "Bijah's Brook." The couple had seven children and became fairly prosperous from farming and real estate. Abijah died in 1794, and when Lucy was 78 years old, she moved to Sunderland, Vermont. But several sources report that every year until her death at age 92, Lucy Terry Prince rode her horse 18 miles over the Green Mountains to visit her husband's grave.[16]

The story of Frederick Bailey, an enslaved man, and Anna Murray, a free woman, is another example of love and marriage withstanding distance and other distractions. Frederick and Anna worked out a plan for him to escape from Baltimore. Anna sold one of her feather beds to help finance the escape, and she helped Frederick borrow free papers and costume himself as a sailor. When he arrived in New York City, she joined him. They married and were known as Mr. and Mrs. Frederick Johnson. The year was 1838. Johnson later changed his name to Douglass, and the couple was known as Mr. and Mrs. Frederick Douglass until Anna's death in 1882.

Frederick Douglass became a professional abolitionist who traveled continually for years. In 1845, he published his *Narrative of Frederick Douglass, an American Slave.* In so doing, he identified himself explicitly as a criminal; that is, as someone who had stolen himself. Being in imminent danger of capture and reenslavement, Douglass fled to England, leaving his wife and children to fend for themselves indefinitely. After he returned home, Douglass was joined by a British woman, Julia Griffiths, who served as administrative assistant for his abolitionist paper, the *North Star.* Many scholars now (as did people in antebellum times) speculate that their relationship was adulterous. As we currently define "adultery," this word may be an apt description. Later in this chapter, though, I will discuss in more detail ways that antebellum African Americans may have defined sexual morality differently than we do today. The point for now is that Frederick and Anna were married until she died. The widower Douglass did not then marry Griffiths (or any of several women rumored to have been outside lovers). He married Helen Pitts, with whom he lived until *he* died.[17]

I have found abundance of printed sources that declare that African Americans, even those who were enslaved, meant for their marriage vows to last for as long as they lived—or beyond death. Some are nonfictional narratives and some are novels. For the antebellum period, however, I believe that the best sources are the newspapers published by, for, and about African Americans themselves. These papers often included regular "Information Wanted" columns that testify to the conviction of marriage surviving long-term separation as well as to desires, often fulfilled, for reunion. For decades after they had last seen one another, we witness husbands still seeking out information about the whereabouts of their wives. Wives are seen advertising for news of their long-lost husbands. Here are a few examples from the *Christian Recorder* between 1864 and 1884:

> Information is wanted of Charles Brisco, who left Virginia, some four or five years ago, to wait upon Lieutenant Fairfax, on a steamer for San Francisco, at the outbreak of this war. Lieutenant Fairfax returned, leaving my husband behind. I am informed that Charles Brisco left San Francisco for Aspinwall, New Grenada, as a cook, or a waiter on a family. Any information concerning him may be left at the Book and Christian Recorder office, No. 619 Pine Street, Philadelphia.
>
> (Signed) Elizabeth Brisco, his Wife.
>
> N.B.B. Charles has a mother and sister in Georgetown, D.C. by the names of Cynthia Brisco and Mrs. Mary A. Dove.
>
> (*Christian Recorder,* March 26, 1864)

> Information wanted by Lucy Walker, of my husband, Anderson Walker. The last time I saw him was on September 2, 1864 at Athens, Georgia. His former owner was Ferdinand Phirwell. Lucy was owned by Marcella Bloomfield. Any information will be thankfully received by the undersigned. Address
>
> Lucy Walker

Care of Rev. Cyrus Boey,
Elder of Bethel Church,
Oswego City, N.Y.
(*Christian Recorder,* March 24, 1866)

Information wanted of my wife Charlotte Guinn, and child. I left them in Baltimore, MD, about 35 years ago. She belonged to lawyer Copeny Jenkins at that time. My name was Francis Guinn. I now go by the name of Robert Green. A knowledge of their whereabouts will be of valuable interest to them. Address Rev. T. A. Cuff, Bristol, PA or Robert Green, Bridgewater, Bucks Co., PA. (*Christian Recorder,* October 5, 1882)

Information wanted of the following named persons, who formerly belonged to Waddle Thompson, of Edgefield District, South Carolina, but moved off 30 years ago: Pyrena, now about 65 years old, and her children, named Eliza, about 45, Celia, about 43; Jordan, about 41; Lange, 39 and Hamp, 33. The above named Pyrena was the wife of William Hill of Newberry District, Sc. William Hill, the husband and father, wishes to hear from any or all of them, if still living. Address W. T. Willie, Independence, Washington County, Texas.

(*Christian Recorder,* January 3, 1884)

This chapter has focused primarily on love and marriage as recorded by enslaved people. Before the Civil War and the subsequent amendments to the Constitution that outlawed slavery and established citizenship for freed slaves, 90 percent of African America was enslaved. But it is vital that we remember two important facts with crucial pertinence for understanding the past. Not all people of African descent were enslaved. And there is a fundamental difference between a "slave" and "an enslaved person." In the chapters that follow, I will discuss these facts in more detail. But before that there is a fundamental question that needs to be answered: "Why should we care about the past?"

T W O

TERMS OF ENDEARMENT

C'est li mo 'oule, c'est li ma pren
—"Aurore Pradère" (African American folk song)

"AURORE PRADÈRE," AN ANTEBELLUM BALLAD SAID TO originate among African Americans in St. Charles Parish, Louisiana, tells a story of one person's determination to choose whom to love. It not only delineates traits that attract the suitor's interest but also reveals a readiness for passionately romantic commitment in the face of opposition. Generally sung in French, the English translation of the first stanza goes like this:

> Aurore Pradère, pretty maid,
> She's just what I want and her I'll have.
> A muslin gown she does not chose,
> She doesn't ask for 'broidered hose,
> She doesn't want prunella shoes;
> she's what I want and her I'll have.[1]

In the quoted stanza, the speaker says that Aurore Pradère is desirable because she is a "pretty maid" who neither asks for nor wears fancy clothes. Prunella and muslin are fabrics more fashionable than practical. Since she does not ask for frivolous gifts, she is, of course, less likely to be a financial burden. But equally important, because she does not try to follow fashion, we can also assume that Aurore Pradère is an independent thinker, someone who also knows what she does and does not want.

Subsequent stanzas declare that "she's not polite," that others say "she's too pretty," and that some say she is "going to the bad." In its context, "going to the bad" suggests a history of mental illness in her family. These allegations suggest that manners, moderate beauty, sound genes, or a good family name are values the community affirms for marriageable women. The lover denies none of the objections. They may or may not be true, but the refrain remains the same, "she's what I want and her I'll have."

Ballads such as "Aurore Pradère," and others, contradict the most commonly told stories about gender relationships in African America. Most often, whether referencing the past or the present, we hear stories about domestic tragedies, thwarted love, and romantic despair. Today we are often told that in African America, women and men distrust and disrespect one another, love relationships are temporary and fragile, marriage is virtually extinct. Though the reasons vary, each seems to go back to slavery and racial discrimination. Slavery, the story goes, degraded, exploited, and coarsened us as human beings. It made people unable to love and be loved. A variation on the theme of degradation, one that was especially popular during the abolitionist period, says that slavery also victimized slave owners. Their marriages disintegrated, their families suffered, and their souls were lost. But these stories suggest, curiously, that the legacy of slavery, this inability to love and to create and sustain intimate relationships, seems to continue to bind African Americans only, while Euro-Americans have gone on to transcend that history.

Stories in which antebellum African Americans choose their own partners and profess unending devotion are nearly absent in U.S. culture. Though they are less often repeated, they have survived. They are circulated in African American folk and print culture. Rediscovering these stories of love in African America can create a new version of our common ancestral legacy in the United States. It can rekindle our sense of the possibilities of enduring marriage and powerful loyalty that can flower in the worst of times as well as the best.

BUT, O, YOUR IDEAS ARE NOT ENTIRELY NEW

The June 2007 issue of *O: The Oprah Magazine* includes an article entitled "8 Entirely New Ideas about Love." The first "new" idea is "It's good to be picky. Very picky." Perhaps being very picky about whom we choose to love may seem a new idea. But it isn't really. Its novelty comes because other narratives are more widely disseminated. Contemporary conventional wisdom has been telling us that many never marry and many marriages fail because we expect too much from our mates. We are too picky. The stories say we need to settle for less because we cannot find, or make, a Mr. Right or a Miss Everything I've Always Dreamed Of. Back in the day, the stories say, folks were more realistic, adjusted their expectations, and simply settled in for the long haul.

Forbidden Fruit: Love Stories from the Underground Railroad, a collection of stories retold by Betty DeRamus, gives historical support for both sides of this controversy. But it clearly demonstrates that antebellum African Americans were very serious about choosing their own mates and went to great lengths to have and to hold spouses of their own choosing. One story which DeRamus calls "Love in the Time of Hate," especially contrasts twenty-first-century ideas with those of earlier times.[2] DeRamus writes:

> Joseph Antoine would have found the twenty-first century as baffling as ballet is to a bullfrog. He wouldn't have understood married couples who split up before their wedding flowers wilt or their new woks and washing machines lose their showroom shine. He wouldn't have understood why black marriage, as an institution, began dwindling so drastically after 1940. He wouldn't have understood why black children, who once could count on honorary "aunts" and "uncles" on every plantation, now, in some cases, boil their own oatmeal and tuck themselves into bed. Most of all he wouldn't have understood why, for some men, falling in love became a fatal flaw, the crack in a man's smooth chocolate-ice-cream cool. (DeRamus 3)

In the story DeRamus tells, Joseph Antoine might have been baffled by the love stories of today, but he would have understood and advocated being "picky. Very picky." When Joseph Antoine found the woman he wanted to marry, he sold himself into bondage for the sake of that marriage. Antoine had been enslaved in Cuba until the 1790s. He left Cuba as a free man, went to Virginia, met a woman, fell in love, and married her. The woman's name is not recorded, but the man who claimed ownership of her was Jonathon Purcell. Apparently, Purcell had no objection to the marriage, and when he decided to move to the Indiana territories, he made a deal with Antoine: If Antoine would agree to serve Purcell for seven and a half years, Purcell would then free Antoine's wife. The deal was struck, and Antoine indentured himself to his wife's owner. However, when the time ended, Jonathon Purcell stated that the agreement had been for 15 years, not seven and a half. The Antoines did not take kindly to this, but Jonathon Purcell was by then a judge of the Common Pleas Court of Indiana. The couple had little choice but to continue to work for him. But next, Purcell took them to New Orleans and tried to sell them. Antoine somehow got Manuel Juan de Salcedo, the governor of Louisiana, to intervene. The sale was stopped, but the 15-year contract with Purcell was upheld. Purcell took the couple to St. Louis and treated them so badly that they fled to Kentucky, where the wife died and the husband was captured and imprisoned. Antoine's case went to court. It took almost a year, but in June 1805, Joseph Antoine was freed. He was then about 40 years old.

This story certainly contradicts the received knowledge that being "picky" is a new idea. Antoine knew who he wanted to marry, and he was determined to stay married despite incredible obstacles. His story redefines what it means to choose whom to espouse and how to love that person absolutely. His story belies casual generalizations that the brutalization of slavery made love and loyalty virtually extinct and that enslaved people had their mates chosen for them by their owners.

The Antoines' story may seem far-fetched; but it is not as unique as it might seem. Records ranging from court documents to personal letters and family histories demonstrate that African Americans frequently chose slavery over separation from their beloveds. DeRamus explains it this way: "They considered freedom a dubious gift, a counterfeit coin, if they couldn't spend it on the people they loved" (DeRamus 10). Fictional and nonfictional accounts of men and women who, like Joseph Antoine, sold themselves into slavery or voluntarily endured brutal situations in order to be with their beloveds or of couples who risked their lives trying to escape together are as much a part of African American culture as those of the solitary fugitive, following the North Star.

In the Antoines' story, we hear the echoes of the Hebrew Bible story about Jacob and Rachel. The Judeo-Christian tradition tells of Jacob working seven years so he and Rachel could marry.[3] At the end, the promise was not kept. Jacob was given Leah instead, and he had to work another seven if he were to marry the woman of his choice. Even then, they did not live happily ever after. It took many years and tears before Rachel and Jacob had a child. But eventually, their devotion was rewarded. Antebellum African American writings often referred to biblical stories about steadfast love, the cause and the reward for being "picky."

In the September 27, 1862, issue of the *Pacific Appeal*, the story "A Marriage of Affection" features Charles and Laura, a couple "like Isaac and Rebecca." Their blissful marriage was the result of suitability, their "union was one of hearts and not convenience, which often occur, when parties are not allowed to exercise their own volition and marry whom they love."[4] DeRamus's story of Joseph Antoine, the evocations of Isaac and Rebecca, of Jacob and Rachel, and of other iconic couples require us to rethink our assumptions about choice, liberty, and love in antebellum African America. "Patrick Brown's First Love" is another tale that challenges assumptions about freedom and enslavement, love and marriage, protecting and providing until death does part. The story, which was published in the April 1859 issue of *Anglo-African Magazine*, begins with two lines of poetry that equate romantic love with happiness:

> Hail, love, young love, cream of all earthly bliss—
> The silken down of happiness complete (*Anglo-African 286*)

"Cream of...bliss," and "silken down of happiness" are astonishingly sensual and sensuous images. Defining love in such physical and yet idealistic poetic terms directly rejects ideas of creatures brutalized and stultified by slavery. It also displays learning in literature and the kind of polish that encourages readers to assume a narrative has been constructed with care.

The narrator follows this lyric with the declaration that slavery has not "blotted out the kingly passion" of a man's love for a woman. Then the author goes farther, to argue that sensibility and finely honed emotions are more characteristic of African Americans than of Euro-Americans. "These children of the sun," the narrator says,

> love as the white man cannot; and in blasted love, anguish as the white
> man cannot.... Many a white man, owner, or overseer, relying on the
> apparently soft and subdued character of their slaves, have invaded
> the slaves' married bed, and met the bloody end they deserved.
> (*Anglo-African 286*)

In the tradition of sentimentality of the era in which this story was published, the evidence of refinement was the ability to feel finely and deeply; the mark of masculinity was chivalrous defense of women's honor. "Patrick Brown's First Love" reverses the usual racial hierarchy.

Evoking the traditions of romance and chivalry with sentimental lyrics coupled with idealized masculinity may seem imitative of European and Euro-American literary tradition. However, if one reflects briefly on other fiction published in the Afro-Protestant press at that time, it is clear that "Patrick Brown's First Love" also fits readily into the African American tradition of heroic bad men. It takes only a slight twist of the plot to make this story a version of Martin Delany's "Blake," also published serially in 1859 in the same magazine, or of Frederick Douglass's "The Heroic Slave," published in 1853.

Patrick Brown is born a slave. He "was never emancipated; he never ran away; was not brought into a Free State by his owner; yet he grew free in the far South. Slavery got tired of him—would have nothing to do with him—while he was young and in his prime of health and strength" (*Anglo-African* 287). Patrick Brown "had been sold many times," but each time his abusive owner had met a mysterious death. Brown was suspected but never implicated. And yes, we learn that Brown did in fact kill each owner. But why? Because of love. "In his early youth," Patrick had loved Keziah with a love that was "passionate and boundless." Keziah loved Patrick, too. "The twain were one in all time and forever, and they were purified in the very depth and truthfulness of their love" (*Anglo-African* 288). But Keziah and Patrick were enslaved. In fact, they were part of a coffle being transported for sale when one of the slave traders began to sexually harass Keziah. First he tried to seduce her, but Keziah ignored him. Then he threatened her. She resisted. Finally, he had Keziah bound, gagged, and carried to a wagon that was set a little way apart from the others. That night the man went in, but no sounds of struggle or resistance were heard. Late the next morning, when still no sounds were heard, one of the other drivers pulled aside the curtain. "There lay the slave-driver, disemboweled; and there, unstained by his guilty touch, with death— beautiful; oh! how beautiful!—on her virgin brow, lay Patrick Brown's first love" (*Anglo-African* 288).

The story leaves no doubt that Patrick Brown killed the man. It is not clear exactly why or how Keziah also died. Since it is an antebellum convention that really pure and pious women would die before submitting to rape, it is likely that readers were supposed to assume she swooned and perished, like all good heroines. Since the story focuses on Patrick Brown, Keziah is a literary device that works better dead. What is important is to see in this story is that Patrick Brown did not watch and meekly hang his head when his beloved was endangered. He took action by killing her assailant. Thereafter, the narrative says, Patrick Brown was a dutiful slave as long as he was treated decently. But if anyone treated him disrespectfully, that person would suffer a fatal accident. Soon no one would buy Brown. He was left free to come and to go as he pleased. Brown's freedom, however, came at a terrible price—the loss of his first and only love. He never loved another woman. So the reader is left at the end to recall words written at the story's beginning: "Most of the deeds of violence perpetrated by the slaves, which reach the newspapers, have this passion [a beloved partner] as their source; and thousands of fierce, brave revenges, which never reach the public ear, are prompted in like manner" (*Anglo-African* 286).

"Aurore Pradère," "Love in a Time of Hate," and "Patrick Brown's First Love" each tells a story in which antebellum African Americans defy the advice of friends and the assaults of foes to claim the lover of their choice. They, and others like them, are love stories of resistance, loving deeply, and guarding fiercely the right to choose the objects of one's affection. Frances Ellen Watkins's "The Two Offers" gives a different angle on one's right to choose and the responsibility of choosing wisely. I do not believe it is a coincidence that the editors of the *Anglo-African Magazine* placed Harper's story immediately after "Patrick Brown's First Love." Much about the two stories seems almost completely contradictory. Brown is the heroic rebel or badman of folktales, while Harper's heroines seem Victorian to the extreme; but both illustrate less than happily-ever-after consequences of choosing whom to love. Both assume that the right to choose one's life partner, or not, is a fundamental human right. Patrick Brown and Keziah choose to love despite the vulnerability of being enslaved. When Keziah dies, Patrick Brown chooses not to love again. "The Two Offers," on the other hand, affirms women's right to choose whether and whom to marry.

When the story begins, Janette is knitting and Laura is writing letters. Laura, in fact, has been writing and tearing up the same letter for more than an hour. Janette asks about this strange behavior, and Laura replies that she has two marriage proposals, and both are "very good offers." Still, Laura confides, "But, to tell you the truth, I do not think that I regard either as a woman should the man she chooses for her husband." Janette replies that Laura should reject both. When a woman cannot decide between two offers, it is a sure sign that something is wrong. Janette says a forced decision or choosing the lesser of two evils does not indicate "a union of hearts" but "a mere matter of bargain and sale, or an affair of convenience and selfish interest." But Laura fears she might not get a better marriage offer. "But then if I refuse," Laura says, "there is the risk of being an old maid, and that is not to be thought of" (*Anglo-African* 106). Laura learns too late the truth of Janette's warning that a more dreadful fate would be "the intense wretchedness of an ill-assorted marriage" (*Anglo-African* 106).

Both women have to make a choice about marital partners under less than optimal circumstances. At first, Laura does not love either man, but she knows that "many a girl would gladly receive" either proposal. She is influenced by external forces, and she convinces herself that she does love one of them. She chooses unwisely and pays with her life. Janette's situation is different. The details are sketchy, as the story puts its emphasis on how her suitor makes her eyes flash and her cheeks flush, how he arouses in her "rich, warm, gushing affections." But earlier she had discovered something that was too serious to overlook, and she chose with her intellect rather than her throbbing heart. Janette had learned that a woman can be fulfilled and can make important contributions without being married.

"The Two Offers" is not antimarriage. It is pro–wise choices. Janette's advice to Laura is both sensible and wise. She once loved "deeply, wildly, passionately," but then a "shock" cast a "shadow" between her and her beloved. She ended their romance. She did not marry but turned her passion and her intelligence toward working as a writer and social activist devoted to antislavery and equal rights. At the story's conclusion, Janette "was an old maid, no husband brightened her life with his love, or shaded it with his neglect. . . . No one appended Mrs. to her name." But "as old age descended peacefully and gently upon her, she had learned one of life's most precious lessons, that true happiness consists . . . in the regulation of desires and the full development and right culture of our whole natures" (*Anglo-African* 114).

"The Two Offers" does not challenge the idea that marriage is a valid and imitable religious and social institution. It does suggest that neither social status nor physical passion should be reasons to marry. "The Two Offers" argues against the idea that marriage is the only or best choice for a woman. And it models a successful, respectable, and happily nonmarried woman whose legitimate domain is in the public sphere. Harper's characters are antebellum African Americans of the free middle class. Accordingly, their options were different from those of enslaved or lower class African Americans. But the message about love and marriage is the same. The best marriages are made when love is freely given and the partners are well chosen.

Harper's story was probably motivated by and in opposition to social expectations that were another kind of enslavement. Historical evidence as well as the frequency with which marriage announcements were published in the African America newspapers show that at least among the free privileged population, African American men, as much as women, probably needed to make heterosexual marriages to establish their respectability. Such marriages could provide children whose labor or social accomplishments could benefit their parents, but they seem also to have been essential symbols of civility.[5] Emma Lapansky's study of African American ideals of "success" and the "good life" in antebellum Philadelphia applies to other free communities as well. Lapansky reports that in 1860 there were more than 22,000 African Americans in Philadelphia. Most "were not literate, not published, not documented in any newspaper, not members of a literary or beneficial society. They owned no real estate...watched no clocks, played no pianos, read no books.... Perhaps as many as half were without mates."[6] But among the "public men," those who wrote, lectured, and generally created and preserved African American print culture, "all but seven were in stable marriages," and both husband and wives were "church organizers, writers, teachers and performers" (Lapansky 8).

Obviously, not all antebellum African Americans were in the position to choose between two or more offers. Not all could choose if or when they would marry. But the literature shows that if antebellum African Americans had the right to choose their mates, they judged it a privilege worth protecting. Often the price was exceedingly high. In his *Narrative*, Frederick Douglass relates the story of his Aunt Hester, who was repeatedly whipped until she was covered with blood.[7] Her crime was that she continually defied her owner by sneaking away to meet her enslaved lover, Ned, who lived on a neighboring farm. Douglass gives a long, graphic description of the first time he witnessed his aunt's torturous punishment. When Douglass writes about his Aunt Hester, one of the few incidents he includes about his relatives, he says he was "terrified and horror-stricken" because he "expected it would be my turn next." He does not elaborate, but his response is clearly related to the cost of choosing one's own love and his knowledge that he, too, would insist on that right. And he did. Although he was an enslaved man with little or no material goods, he chose to consort with free African Americans. He met Anna Murray, a free and self-supporting woman of color, at a literary society. As a free woman with property, Anna Murray was outside of Douglass's social class, but they shared a certain predisposition to defy convention and law. Anna helped Frederick escape to New York, where they married. Frederick was not always able to provide for or to protect his wife and five children. At times, they were separated for weeks, months or years. But Frederick and Anna had chosen one another, and they also chose to remain married until her death did them part.

When they could not marry whom they chose under circumstances of their own choosing, some enslaved people chose not to marry at all. The man Harriet Jacobs—an enslaved woman—loved was a free man and a carpenter. He would have purchased her if he could. He would have married her regardless of whether she was enslaved or not. But her owner refused permission for them to marry. Instead, he told Harriet she could choose a husband from among the enslaved men he owned. She retorted, "Don't you suppose, sir, that a slave can have some preference about marrying? Do you suppose that all men are alike to her?"[8] Her enraged owner threatened that if her carpenter and she were ever seen together again, he would shoot them both. The owner could keep them apart, but he could not control their hearts. Jacobs never married.

William Wells Brown had a different problem. Mrs. Price, the woman who claimed to own him, wanted Brown to marry because she believed marriage made enslaved people less likely to try to escape. Brown thought so, too, and for that reason, he was determined not to marry as long as he was enslaved. But Mrs. Price was determined to get him a wife. She first tried to convince him to marry Maria, an enslaved woman she owned. Brown observed: "getting married, while in slavery, was the last of my thoughts; and had I been ever so inclined, I should not have married Maria, as my love had already gone in another quarter."[9] Believing that Brown loved Eliza, another enslaved woman, Mrs. Price purchased her and tried to arrange their marriage. William Wells Brown writes that "the more I thought of the trap laid by Mrs. Price...by getting me a wife, the more I determined never to marry any woman on earth until I should get my liberty" (*Brown* 412). Brown doesn't say how much choice Eliza had, but the point here is something else: sometimes enslaved people could exercise some freedom as to whom they would marry and when. Eventually Brown was able to escape (without Eliza). After that, he chose a bride for himself.

Noah Davis shows that religious compatibility was vital to his choice. He had known for many years the woman he eventually married. They had the same circle of friends, but he declares "nothing of a special liking had manifested itself until the day she was baptized."[10] He regards his wife "as the special gift of God to me" and testifies that though they were both enslaved and to different owners at that time, they have "lived happily together, as husband and wife, for the last twenty-eight years" (*Davis* 27). That the Reverend Noah Davis suggests that God chose his partner for him may be marked up to his writing his personal history as "Pastor of the Sarasota Street African Baptist Church [in] Baltimore"; except that his attitudes are echoed in the narratives of others who were not church officials.

UNSPEAKABLE THINGS UNSPOKEN

Some stories about love and choices were deliberately suppressed at times by antebellum African Americans themselves, for as William Wells Brown wrote, "people, generally, don't like to tell their love stories to everybody that may think fit to ask about them" (*Brown* 412). Other times, stories embarrassed or offended sensibilities. Some were rude, crude, or pornographic. Some were politically counterproductive. For example, virtually every recorded story of deliberate and defiant choice of spouse from the antebellum period, whether it is of African Americans or other Americans, refers clearly and unambiguously to heterosexual, monogamous marriages. But was love limited to heterosexual couples? Did marriage only mean one man and one woman? When we ask such questions, the silence is thunderous. While early African American print culture is replete with references to love, courtship, marriage, gender, and parenting roles, it is seriously silent about questions of sexual orientation. Yet it is common sense to assume that not all African Americans were heterosexual and not all marriages were monogamous.

The silence in African America is complicated by the silence that prevails in U.S. history more generally. While common conversations among antebellum Euro-Americans and a good amount of everyday discussion in African America concerned morality, modesty, and chastity, "mum" seems to have been the word when it comes to same-sex relationships. As in other segments of antebellum U.S. society, there are hints that African American communities recognized enduring, personal relationships that were not heterosexual. It is not clear, however, to what extent homosexual or lesbian relationships were actually sanctioned in African America. In her article "Female World of Love and Ritual," Carroll Smith-Rosenberg explains how feelings and physical behaviors between women that we today would consider as sexual or erotic were not so interpreted in the nineteenth century.[11] And Carolyn Sorisio affirms, in *Fleshing Out America* that "until 1880 most same-sex relationships, even when extremely close or sensual, were assumed to be 'devoid of sexual content.' "[12] But until recently, scholarship on sexuality in antebellum African America was virtually nonexistent. What exists thus far has yet to offer much beyond speculation based on hypotheses, factual fragments, contemporary connotations, and the fervent desire to approve or disprove a particular thesis. For example, some stories insist that homosexuality is a learned behavior resulting from European pollution of the African. But neither biological science nor social science supports the idea that desires for love and family are, or ever were, restricted to unions between females and males. Sociologist Orlando Patterson acknowledges that "in every known human society, a small minority of men are homosexuals," and that "Southern society was highly honorific, with a considerable degree of male bonding and homoerotic male play." He says this, however, in relation to the scant references to homosexual assault. He may have meant only to suggest that enslaved men were not exempt from sexual exploitation. Biographers have sometimes hinted at same-sex sexual abuse. William S. McFeely implies that Frederick Douglass was sexually abused by his master, and Nell Painter Irwin suggests that Sojourner Truth was sexually abused by her mistress. Basically, speculation on same-sex relationships, especially by African American scholars, seems limited to instances of sexual exploitation.

James Oliver Horton, former president of the Organization of American Historians, is one of the few African Americanists who alludes to homosexuality as a normal aspect of culture. In writing about same-sex organizations, Horton notes the possibility that disciplining heterosexual interactions was but one reason for gender segregation. He describes the numerous male-only organizations, the camaraderie among sailors and other workers who lived in male-only boarding houses, and other informal congregations such as those at barber shops and hotels as sites where masculinity was defined and explored. "The informal groups generally built their activities around card playing, drinking, and storytelling,— all-male activities that created a bond." Horton notes also that especially among free working-class African Americans, marriage was viewed with ambivalence. He tells, for example, of a man named Fletcher who married and moved from Boston's North End, where he had lived with his male friends, to "the more family-oriented black residential area of

Beacon Hill." Horton says that Fletcher's friends were both "amused" and "saddened" when Fletcher 'got married, got religion, and moved to the hill.' "[13] Horton does not explicitly state that the bonds of what he calls "black male groups" were anything more than fraternal; however, he leaves open the possibility that then, as now, they provided havens for men who preferred to be with men. We might safely imagine that if homosexuality and bisexuality were not accepted, they were, especially if discreet, at least tolerated (Horton 111–12).

Analysis of court cases and laws discovers suggestions of consensual interracial or homosexual relationships. A. Leon Higgenbotham Jr., writes that a 1662 statute reads "if any Christian shall commit fornication with a Negro man or woman, he shall pay double fines." He interprets this and other examples as ways that interracial marriages and sex were proscribed in the colonial period.[14] Higgenbotham was not focusing on same-sex relationships between African Americans, but the law indicates that fornication occurred with men and with women. It forbids "Christians" from having sex "with a Negro man or woman." It does not forbid Christian men from fornicating with "a Negro...woman" and Christian women from fornicating "with a Negro man."

Analysis of legal history discovers many indictments or prohibitions against "sodomy" generally. However, Jonathan Ned Katz notes, "two sodomy case reports and two sodomy statutes are the only relevant early colonial documents known to refer to the presence of Blacks, though by about 1680, Africans constituted the second largest occupational group after yeoman farmers"[15] In legal history, same-sex relationships are treated as deviant and criminal. But Katz also notes that certain acts of sexual violence, such as the rape of a black woman or servant women, were not considered criminal. This might explain some of the legal silences.

We should not interpret silence, however, as proof of absence. As Katz eloquently writes, "the interdiction, suppression, prohibition, and taboo—the silences about the same-sex erotic—are not accidental absences, but are produced, like speech" (Katz *Almanac* 163). To understand realistically ways freedom of speech confronted censorship, how decorum closeted libido, Katz counsels us to think about "sex-talk, sex-silence, and sex itself." Such meditation is vexed by time and intents. One reason little discussion of homosexuality is found in antebellum writing is that the very concept of "homosexuality" as it is known today was invented in the postbellum period. The deeds may have been the same, but the words were not. As I read antebellum writings, I am struck by how the same words or associations are used for the despised and disreputable, the poor and the outcast. For example, I notice that "degraded," "degenerate," and "depraved" are regularly used in the antebellum United States to describe same-sex relationships and to describe African Americans. The continued equation of African American women and men with lust, promiscuity, and sexual excesses could include some homoerotic calculations as well. In thinking about same-sex love, homoerotic relationships, wedlock, bonding, and lifelong commitments, we need to remember that the words used in the antebellum era are not necessarily those we use now. The words we use today to describe certain behaviors may not be appropriate for how that behavior was interpreted or intended then. Accurate interpretation requires careful attention to historical context. Still, the effort expended is rewarded by our enhanced ability to tell the stories that somehow must be told.

DO ADDIE AND REBECCA PRESENT A PROBLEM?

In the early 1990s, Karen V. Hansen found a cache of letters written between 1859 and 1869 by Addie Brown and Rebecca Primus, two women of free African America.[16] Primus's letters were to her family and are very useful for their depiction of the day-to-day life of a middle-class African American schoolteacher during the Civil War. The majority of the letters and the ones that have created the most stir are from Brown to Primus. Since Primus's letters to Brown have not been found, we have only Brown's version of their relationship. But Addie Brown's letters are provocative and suggest ideas about physical intimacy and marriage that literature written for publication does not. For example, Addie wrote to Rebecca:

> O my *Dear* Friend how I did miss you last night I did not have any one to hug me and to kiss Rebecca don't you think I am very foolish I don't want anyone to kiss me now I turn Mr Games away this morning no *kisses* is like yours....you are the first Girl that I ever *love* so and you are the *last* one. Dear Rebecca do not say anything against me *loving* you so for I mean just what I say O Rebecca it seem I can see you now casting those loving eyes at me if you was a man what would things come to they would come to something very quick what do you think the matter don't laugh at me I not exactly crazy yet. (*Beloved* 21)

And on November 17, 1860, Addie wrote:

> O my Dear Dear Rebecca when you press me to your Dear bosom...happy
> I was, last night I gave any thing if I could only layed my poor aching head on
> your *bosom*. O Dear how soon will it be I can be able to do so....Dear Rebecca
> when I am away from you I feel so unhapy the hours and days are like weeks
> & month will that day ever come when I can be with you oftener....I rather
> have my head on your lap then pencil the few lines to you We can't always
> have what we want can we My Dearest love! (*Beloved* 24–24)

Is this evidence of what we today define as a lesbian relationship?
Maybe. Maybe not. As we know from experience and as many scholars
have reported, same-sex relationships have different modes of expression and interpretation in different cultures and different times. Clearly
these two women enjoyed what Karen V. Hansen calls "bosom sex." That
is, they shared passionate kisses, cuddled, and slept together, but there
is no evidence that they ever shared or desired genital contact. Does les-
bianism as it is known today require genital contact? The editor of the
Brown-Primus letters, Farah Jasmine Griffin, writes: "there are things
about Rebecca and Addie that remain mysterious. Hopefully they will
continue to be taken up by readers, historians and poets, and other such
mythmakers and image weavers" (*Beloved* 194).

Other letters from Addie describe flirtations, courtship, and her marriage. She wrote to Rebecca on March 5, 1862, "My Dear my old Lover
was here that eve after the company had [disperse] father was teasing
me and said he was going to tell Mr. Lee about him and I my Darling can
I help if the Gentleman will pay me attention" (*Beloved* 62). In another
letter about that same time, Addie wrote Rebecca:

> I rec two letters from Mr Lee they both came at once...he will remain
> in key West two or three months....He inquired very particular for your
> health and what do you think he wants to know what do you think of me
> tramp over his *heart* weather you approve of it are not he write very nice
> letter he said it will not be long before he will return and make me his wife
> he said that he has met with great many Ladies since he is begone but none
> compare with his sweet Addie he says his love is stronger than ever. Dear
> Rebecca I never shall love any person as I do you. (*Beloved* 63)

Another letter to Rebecca from the woman Addie calls "Aunt Chaty" suggests that Addie's relationships with Primus and with Lee were socially
acceptable and complementary. Aunt Chaty wrote that without Primus

or Lee, Addie looks "so sad and melencahly," as if she had lost all her friends. But, Aunt Chaty wrote, when Addie got two letters from Lee, "I never seen anyone so overjoyed as she was…you say you do not know what love is Addie does I can assure" (*Beloved* 63). Addie's letters to Rebecca are full of protestations of love and affection, descriptions of physical intimacies of the past and future. They also describe similar intimacies or invitations to such from other women. But Addie begins her letters to Rebecca with salutations such as "My Darling Sister," "My Dear Sister," and "My Beloved & Cherish Sister." She regularly closes her letters to Rebecca with "From your Darling Little Sister," "Your Darling sister Addie," and "Your affect daughter & Sister R. P."

A letter of August 31, 1861, is important to our interpretation of this relationship. Addie addresses Rebecca here as "My Dear Friend." Apparently, they had argued about the reciprocity of their emotional attachments. Addie wrote:

> You would like to know my feelings towards you…it seems strange that you should ask such a question did you think that I did not *love* you as much as I profess or what was it?…I felt hurt.…I try to forget it as you ask me to do but ever time I come near you I thought of it and thought perhaps you did. you spoke in the manner that you could not trust me out of your site for that I would do most anything if I did not think you would hear of it my Darling that not so for I'm not ashamed to do anything that was proper in your site or out of your site.…I tell you how I feel towards you that is this like a Child would feel toward a Mother [who] has forbidden any Gentlemen to go with her Daughter and she *loves* her *Mother* to that extent that you don't want to displease and still she would like to have her say in that line…(*Beloved* 44–45)

There are about 150 letters from Addie to Rebecca written between 1859 and 1868. They describe numerous dates, conversations, courtships, and engagements with men. In 1867, Addie is engaged to Joseph Tines and writes of a rival "Miss L." "I write a very plain letter to Joseph about Miss L.," she confides to Rebecca. "He got to do one thing or the other. Think he was not to go and see her or even correspond with her, if so I should give him up.…so he has promise not to have anything to do with her" (*Beloved* 227). Addie Brown married Joseph Tines in April 1868. Apparently it was a happy marriage but brief. Addie Brown Tines died January 11, 1870. Rebecca later married Charles Thomas, a close friend she had made when she lived in Maryland.

To interpret the relationship between Addie and Rebecca as lesbian, homosexual, bisexual, or even sexually experimental would be fraught with difficulty. Most scholars agree that what we define as homosexual today in the United States is not defined as such in other parts of the world and was not defined as such in U.S. culture in other eras. It is clear, however, that African Americans were no lest apt than other people to have intense, lasting, and emotionally fulfilling same-sex relationships. Kevin Everod Quashie's discussion of the "idea of the girl friend" in contemporary African America can be helpful only if applied cautiously. Quashie writes: "to be loved, to be held, to remember: these basic human impulses, sprawling and imprecise, are each metaphors of selfhood."[17] He argues that preservation of one's essential humanness often requires the rejection of externally imposed definitions or disciplines and the acceptance of personal and interpersonal identities and relationships that fulfill human impulses to loved, held, and remembered. One way this can be done, Quashie argues, is through a "loosely conceptualized lesbian identity" that "disrupts the idea of an oppositional and narrowly defined Black femaleness that is in complete service to intersections of whiteness and maleness—and, instead, offers an expression of Black female relationality, a kind of self-centeredness that is a necessary political gesture" (Quashie 5).

The silences around interracial and multiple-partnered or shared marriages are a bit different. It is more akin to seeing two elephants in the middle of the bedroom, pretending not to see them, but walking around them with such care as to call forth attention. The white elephant does provoke *sub voce* stories focusing on rape and coercion as the reasons for certain people being treated better or worse, being sold or not sold, and being isolated from or marginal to the African American communities. But it takes only a little searching to uncover a fairly regular series of cautionary tales in which love across the color line exists generally briefly and tragically.

Fiction such as William Wells Brown's *Clotel* (1853) and Frank J. Webb's *The Garies and Their Friends* (1857) suggest there is no inherent reason to prohibit love and marriage between people of different ancestry, but in U.S. society such affairs are doomed. Emily Garie's African ancestry is barely visible, but she and her Euro-American husband, Clarence, live and work in African America. The Garies are well-educated, well-to-do financially, and the proud parents of two well-behaved children. They seem to have an ideal personal relationship, but both die as a result of racially motivated violence. Although Clotel is reputedly the child of Thomas Jefferson, she does have African ancestry and thus cannot legally marry her white lover, Horatio. However, they make promises to one another that allows Clotel to consider herself married in God's eyes and she lives happily in the cottage he bought her. They have a child and for a while, their relationship is fairly Edenic. But, Horatio eventually marries a Euro-American woman who can be the wife required by his social and political ambitions. Clotel considers her marriage defiled and though she loves him, she refuses to live as a concubine. Clotel's unhappy existence ends when she jumps off a bridge. However, their daughter, Mary, does find happiness and legal marriage with a white man in Europe. Julia C. Collins, writing during the war years, may have intended a different ending for her interracial couple in *Curse of Caste* (1864); however, she died before completing the serialized story. William G. Allen's book *The American Prejudice against Color* (1853) is an autobiography. William Allen, a professor of Classics, meets the daughter of a colleague and becomes engaged to her. This romance, too, is thwarted by the violent reactions of those outside his circle of friends. His fiancé Mary King is kidnapped and imprisoned in her room. Allen narrowly escapes being tarred and feathered. Allen's memoir is unusual in that it explicitly argues against racial discrimination and for interracial marriage. Allen attributes the couple's sad situation, not merely to ruffians and ignorant racists. He indicts hypocritical abolitionists and liberals who would hire an African American professor to teach interracial classes, socialize with him in their homes, but refuse to support an interracial romance.

The second elephant is black, an African elephant. It was generally believed in antebellum U.S. America that sexual promiscuity and polygamous marriages were common in Africa. Allegedly, African men took many wives, including the widows of their near kin. When a woman's husband died or disappeared, she quickly found another mate. Some argued that licentiousness was a biological trait. Some declared that Africans were simply incapable of long-term affection or deeply held emotions. Common wisdom was given such practices and proclivities, African Americans had to be carefully controlled and ought never be allowed to mix freely in civilized society. Such notions gained some credibility from court cases, the writings of travelers, public officials, and self-styled experts on "the Negro." Documents and testimony from itinerant preachers, teachers, and even the Freedman's Bureau and the Union army, supported such notions with examples of freed slaves who had to be forced to give up their multiple spouses, marry legally, and stay married. Ira Berlin cites one such example in *Many Thousands Gone: The First Two Centuries of Slavery in North America,* as follows.

> Polygamy persisted. An Anglican chaplain in New York maintained that black people shunned Christianity "because of their polygamy contracted before baptism where none or neither of the wives also will accept divorce." The commitment to multiple wives became a point of conflict between black New Yorkers and Elias Neau, who, by his own admission, repelled potential converts "because they know that I often insist on the 7th commandment, and that I thunder against polygamy."[18]

Early African American print culture rarely addresses sexual behavior or polygamous or polygynous marriages directly; but, it does discreetly acknowledge some of the complications that stem from them. For example, statements about the propriety or circumstances for divorce or to the surprising reappearance of partners assumed dead or otherwise permanently departed imply that multiple or polygamous marriages did occur. Article 36 in the *Doctrines and Discipline of the African Methodist Episcopal Zion Church* decrees:

> No man who has two or more living wives, or woman who has two or more living husbands, shall be admitted a Member of our church, except they were unavoidably separated by slavery, so as to have not the least prospect of being together again in this life, or except the separation occurs on Scriptural grounds.[19]

To discern the stories by African Americans themselves about polygamy, polygyny, and other such sexual and marital practices, we must listen to the silences and we must read between the lines. This is best accomplished by understanding something about African American ways of communicating. For instance, knowing that what we see is not always all there is, understanding habitual uses of indirection, dissemblance and diversion, and always considering the source and the situation are necessary. Recalling that African America was forced into existence by a series of necessities and often shaped by creative expediency, we can reconstruct a context that might explain why some things were said or not. Meditating upon what we know from many sources, it seems incredibly ingenuous to think that the only modes of matrimony were monogamous and heterosexual. Some African Americans were Islamic or from tribal cultures that accepted or even advocated multiple wives or husbands. Enslaved people from cultures where polygamy had been restricted to those of the ruling classes or available only to those who could afford to support more than one household, ironically, were now able to emulate those whom they may have envied. Free or enslaved, extended families and multiple spouses could be the most practical way to live. Adults could pool their material possessions, share responsibilities for rearing children, and generally enhance the status of each individual through membership in a family unit that offered emotional and physical support. Under such circumstances, polygamy or polyandry would not necessarily offend or violate the cultural consciousness of all people of African heritages.

On the other hand, Africans in America sometimes found themselves between the rock of cultural values and the hard place of isolation. Scholars frequently note that exogamy taboos were more stringent among people of African ancestry than for many other U.S. groups. Whereas among the very wealthy, the very poor, and the very isolated peoples of European heritage, marriage between cousins or within a particular class, religion, or region might be preferred to mingling with outsiders, African American cultural norms strictly forbid such alliances.[20] Sometimes this taboo extended to fictive kin and tribal members. Herbert G. Gutman notes that folk songs and folk tales helped perpetuate a fairly extended incest taboo and cites several versions that warn of inadvertent marriages between mothers and sons or sisters and brothers. He cites songs such as the following:

> Sally's in de garden siftin'sand,
> And all she want is a honey men.
> De reason why I wouldn't marry,
> Because she is my cousin. (88)

Sometimes the supply of marriageable mates could not possibly meet the demand. Large plantations were actually the minority of slaveholding situations; most slaveholders owned from 5 to 20 slaves.[21] Often, those in small communities might all be one's kin. We can imagine, therefore, that in cases where ancestry or family connection was uncertain, many people would err on the side of caution rather than violate exogamous beliefs. Such caution would reduce the pool of eligible mates and increase the attraction of sharing.

Evidence suggests that polygamy was probably not a frequent arrangement, but that heterosexual monogamy was not always a viable option.

Putting the pieces together, we can reasonably assume that even though antebellum African American texts rarely, if ever, discuss polygamous or polyandrous marriages, some forms of shared marriages were at least tolerated.

The silence gets louder as we consider the social context of antebellum United States. As the nineteenth century progressed, conflicts increased over legal forms of marriage and circumstances of divorce. In the early 1830s, Joseph Smith founded a sect based upon his revelations, which included the legitimacy of polygamy. Purportedly, Smith himself married between 25 and 30 women, some of whom were sisters and some who were already married to other men. Plural marriage was not welcomed by the majority of U.S. citizens, thus the early Mormans, as they came to be called, were forced to migrate further and further into the frontier. There were numerous violent confrontations and in 1844, Joseph Smith was killed. However, neither the westward exile nor his assassination stifled belief in "celestial marriage" and other variations and the United States government was slow to enact legal sanctions.[22]

Mormons were but one of many religious or communal sects that resisted or refuted that definition. The Oneida communities, for example, adopted "complex marriages" and "ascending fellowship."[23] With "complex marriage," every female member of the community was married to every male member, and vice versa. If one wanted to live with another person, one had to use an intermediary to negotiate mutual consent. But a couple could not have an exclusive relationship. "Ascending fellowship" was a practice wherein young males and females were assigned mentors for their spiritual and sexual educations. These mentors were called Central Members and were generally much older. Female mentors, in fact, were postmenopausal. This was to avoid unwanted pregnancies while their male protégés learned to practice Male Continence, or sexual intercourse without ejaculation.

For most U.S. citizens marriage was a legal and usually religious union of two consenting adults. Neither Afro- nor Euro-Protestantism approved officially of such alternative arrangements. The Euro-Protestants and the general media were often hostile, if not inflammatory, against them. The Afro-Protestant press in contrast, seemed to avoid mentioning dissenters. In part this may have been because the sects and utopian movements were racially exclusive. There were exceptions, though, that prove the rule. Sojourner Truth lived for a few years at the "Kingdom of Matthias," a community whose leader, Robert Matthias, determined "match spirits" that ignored existing marriages and sometimes even the wishes of one partner. Matthias decided who would marry whom and for how long. Only two members were not match married. One was Sojourner Truth. Her biographer Nell Irwin Painter declares that both unmatched individuals "regretted being left out."[24] The point is not how many African Americans were actually involved in the experimental and alternative marriages and sexual relationships that cropped up all over the antebellum United States. The point is that Afro-Protestants were promoting their particular views of love and marriage within a larger social context that was not entirely unified on the topics of monogamous, lifetime marriages, and they were not unaware of this.

As twenty-first-century seekers of the truth, we will only discover portions thereof. We can never know precisely or unquestioningly what African Americans thought about love and marriage, about family and sexual morality, about their deepest, most personal desires and the expressions of those desires. Not only is historical reconstruction an impossible task, but African Americans found discretion the better part of valour. They didn't tell everything they knew, and what they did tell, they sometimes told slant. Still, their writings, especially when read in context and with an eye to what is not told, have much to teach us all. Without their perspectives, our mythologies and our histories will never be as complete as possible.

MARRY IN HASTE, REPENT AT LEISURE

Regardless of actual practices, the public story told in early African America was that marriage was a lifetime commitment made voluntarily by a woman and a man and that choosing a mate was critical for one's happiness. Bad choices made for bad lives. The Afro-Protestant press was replete with suggestions and lectures about how to choose a mate and how to make well-informed consent. It worked assiduously to warn the would-be married of the consequences of ill-informed choice. If tales were told about being married "until death—or distance" parted, it was to acknowledge the strength of the specter of involuntary separation, not to approve the act of separation. Every couple married knowing that circumstances could change and they might be parted by reasons other than death. The Afro-Protestant media acknowledge this in articles that wrestle with the consequences of involuntary separation. Antebellum

African American print culture more generally, in letters and memoirs, songs and court petitions, acknowledges that uncontrollable circumstances can and do intervene. But such acknowledgments are not the same as passive acceptance. Repeatedly, the historical narratives feature marriage as a lifetime commitment. In general, such writings support W. D. W. Schuremen's warning that "the disposition of the person selected cannot fail to fix your destiny." It urged careful consideration and informed decision making.[25]

Sometimes the harsh practicality of choices was decorated in effusive and sentimental language. In a letter published in the January 11, 1828, issue of *Freedom's Journal*, "E" advises that an ugly educated woman makes a better wife than "the illiterate beauty" and asserts:

> I am very much opposed to that state which is so emphatically termed single *blessedness*, and am of the opinion, that mankind do not arrive at that height of felicity allowed them in this world, until they have entered the Elysian grove of Hymen; yet I look upon marriage as the most solemn of all earthly engagements; it is a step on which depends the happiness for life of two rational beings, and should only be entered into after serious reflection on its consequences, and where two hearts are inseparately [*sic*] united with the bond of mutual and tender love. The vices and virtues, failures and imperfections in the characters of both parties should be familiarly known to each other; and opinion if this acquaintance has no influence in discovering the attachment, there is a promise of all that happiness, which the nuptial tie is eminently calculated to bestow.
>
> Where an union is effected under other circumstances, and merely for the sake of the magical charm which (in the heated imagination of youth) is connected with the names of *husband* and *wife*, the unexpected disclosure of casual faults, will beget disappointments; disappointments will beget inquietude; inquietude, distrust; distrust, jealousy; and jealousy exterminates love, gives birth to shame, and misery follows.

The author of an essay in the *Christian Recorder* for March 16, 1861, entitled "To Avoid a Bad Husband" uses more spare language but essentially argues the same point: marriage lasts for a lifetime, so choose wisely. The writer offers 10 rules to women. First, "Never marry for wealth." The list that follows warns against marrying an alcoholic, a man who is too handsome, or "a fop, or one who struts about dandy-like, in his silk gloves and ruffles, with a silver cane, and rings on his fingers." The final line of the essay addresses women indirectly but seems to sum up all necessary advice on how to become or how to choose a good wife: "In the choice of a wife, take the obedient daughter of a good mother."

The seriousness of marriage as a lifetime commitment and the consequent necessity for careful selection did not mean that writers never used ridicule or humor to make their points. Indeed, in the periodical press, jokes, satire, and sometimes just a bit of cynicism seem to greatly outnumber instances of more learned or reasoned discussions. A good example is this brief verse, written for *Freedom's Journal* of July 27, 1827, that defines some fairly common, if not valid, reasons for men to marry.

In youth, age, and manhood, three wives have I tried.
Whose qualities note have my wants all supplied:
The first, goaded on by the ardour of youth,
I woo'd for the sake of her person forsooth;
The second, I took for the sake of her purse;
And the third—for what reason? I wanted a nurse.

Frances Ellen Watkins's "Advice to Girls" puts the advice of many more ponderous editorials humorously and succinctly.[26]

Wed not a man whose merit lies
     In things of outward show,
In raven hair or flashing eyes
     That please your fancy so.
But marry one who's good and kind,
     And free from all pretence;
Who, if without a gifted mind,
     At least has common sense.

The antebellum Afro-Protestant press balanced advice about how to choose with examples of how not to choose. It frequently used as negative examples single individuals whom it calls "old maids" and "old bachelors." In "The Old Maid's Diary," published November 2, 1827, in *Freedom's Journal,* the supposed excerpts begin at age 15: the young girl is "anxious for coming out and the attention of the men." At age 23, she "flirts with every young man she meets" and at age 24 "wonders she is not married." An old maid, the wise reader learns, makes a series of mistakes that start with being overly anxious to begin the courting ritual. Marriage is for adults. Fifteen-year-olds are too young for such concerns. Anxiety to begin courtship can translate into indiscriminate flirting. Such behavior leads to antisocial behavior and does not attract husbands. At age 38, the "Old Maid" "likes talking of her acquaintances who are married unfortunately and finds consolation in their misfortune." Being single leads to debauchery for some. At 41, the story says, "if rich, as a *dernier resot* [*sic*] makes love to a young man without fortune." The fate of those flirts who are not rich is left unspoken. At 50, the never-married woman "becomes disgusted with the world." And one might assume that the world is disgusted back or has forgotten she exists.

A week after "The Old Maid's Diary," *Freedom's Journal* published the tale "A Bachelor's Thermometer." A 16-year-old youth has "incipient palpitations towards the young ladies," and at 17 he experiences "blushing and confusion in conversing with them." At age 23, he "thinks no woman good enough for him." For the male, courting interest begins a bit later, but as with the girl who becomes an old maid, he starts to think about it too early and does not make a good impression. Courtship and marriage are concerns for adults, not children. At 23, the bachelor is arrogant, perhaps because indiscriminating flirtatious women distort his self-image and common sense. Whatever the cause, he fails to find an appropriate mate and at 35 "falls deeply and violently in love with one of seventeen," which at 36 ends with "*au dernier desepoir* another refusal." Equivalent to women's indiscriminate flirting is men's excessive egos. In either case, the problem is employing inappropriate standards for choosing a mate. At 46, the bachelor is "gouty and nervous symptoms begin to appear." Being single is unhealthy, as it is for the "old maid." Fearing to live alone and because gender allows different compensatory choices, at 51, the bachelor "hires a housekeeper as a nurse." But hiring a helper is not equivalent to having a helpmate. At 55, the bachelor is "completely under her influence and very miserable." The miserable old bachelor falls in love with his nurse; he wills her his property, but he dies before "espousing her." Delay in making a proper choice leads to loss of possessions and of male privilege. For both men and women, incorrect approaches to courtship make marriage less likely, but the single life does not fulfill the "Divine Mandate." Becoming an "old maid" or "old bachelor" leads to loss of health, happiness, and relevance in the world.

SIGNIFYING INSTANCES

African American storytellers mastered the art of making the desired moral plain by avoiding details. Another technique was to reverse the prevailing practice of racial markers. If the paragons of virtue, the heroes and heroines of their tales, were not assumed to be African Americans, nonetheless they could be. The tales did not usually mark the villains, the ignorant, and the pathetic as white, but they did describe ethnic or cultural contexts that identified ignorant or disreputable conduct with people of the lower classes, people of European descent, and people from exotic places. In other words, antebellum African Americans, especially in the Afro-Protestant press, used the rhetorical technique that linguists and anthropologists such as Claudia Mitchell Kernan and Geneva Smitherman define as "signifying." The papers published doubled-edged, multilayered messages that came cloaked in lamb's clothing. Like the Brer Rabbit stories, the press's coverage of inappropriate courtships is less naive and well-intentioned than is apparent to the uninitiated.

The very first issue of *Freedom's Journal* includes a report that "Ann W. Cheeny, of Onondaga country, has recovered $600 of Samuel R. Matthews, for a breach of marriage promise. He had visited her as a suitor for eight years, and it is said he is worth from 25,000 to 30,000 dollars." This story suggests, but does not spell out, an obvious caution. The article "Chinese Fashions" describes the bound foot as measuring "two inches and three fourths"—an example from abroad of the harm that ideas of beauty based on distorted marriage values can do. Similarly, "Choosing a Wife by Proxy" describes another harmful tradition, explicitly identified as Moravian.

The following notice provides humor but also demonstrates the absurdity of either sex thinking that "to have and to hold" means owning ones spouse:

> LOTTERY–Dangle, jr. of Virginia, offers himself as the Prize of a lottery, to all widows and Maids under 25—the number of tickets to be three hundred, at one Hundred Dollars each but one number to be drawn from the wheel, the fortunate holder of which is entitled to Himself and the thirty thousand dolls [*sic*]. (*Freedom's Journal*, January 24, 1829)

"Old Bachelors" (*Freedom's Journal*, February 21, 1829) begins: "A writer in the Ohio State Journal proposes instead of levying a tax on old bachelors, to declare them by law ineligible to any office of either power or profit." The social status of an "old" single man is that of being regarded "as our ancestors did a Jew, as one who has no claim to any favor or generosity at their hands." The editors of the paper say the source of this story is the *Dayton (Ohio) Journal*. Since the ancestors of African Americans were not likely to have treated Jewish people as their inferiors, referencing a

Euro-American publication suggests that "old bachelors," regardless of ethnicity are regarded as socially inferior.

The June 10, 1837, issue of the *Colored American* in New York City prefaces "The Intemperate Husband" with the note that it is excerpted from Mr. Charles Sprague's address, delivered before the Massachusetts society for "suppressing Intemperance." The *Christian Recorder* reports a discussion in the *London Times* that points out the foolishness of women who seek wealthy or handsome husbands, rather than "good" ones, These are all examples of the written version of the oral tradition known as signifying.[27]

So what does it matter that songs such as Aurore Pradere demonstrate that being "picky" is not something new for African American love and marriage and that some antebellum African Americans were "picky. Very picky"? Should we admire those like Joseph Antoine who were so besott by love that they would give up their freedom? True, slavery and indenture were not quite the same. An indentured servant was bound for a specified amount of time; enslavement was a life sentence that passed on for generations. But as the Antoine myth reveals, indentured service can sometimes become slavery. Is Antoine's a kind of love we should take as a model? Was he heroic or stupid? If you can't be with the one you love, then love the one you're with, right? Maybe not.

What does it earn us to know that antebellum African Americans took marriage very seriously? Perhaps knowing that marriage was highly valued in antebellum African America's primary investments will make us reconsider what the legacy of slavery is for African Americans. It encourages our resistance and perseverance today to know that in a time when slavery and racial discrimination ruled, when law, custom, political power, and theological teachings united to kill the spirits of people of African descent, some still chose the person they wanted and were determined to remain at that person's side, enabling not only survival but also resistance and the engendering of sustaining families, communities, and ultimately a nation. Love is one of the only experiences that an external force, regardless of its powerful ways and means, cannot deny people or dictate for them against their wishes. Such knowledge should be mulled over for its potential power to change or to encourage our behaviors and attitudes today.

THREE

Practical Thoughts, Divine Mandates, and the Afro-Protestant Press

We will remember November 4, 2008, as the day Barack Obama, a symbol of hope and unity, was elected president of the United States. But in California, many voters celebrated with mixed feelings. Californians had, as expected, voted for Obama; but the state had, as not expected, defeated Proposition 8, a measure to add these 14 words to the California State Constitution: "Only marriage between a man and a woman is valid or recognized in California." Anti–Proposition 8 proponents had tried to avoid religious issues and had campaigned instead on issues of civil rights, proclaiming that the proposed constitutional amendment would discriminate against homosexuals in the same ways other laws had oppressed African Americans. The strategy didn't work. Many, if not most, proponents of the measure believed they were involved in a holy war. Numerous reports detailed the immense financial contributions, multitude of volunteer canvassers, and the many sermons preached to help pass the measure. Post-election analyses identified the money and energy invested by the Church of Jesus Christ of Latter Day Saints and the Catholic Church proved to be major, maybe the primary, reasons the proposal passed. For example, in an article headlined

"Mormons Tipped Scale in Ban on Gay Marriage," the *New York Times* reported that the Roman Catholic archbishop of San Francisco persuaded Mormon leadership in Utah to join the political fight in California. Consequently, it was not particularly illogical that postelection analyses touted statistics that identified African American churchgoers as a significant voting block for the proposition.

Still, it is revealing that while they were unsurprised by the predominantly white Christian groups' behavior, many opponents of Proposition 8 saw the 70% approval rating of African American voters as an unfathomable betrayal. They had expected that a group long oppressed by laws that had thwarted their enactment of love and denied them marriage would respond to the calls of others identifying themselves as similarly oppressed. A comment included in an NBC newscast is typical of many: "I understand the African-American and Latino communities voted heavily in favor of Proposition 8. To them I say, shame on you because you should know what this feels like." The campaign against Proposition 8 underestimated the role religion plays in African American politics and ideas about marriage. Proposition 8 opponents' anger and disappointment toward African American voters could be mitigated were they to understand more about Afro-Protestantism.

In the twenty-first century, we tend to stress marriage as a legal contract with enormous practical implications. But historically Afro-Protestants have also believed that marriage is a Divine mandate. Laws can say what they will, but African Americans have long insisted on their own definitions and recognitions of marriage. This has been part and parcel of their determination to be free to love whom and how they wish. Many stories are told to support, to explain, and to enable African Americans' determination to carry out this Divine mandate while living in a society run by men who rejected this belief.

"A FEW PRACTICAL THOUGHTS"

On February 9, 1861, the *Christian Recorder* published a letter from W. D. W. Schureman that began this way: "Mr. Editor:—I propose writing a few practical thoughts on [marriage]....Marriage is the union of sexes, under matrimonial obligations. It is the proper mode to carry out a Divine mandate." Like *Freedom's Journal*, the *Colored American*, the *Repository of Religion and Literature and Science and Art*, the *Pacific Appeal*, and virtually every periodical published in antebellum African America, the *Christian Recorder* is part of the antebellum Afro-Protestant press, the institution that was the heart and soul of African American publishing.

The term Afro-Protestant press encompasses publications and publishing companies, editors, owners, authors, sales representatives, printers, and other employees. From its beginnings in 1827 to 1861 and afterward, the Afro-Protestant press gave particular attention to education, morality, and civic responsibility. Letters to the editor, such as that by W. D. W. Schureman, regularly advertised, advised, admonished, and taught about love, marriage, weddings, and other aspects of domestic life. They were part of an arsenal of literary forms that included reports and essays, sermons, advice columns, announcements, stories, poems, and jokes, all of which defined and encouraged a pragmatic politics of respectability and education as well as ideals, visions, dreams, and theological directives.

W. D. W. Schureman's "Thoughts on Marriage" is fairly typical of the ideals or official positions taken by antebellum African Americans on this topic. But the official or ideal, as even Schureman acknowledges, was not that popular. "How few understand the great and important object of matrimony," he wrote. "Some think it is to unite with a pretty or handsome person, or to satisfy amative desire; to accumulate riches, to show our independence, and thereby spite others; to have a home, to have a cover, to appear like others." Trying to teach readers the dangers of popular attitudes and behaviors, Schureman focuses most of his essay on the grief that comes from marrying for the wrong reasons and thus choosing the wrong mate.

The basic assumption in Schureman's letter, as in the numerous examples given in chapter 2, is that marriage should be lifelong commitment. It follows that he would declare "a misstep in marriage" to be "one of the greatest curses known to domestic life, or the public community." His essay is an effort to help readers avoid such tragedies by reminding them of the real purpose of marriage. "The object of matrimony," he explains,

> is to glorify God; under its varied facilities to serve him with our body and spirit, which are his. Thus preparing ourselves for usefulness here and heaven hereafter; to train up our children in the way they should go, so that when they become old they may not depart from it.

In 1861, when Schureman wrote his "Thoughts on Marriage," gender and family issues were frustrating most people in the United States.

The exigencies of the Civil War, like those of all wars, required extreme changes in gender expectations. That war, perhaps more than others, also fractured families in unexpected and irrevocable ways. Relationships between and among men and women, males and females, single, married, and divorced demanded increasing attention, discussion, and negotiation. But race, always an underlying, generally unacknowledged presence, formed a *ménage a trois* with sex and marriage, complicating ideas about piety and purity, especially. The Afro-Protestant press had to navigate with special skill these choppy domestic waters. Much of what it would condemn was the very behaviors it did not want to acknowledge publicly. Respectability was essential for nonviolent political change. Writing about sex and reproduction, marriage and family, and morality overall was akin to fiddling on a roof covered with razor blades and broken glass.

Like other African Americans who sought with their writings to define and to discipline marriage in antebellum African America, Schureman believed marriage was a sacred and a sexual obligation. Mingling theology and common sense in didactic narratives, he tried to minimize the risks to social respectability and political equity that full revelation of the dissenting behaviors posed. Like many African American writers, he relied on his readers' abilities to understand the cultural connotations and contexts allowing them to decode deliberate understatement and ambiguity. "Marriage is the union of sexes, under matrimonial obligations. It is the proper mode to carry out a Divine mandate." Marriage is not intended "to unite with a pretty or handsome person, or to satisfy amative desire." In the context of "matrimonial obligations" and "amative desire," "union of sexes" clearly carries sexual connotations. "To have a cover, to appear like others" may allude to homosexual people as well as to those misguided into believing in "single *blessedness.* Reading this essay in its antebellum, "to show our independence, and thereby spite others" can refer to laws that forbid enslaved people to marry, as well as pointing to conflicts between African American leaders and Euro-American leaders over the proper forms and proper persons to authorize and to conduct marriages. This problem began in the colonial period and was still unresolved. These last few interpretations of Schureman's statements might seem a bit farfetched for what at first may appear fairly conventional, even conservative, assertions, until one considers them in relationship to others, such as "Matrimony," by Daniel Allen Payne ("D. A. P."), serialized in the "Young Ladies Lecture

Room" section of the *Repository of Religion and Literature and Science and Art* in 1859.[1]

Payne, a bishop of the AME Church, was without a doubt the most prolific and prescriptive writer about marriage and domestic life in African America. Like Schureman, Payne combined lofty theology with attention to physicality. Since Bishop Payne was a frequent contributor and a member of the *Repository*'s editorial corps, readers would have readily identified D. A. P. and invested his pronouncements with clerical authority. At the same time, "D. A. P.," being less formal than "Rev. Bishop Daniel A. Payne," has the immediate effect of decreasing the social distance between reader and writer and encouraging more intimacy and more personalized interpretations. Nonetheless, it strikes a discordant note, given the lofty tone of the overall essay. It is the first of several signals that the entire essay is consciously constructed toward particular ends. We would do well to remember Brer Rabbit, signifying, and other African American rhetorical conventions as we read.

Payne begins by describing the wedding preparations and preoccupations of engaged couples. Then he critiques them. Marriage, Payne admonishes, is more than ceremony and setting up housekeeping. It is more than a social or legal status. It is, Payne declares, "God's *Design*." To illustrate the divinely created marital prototype, Payne relates a story about the marriage of the first woman and the first man.[2] He begins with the substance of Genesis 2:21–22, describing God forming woman from the rib of sleeping man. He says that God brought the woman, "blooming in grace and beauty," to the man "for his helpmate, and gave them this command: 'Be faithful, multiply, and replenish the earth.'" These words are inaccurate and are quoted out of context. According to the King James Version of the Bible,[3] the language is "Be fruitful, multiply, and replenish the earth." Afro-Protestant theology favors fidelity to God's design or mandate as the first commandment of marriage; accordingly, Bishop Payne emphasizes the importance of being faithful, to God and to one another.

Payne's matrimonial origins story is important for more than the coupling of "faithful" and "fruitful." It deletes a critical part of the verse he quotes as God's mandate and blends two separate Edenic stories into one. The first part of Payne's narrative, which has Eve formed from Adam's rib comes from Genesis 2: 21–22. The second part comes from Genesis 1:26–31, which says God created male and female at the same time and blessed them both, giving them the same responsibilities. In

Genesis 1:28, God says "Be fruitful, and multiply, and replenish the earth, and subdue it: and have dominion over . . . every living thing that moveth upon the earth." Payne may have ignored the dominion requirement out of deference to the subordinated status of African Americans. In the antebellum United States, it would have seemed an impossible dream (or nightmare) to imagine that African Americans could or would subdue the earth and dominate every living thing, at least any time soon. To preach such would have been suicidal—and would not have won many converts to Christianity.

On the other hand, Payne waxes poetic, even erotic, about "God's *design*" for marriage: reproduction. He writes in terms that mingle the sensual with the sacred. Marriage is for procreation. The proper work of a wife and a husband, Payne asserts, is to create "holy beings like themselves, full of intellect, and full of love." This portion of his essay advances with quiet sensuality. Marriage was instituted in a place of "pristine beauty and purity." It was in "a garden filled with luscious fruits, and decked with flowers as beautiful as they were fragrant, gay with the perching, the flying, and singing of birds, whose plumage vied with the hues of the rainbow—the seat of happiness and immortality." The first man and the first woman loved God passionately, with all their hearts, souls, and might. The "breathing of their lips was praise; the pulsations of their hearts were adoration." Payne's narrator sounds as seductive as the serpent of Eden in this passage:

> Young woman, wilt thou be wise? Hear me then; sister, daughter, listen while I whisper in your ears the teachings of our holy religion. . . . Let me stir up in thy minds thoughts which will never sleep nor slumber—emotions which, swelling up from the heart's deep fountains, shall impel thee to such a course of action, as will result in good to earth, and glory to heaven . . . sweet one. . . . Mind I tell you there is a mystery in matrimony, which none can read but the initiated; which none can fully understand but the soul which is taught of heaven.

Close analysis of Daniel Payne's essay reveals several rhetorical strategies that combine to offer a biblical interpretation that is both lofty and earthy, idealized and realistic, candid and crafty. Had Payne been an unlettered preacher or inexperienced writer, it might be plausible to dismiss his word choice, selection of details, and conflation of two stories into one as an accident. But Daniel Payne was extraordinarily well educated and an inveterate writer skilled in several genres. A likelier reading is that Payne's "Matrimony" as an example of one of Afro-Protestantism's essential characteristics, "the combining of (1) biblical interpretation, with (2) magical transformation," the result of which is "a remarkably efficacious use of biblical figures, with a historically transformative and therapeutic intent, in the social imagination and political performances of black North Americans."[4] Gayraud S. Wilmore describes a combination of improvisation, realism, and critical silences that he calls a "curious mixture of zeal and carelessness." Wilmore notes that in antebellum Afro-Protestantism, the "dominant motif...was affirmation and joy—even carnal pleasure had its prominent place. Such a religion bound men and women to the organic, vitalistic powers of creation—to the powers that they believed could provide for and sustain [them]."[5] Such a religion underlies the definition of marriage, its goods, and its goals that Payne and other theologians preached.

Dissertations such as those by Payne and Schureman were not the only source of such stories. George Moses Horton's poem "The Cheerless Condition of Bachelorship" tells a similar tale. Horton begins by describing Adam as frustrated and ill at ease:

> When Adam dwelt in Eden's shades alone,
> He breathed to heaven a sad and piteous tone;
> For nothing pleasing yet the world displayed,
> Though he the blooming garden well surveyed.[6]

Horton, like many antebellum Afro-Protestants, combines pagan and Christian stories. He uses the second version of the Genesis creation story as the plot but includes Greek mythological characters such as Hymen, the god of marriages and weddings (son of Dionysus, god of wine), and Philomena (alternate name of Philomela, the nightingale). In Horton's poem, the biblical story of God causing a deep sleep to fall over Adam is detailed as God giving Adam an "opiate" before extracting one of Adam's bones. While asleep, Adam dreamed of a "queen of pleasure." When Adam awakened, "he gazed with rapture and surprise" upon a smiling "bridal vision." Horton describes what happens next:

> The birds of Hymen struck the wondrous song,
> And fragrant breezes flowed with peace along;
> Myriads of beasts flocked round their festive place,
> Which pranced and bellowed round the scene of grace.
> The Philomena tuned her lyric tongue,

And rung all night the hymenial song;
Such is the happy change of single life,
And such the pain of man without a wife;
No smiling dame his pleasure to divide,
A perfect stranger to a loving bride.

After extended description of the eroticism of marriage, Horton concludes his poem with descriptions of the frustration, loss, and "melan-
choly wile" that "man alone" experiences.

In part, because he was a poet and he was not writing for publication
in an Afro-Protestant periodical, George Moses Horton's Eden is explicitly sexual and the rewards of marriage are, too. Poetry, song, and folklore allow more metaphoric ambiguity and linguistic slyness. But social
change was also a factor. As time passed, the elation of the American
Revolution gave way to practical issues of national unity. Social fissures
and fixes were everywhere. Ralph Waldo Emerson describes the situation
in 1840 this way: "We are all a little wild here with numberless projects
of social reform. Not a reading man but has a draft of a new community
in his waistcoat pocket."[7] Gender, race, and class exacerbated the clashes
between the newly emigrated and the sons and daughters of the American Revolution.

In the antebellum period, marriage posed an increasingly complicated
political dilemma. The United States governing system was organized
around families. Marriage was a sign of social and civic responsibility.
Husbands were to be heads of households and wives were to stay inside
and turn houses into homes. But how could those who were poor and
couldn't afford even a cabin, who were women but had to toil in public spaces, who were politically vulnerable and without the vote fulfill
the obligations of marriage and family, and thus the state? Then again,
an acknowledged purpose of marriage was procreation. Wives would
be mothers. Husbands would be fathers. In this era, people of African
descent had far less control over their reproductive and sexual experiences than did Euro-Americans (whose practices in reality were not particularly commensurate with their theories anyway).

The Afro-Protestant press sought to replace popular stereotypes of
Africans as primitive, irresponsible, and lustful with proof of their civilized, disciplined, and moral behavior. But marriage meant reproduction,
and reproduction required sex. Writers such as Payne and Schureman
responded to increasing crises that came from slavery and from racist
science enabled by popular forms of eugenics and evolution by writing

more theoretically about marriage. As in other publications, discussions of the goods and goals of marriage were usually implied and interwoven with ideas of education, morality, politics, economy, and other aspects of life both private and public. The idea of marriage and reproduction, in Payne's words, as "God's *design*" or, as Schureman writes, "the proper mode to carry out a Divine mandate" was widespread in the United States generally. But Schureman laments, "few understand the great and important object of matrimony. Race, sex, gender, class, and good doses of independent spirits and just plain contrariness made definitions and discipline especially difficult. In nineteenth-century U.S. writing, marriage was again and again depicted as a communal or political contract and as an individual or religious covenant.

WEDLOCK AND REPRODUCTION

Afro-Protestantism and other African American religions, then as now, encouraged their adherents to appreciate marriage as the "proper mode to carry out a Divine mandate." Their communities sanctioned it and generally conferred preferred status to married couples. Autobiographical writings by African Americans provide helpful examples of how some negotiated the problems of respectability and fertility. The Reverend Samuel Ringgold Ward wrote in *Autobiography of a Fugitive Negro*, that

> in Newark, New Jersey, where I was living in January 1838...I was married to Miss Reynolds, of New York: and in October 1838 Samuel Ringgold Ward the younger was born, and I became, "to all intents, constructions, and purposes whatsoever," a family man, aged twenty-one years and twelve days.[8]

Ward's precise chronology has a purpose. He became "a family man" at the appropriately respectable age of "twenty-one years and twelve days." From January to October is 10 months, a precisely appropriate point in time for a respectably married couple to become a "family."

Marriage and children were inextricably bound in the minds of most nineteenth-century African Americans. Their writings show that children were important and proper parenting was a major priority. Their writings also reveal that many enslaved people refused to marry because they did not want to replenish the earth with enslaved people. By law, a child's status was determined by her or his mother's legal position.

Enslaved women's children were enslaved also. Some women did not have choices about whether to conceive or not. But for those who did, consent and consequences were central. Marriage was one small area in her life wherein a woman could usually exercise choice. She could "Just say no"—or "yes."

Elizabeth Keckley's *Behind the Scenes* (1868) demonstrates that refusing to marry was a form of birth control.[9] She does not specify exactly when she met George Keckley, the African American man she loved. She does relate that they were separated when her owner moved her from Virginia to Missouri. However, a two-year separation did not abate their love. She writes: "Mr. Keckley, whom I had met in Virginia and learned to regard with more than friendship, came to St. Louis. He then sought my hand in marriage; for a long time I refused to consider his proposal, for I could not bear the thought of bringing children into slavery" (Keckley 29). Spurred by her desire to marry George Keckley, Elizabeth badgered her owner to let her buy her freedom. Despite his vehement refusal and threats, Keckley persisted until Hugh Garland agreed to a price. She did not have the money. But she was a talented seamstress and believed she could earn it. As soon as she could foresee freedom—"taking a prospective glance at freedom" is how she phrases it—she "consented to marry Keckley" (Keckley 29).

As a married woman, Elizabeth Keckley, like other women, was still vulnerable to rape and coercion. In fact, when Elizabeth Hobbs agreed to marry George Keckley, she already had a son whom she loved dearly. Keckley felt sorrow but not shame about the circumstances of his birth. She dismisses in one paragraph four years of forced intimacy with a white man:

> I was regarded as fair-looking for one of my race, and for four years a white man—I spare the world his name—had base designs upon me. I do not care to dwell upon this subject, for it is one that is fraught with pain. Suffice it to say, that he persecuted me for four years, and I—I—became a mother. The child of which he was the father was the only child that I ever brought into the world. If my poor boy ever suffered any humiliating pangs on account of birth, he could not blame his mother, for God knows that she did not wish to give him life; he must blame that society which deemed it no crime to undermine the virtue of girls in my position. (Keckley 24)

Her child, she wrote, "could not blame his mother." Apparently others did not blame her either. The fact that Elizabeth had a child by a white man did not deter courtship. Nor did it impugn her respectability within Afro-Protestant society.

Running a Thousand Miles for Freedom shows that Keckley's evaluation of marriage and children was not unusual. William Craft wrote that the woman he loved, Ellen, refused to marry him because she

> had seen so many other children separated from their parents…that the mere thought of her ever becoming the mother of a child…appeared to fill her very soul with horror; and as she had taken what I felt to be an important view of her condition, I did not, at first, press the marriage, but agreed to assist her in trying to devise some plan by which we might escape from our unhappy condition, and then be married.[10]

Finally, when no escape plan seemed immediately feasible, while keeping "our dim eyes steadily fixed upon the glimmering hope of liberty, and earnestly pray[ing] God mercifully to assist us to escape from our unjust thraldom" (286), Ellen and William married.

Thomas W. Henry's narrative *From Slavery to Salvation* is yet another testimony to the fact that Elizabeth Keckley's and Ellen Craft's fears were neither uncommon nor unfounded.[11] Thomas W. Henry was a free African American, married to an enslaved woman. According to her owner's will, Thomas W. Henry's wife would be freed when she became 31 years old. However, any children she bore while enslaved would themselves be enslaved for life. The couple had four children before Thomas W. Henry was able to purchase them. He raised $900 and paid for his wife and the two youngest children. But then, Henry tells us, "the price of the poor colored people had increased, and the remaining two of my children (who were yet slaves) were sold. The last two that were sold were a boy and a girl" (Henry 61). For those to whom the concept of marriage was inseparable from reproduction, the additional sorrow of bringing children into a hostile world could serve as another reason to avoid marriage; however, even this did not stop lovers from making public vows of commitment or community leaders from advocating marriage.

AND THE MORAL IS?

Nineteenth-century African American newspapers and journals understood marriage as evidence of morality and godliness. Humorous articles, advice columns, letters, poetry, and stories about marriage written by women and men for Afro-Protestant publications and those reprinted from other sources are numerous. However, it seems that ministers were the primary authors of discussions about the whys and wherefores of marriage. Afro-Protestant ministers tended to define religious fidelity and marital happiness as inextricably joined. Marriage was "God's *design.*" It was a lifetime commitment and the prequel to creating families on and for which African America itself should exist and thrive. Legal or social conventions of other groups were secondary and binding only insofar as they were biblically based. At the same time, in many ways, the Afro-Protestant press defined the goods and goals of marriage similarly to those being espoused in Euro-America. Marriage was a "union of sexes" for the sake of procreation. Scenes of happy homes repeatedly feature a husband, a wife, and adorable young children around the hearth of a clean and nicely furnished home. Writers projected the ideal family as preferably Afro-Protestant but certainly Christian people whose daily prayers were for one another, their community, their country, and the world. Each member of the family had a defined role and a clear purpose in God's creation.

What these "thoughts on marriage" do not argue, however, is that the U.S. government or any other human authority has the final say. Laws of the land that proscribe or prohibit a marriage do not take precedence. Like Schureman, they, antebellum Afro-Protestants especially, defined marriage as a "Divine mandate." If the laws of the land or popular opinion were more permissive, Afro-Protestant spokespersons urged adherence to the more stringent rules they found in the Bible. For example, consider the words of the author of "The Subject of Matrimony and Divorce,"[12] a regular contributor to *Christian Recorderl,* who signed himself "Itinerant." "There are those among us who would have a popular church," he writes, "and in order for this, they say the laws of the land tolerate 'divorces," and allow persons to marry [again]." "Itinerant" even elaborates on the biblical injunctions by saying that while a spouse can be "put away" for specific transgressions, neither can then marry again.

This public position on marriage was quite similar to the view held in the larger nation. However, African Americans tended to be especially clear about the political risks that bad marriages brought. Bad marriages are detrimental to the entire community; thus, good choosing of spouses is imperative. At first reading, values in the Afro-Protestant press may seem much like those of middle-class Euro-Protestants, they are, however, subtle, significantly different in details, emphases, and interpretations.

For example, the goods of marriage were not so much the acquisition of property or consolidation of wealth as history says they were in Europe, Africa, and other parts of America. This is not to say such considerations were irrelevant. Even among the enslaved, marriage certainly could improve one's economic position. Many antebellum African Americans, including those in bondage, were industrious, ingenious, or lucky enough to be able to provide more for themselves than what they were given. Some became quite wealthy. While it might seem odd, even within slavery there was a class system that permitted skilled workers, including blacksmiths, nurses, cooks, and carpenters to acquire necessities, and sometimes luxuries, for themselves and for their loved ones. Being enslaved did not prevent some people from cultivating gardens, hunting, or fishing to supplement their diets and bartering or selling other goods. Enslaved people sometimes raised enough money to purchase livestock, real estate, themselves, or their loved ones. In antebellum African America, marriage to the right kind of person was very helpful, whether one was free or not.

Gender relationships were likewise more complex than the term *patriarchy* suggests. D.A.P.'s God may have created the female for the male, but He gave them equally the same mandate. They were to be "faithful (or fruitful), multiply, and replenish the earth." Such reproduction was not explicitly linked to sexual repression or monogamy. African American writers emphasize marriage as "the proper mode" within which reproduction should occur. They do not, however, emphasize biological paternity. Their stress was almost always on the responsibilities of married people to be good parents and to rear children "in the way they should go." It simply didn't make sense for them to embrace Euro-American laws about the legitimacy or value of children promulgated by the same legal system that defined 90 percent of African Americans as three-fifths human. This is not to say that antebellum African Americans did not value fidelity and family lines. Rather, they interpreted *fidelity* and *family* realistically. It also suggests that the decision to marry was more fraught for them and that choosing marriage in the face of so many complications meant that they really valued the ties that bound them together as couples and as families.

In the twenty-first century, we might mistakenly interpret such values as imitative of or acquiescent to Euro-centric ones. We must, however, remember that circumstances were quite different in the antebellum period. For example, "Am I not a man and a brother?" and "Ar'n't I a woman?" were not rhetorical questions. Many antebellum Americans were, at best, uncertain about that. Antebellum Americans were not happy about individuals who did not know or who challenged their "place" in society. Under those circumstances, those who mimicked their betters or consorted with their social inferiors were treated without sympathy. Harriet Beecher Stowe was an obvious example. Because she dared write publicly about political issues, she was branded as having "unsexed" herself. In such an environment, people of African descent who dressed, behaved, or spoke as Euro-Americans did were considered audacious and threatening. Even if an African American slavishly imitated ideals of marriage or family assumed to be Euro-American, that hued imitation was interpreted as bold and dangerous to the social order. And the situation is even more complicated than that. Some ideas and ideals have no provenance. Monotheism and capitalism, self-respect and communal responsibility with clearly defined roles for gender, age, and community or tribal status are essential values in cultures and countries around the world. It is ingenuous, parochial. and deeply ethnocentric to try to locate honesty, industry, respect, frugality, cleanliness, morality, literacy, and love exclusively in European or Euro-American cultures and to assume that others assimilated or converted such values from them.

As Africans became African Americans defined outside and against what was called "Americans," part of what they became was externally imposed. But a great part of what they became was consciously negotiated. It takes a lot of explanation, persuasion, and practice to create cultural consensus among thousands of people. In African America, as in other cultures, men and women did not always have compatible gender expectations. Parents and children did not always see eye to eye. Relatives and friends might interfere in marital matters. Politics, religion, economics, and education all influenced perceptions and opinions. Time, place, and circumstances all change continually, but not everyone wants to change along with them. All of this is perfectly normal and is one reason why humans have governments and other institutions to mediate and legislate.

For many people of African descent, their most obvious commonality was an alien concept called "race." Left to themselves, they could self-identify more by class, gender, ethnicity, region, or other factors. But they were not left to themselves. People who were not of African descent were quick to offer advice or to impose their ideas on intimate matters. Some were paternalistic, others condescending. Preachers, teachers, and philanthropists tried to enforce alien or alienating regulations and rituals. Some were imperial, tyrannical, or just plain malevolent—for example, the rules enslavers imposed about who would marry whom and under what conditions. The powerful sometimes imposed their wills over those of parents, friends, or even their own common sense. All of this certainly had great effect on African Americans' ideas about and practices of marriage. And it clearly influenced how they discussed such topics in print.

I know that what is reported in early African American print culture is not necessarily what happened, or all that happened. As African American elders have said for generations, "Every shut eye ain't sleep." But early African American print culture records the story as it was told. This chapter has discussed the ideas of marriage as revealed by the documents of antebellum African Americans and focused on the stories that run counter to common opinion today. It concludes, as did Ann Patton Malone, that "made careful distinction between a marriage and a wedding."[13] Malone is referring to enslaved people here; however, this statement aptly sums up the attitudes and behaviors of many, if not most, people in the antebellum United States. An appropriate understanding of the history of marriage in this country rests on our acknowledging that to marry and to have a wedding is not the same thing.

Received wisdom that antebellum African American marriages were often enacted without benefit of clergy or proper paperwork is inaccurate. It conflates different times, places, and circumstances into a monolith that obscures, especially, rites and rituals of free people. It tells only part of the story. Out of context, one tends to interpret this perception as evidence that marriage was not a highly regarded institution in African America. To declare that the laws of the antebellum United States prohibited marriage between enslaved people does not prove that these people did not marry. It ignores evidence that for many people, regardless of racial classification, common law marriages were viable, even preferred options.

Similarly, to avow, as many do, that if or when African Americans married, their status as slaves or their vulnerability as victims of racial oppression eliminated any hope or intention that their union would last until death is both disingenuous and destructive. The specter of involuntary separation haunted many marriages. True: the tensions that an enslaved couple might feel about their ability to determine the permanence of their union certainly impacted their decisions to wed and no doubt cast a shadow on their marriages. Fact: many marriages in the antebellum United States, including those among free people, were disrupted or destroyed by a spouse going to a distant place and the couple knowing or believing the separation was final. But again this is only part of the story. When we consider the realities of marriage within their general historical context, the odds of lifelong cohabitation in African America seem more similar to the odds of lifelong cohabitation in the antebellum period generally. In fact, if we compare twenty-first-century marriage rates and divorce rates with the extant data for antebellum African America, statistics show that in the past, more African Americans married and fewer divorced than is true today. In antebellum African America, those who were free could, and many did, contract formal or legal marriages. Wedding celebrations, complete with feasting, dancing, and honeymoons, even among the enslaved, were not uncommon. But perhaps then, more than now, weddings were not "so much more significant than marriages" (Jordan 1). Basically, what people of African heritage in America had in common with people of non-African heritages in America was this: there was the official way, and there were alternatives. In practice, marriage was not a singular, one-size-fits-all construct. Marriage was a malleable and diverse institution formed as a synthesis of memory and imaginations, needs and options, desires and realities, theories and theologies, pragmatism and practicality. And early African Americans married because they wanted what most human beings want: to love and to be loved, to have and to hold, to combine one's destinies and resources with someone one holds dear. And they wanted this to last a lifetime.

FOUR

RIGHTS AND RITUALS

MARRIED. In this city, on Thursday evening 27th ult. by the Rev. Mr.
Parois, Mr. BENJAMIN MERMIER, of Philadelphia, to Miss
ANNA BELLEVU, of St. Pierre, Martinique.

In St. Phillip's Church, on Wednesday, 2nd inst. By the Rev.
Peter Williams, Mr. ANDREW WILLIAMS, of Salem, Mass. To
Miss JULIA SEABRE, of this city.

In this city, on the 31st ult. By the Rev. S. E. Cornish, Mr. JOHN
W. FREEMAN, to Miss DIANA THOMPSON.
—Freedom's Journal, *January 11, 1828*

These announcements were published together in one issue of one antebellum African American newspaper. They represent countless other
published advertisements and marriage banns announced in churches.
Each outlines a personal story and represents communal ones. The
Bellevu-Mermier merger joins the diasporic. She is from Martinique,
while he is "of" the United States. Their names, as well as the minister's,
suggest a Francophone heritage. They were probably bilingual. The
Seabre-Williams wedding unites residents from neighboring states. The
bride was "of this city." These two announcements remind us that African
America was national as well as international. Long-distance transporta-
tion in the early nineteenth century was rudimentary, and telephones,
telegraphs, and text-messaging did not exist, but African American communities were not necessarily insular. The third ad represents another

kind of diaspora. Freeman is a surname commonly assumed by African Americans who were not or were no longer enslaved. Freeman evokes slavery as an antithesis. Quite probably, John W. Freeman or his father was a former slave. Thompson, on the other hand, is a name common to northern England and Ireland. All three couples were married by ordained ministers. We have to imagine the details of how couples met, but clearly marriages in African America united couples of various heritages and histories.

These ads also reveal some of the history of antebellum African American demands for civil rights. Like virtually every Afro-Protestant congregation of the time, St. Phillips Episcopal Church in New York City had begun in political protest. Ten years before the Williams-Seabre marriage, its congregants had rejected the increasing racial discrimination in the Trinity Episcopal Church by splitting off and forming their own separate congregation. The church members were not segregationists, and they continued to work with Euro-Americans of good will. For example, they collaborated with a white abolitionist group and with others who supported civic and educational advancement for everyone. Like most Afro-Protestants, the people of St. Phillips did not believe themselves inferior beings, and they would not accept treatment from others that suggested as much. Under the leadership of Peter Williams, one of the first ordained African American priests and a founding member of the African Association for Mutual Relief, St. Phillips helped to establish schools and a community center, and to organize social and civic activities for African Americans. The Reverend S. E. Cornish, who married John W. Freeman to Diana Thompson, also linked the sacred and the secular in other ways. As editor of *Freedom's Journal* and later the *Rights of All* and the *Colored American*, Cornish was an intellectual, a preacher, a community leader, and a political activist.

The brief wedding announcements also carry complex association: they signal the fundamental union of politics and respect. The masthead of *Freedom's Journal* displays this in its motto, "Righteousness Exalteth a Nation." Righteousness included respectability, but even more it represented morality. Almost every antebellum African American periodical proclaimed itself dedicated to the advancement of moral improvement via literacy and liberty. The idea of morality included sexual behavior, but this was just part of the larger concept of righteousness, ethics, and manners. Morality was about respectability, given and assumed. It was the basis for claims to civil rights and to religious practices. One common instance is the scrupulous use of honorifics, "Mr." "Miss," and "the Rev." In an era when humanity and respect were not voluntarily offered people of African descent, they seized and defended their rights to titles, to surnames, and to the performance of such rituals and roles as they chose to enact.

MARRIAGE AND THE BIRTH OF
AFRICAN AMERICAN CULTURE

To understand more fully the union of civil rights and marriage rituals, it helps to think more about how African America came to be.[1] Between 1827, when these wedding banns were announced, and 1624, when Isabella and Antoney's son William was born in Jamestown, Virginia, were two centuries of individual and institutional births. During that time, people of African origin organized themselves into a number of mutual aid and union societies, fraternal and sororal clubs, and literary and civic groups. One of the earliest documented groups was the African Union Society of Philadelphia.

On April 12, 1787, several men gathered to form a brotherhood that would provide mutual economic and spiritual support for themselves and their families.[2] Among their number were Absalom Jones, later the founder of the African Episcopal Church, and Richard Allen, later the founder of the AME Church. Like their colleagues in Newport, Providence, Boston, New York, and other cities, the founding members of the African Union Society of Philadelphia immediately created a fund to help members who became sick or destitute and to ensure that their widows and orphans would have food, shelter, and education. Financial resources were essential to the welfare of the African America that was being born from unions of people from various tribes, cultures, and religions in Africa. But the mission statements and the activities of these early African Union societies make clear that they also banded together in order to establish consensus on morality. One of the first actions of the African Union Society of Philadelphia was to establish an oversight committee that would regularly visit each member, provide necessary financial assistance, offer advice, and report "to the group any concerns about the sobriety and orderliness of their lives" (Douglass 19).

Marriage and sexual ethics were immediate concerns. The minutes of the Society's meeting on January 15, 1788, report the following resolution: "That no man shall live with any woman as man and wife without she is lawfully his wife, and his certificate must be delivered to the clerk to be put on record" (Douglass 20).

The members approved the resolution, but everyone agreed that their private affairs were also public concerns. One of the first disciplinary cases recorded in the Society's minutes involved a member who had left his wife and family and was living with another woman. He was unrepentant. The African Union Society expelled him.

Subsequent entries in the records of the Society reveal other stories. In 1790, its records say that "the minds of divers members for several years" has been directed toward regularizing "modes of procedure" for marriage. The Society created a committee charged with recommending a "a sober and reputable way, taking care that parents and others concerned be consulted and consent obtained, and everything else connected with such a proceeding made as comfortable to propriety as might be" (Douglass 36). The Society also charged the committee with creating "a proper form of the necessary certificate and book of records thereof" (Douglass 36). When the marriage committee presented its report, it stressed the care with which its members had deliberated. It also stressed the tentativeness of its recommendations, which it expected the entire Society to debate: "Your committee, after several sittings, and weightily considering the subject referred to them, have freedom to offer for your deliberation the following mode of procedure proposed to be adopted and continued in, until experience shall point out amendments therein" (Douglass 37)

Here again, to understand the reasons for such a committee, for its extended deliberations, and for the obvious tentativeness of its recommendations, we must understand the circumstances within which the Society's members were living. Individual members had disparate philosophies, cultural models, and personal circumstances. These few words from the preface to the Society's rules and regulations speak volumes: "There being too few to be found under the like concern, and those who were, differed in their religious sentiments, with these circumstances they labored for some time" (Douglass 15). But "after a serious communication of sentiments," the individuals agreed that they could have a viable organization that looked to the general moral improvement despite their varied personal and religious beliefs, the only criteria being that each person must live "an orderly and sober life" (Douglass 15).

The challenges Africans had in uniting were not entirely different from those of others in the newly united states of America. Even then, diversity—the *pluribus*—was a challenge to creating and maintaining one nation, the *unum*. Still, with some notable exceptions—such as the conflicts between the immigrants and the indigenous peoples, the Puritans and those they claimed practiced witchcraft, the Californians and the Chinese they imported as labor, and the antislavery and proslavery groups—pre–Civil War America was a fairly tolerant place. New World people had come from various old worlds and brought with them distinct identities and traditions, but they were quick to trade them in for ways and means that worked in new circumstances. To get along, they often had to go along. They allied themselves with various congregations, colonies, states, and territories with similar ideas and ideals but generally left others to their own devices.

Those who came to the New World from Africa were similar. Nowhere is this more apparent than in ideals of marriage and morality. Many traditional religions of Africa did not separate life, afterlife, spirit, and body as did the Europeans. As the African Union societies demonstrate, given the opportunity, African Americans continued to mingle what we might call the secular and the sacred even when they had converted to some form of Christianity or other religion. On the other hand, Africans in America and those born to them were not untouched by the religious fervor of the Great Awakening. They, too, were influenced by that "moral earthquake" (Douglass 11) that characterized the antebellum period. Like other Catholics, Quakers, Congregationalists, Anglicans, Baptists, Methodists, pagans, atheists, Jews, and Muslims, people of African descent were not opposed to a separation of church and state that allowed groups to coexist within a vaguely humanistic national morality. For one thing, it allowed them to conduct their religious services as they wished. In general, free Africans could accept separate as long as it was equal.

But these groups' stories were also markedly different. British, German, French, Spanish, and others were becoming Euro-Americans by defining themselves as "white," in opposition to both the indigenous people of North America and the dark-skinned people being imported as three-fifths human. From their arrival in the Americas until the Civil War, settlers formed various Creole nations within the new nation that was forming. The process was difficult for everyone. For people of African descent, it was excruciating.

The vast majority of Africans had not chosen to immigrate to a new place or to abandon their cultures in favor of new group identities. But as they were loaded onto the big ships, they were renamed and reassigned roles and relationships. Whereas they had identified themselves by family, tribe, religion, class, or gender, the Middle Passage defined them as African, black, Negro, slave, and so on. To be considered things and not people was an entirely new concept and condition for Bambara, Yoruba, Senegambians, and others who knew their ancestral histories from the origins of the earth until their arrival on those strange ships. Women, men, and children of various ethnic and religious traditions on the African continent found themselves forced into alien roles that often violated their most basic taboos. Many, no doubt, believed that their gods had stayed in Africa and left them entirely on their own. They no longer practiced ancestral rites and customs. They accepted different food, clothing, and daily routines. Some suppressed their protests and eventually their heritages. Others never forgot the stories of their people. In either case, survival required creativity, courage, cunning, and strength. Some recognized similarities or small loopholes where they might retreat and made pragmatic adaptations. Some didn't have enough of the right stuff. Their bodies survived, but souls were murdered; they became slaves, chattel, property, and things. But many, many, many others not only survived but lived, loved, married, and reproduced—they just kept on keeping on. Their children born in this culture were African Americans, a novel idea. The culture they produced was unprecedented, hybrid, syncretic, and ingenious. Born of the union of Africa and North America, now there was African America.

African Americans created themselves by combining varying qualities of gender and geography, religion, tribal origin, health, and economic resources. People of African origin were influenced by their proximity to and the nature of their relationships with people of other cultural origins. People of African origin also influenced those among whom they lived and worked. The process was reciprocal, though not necessarily equally so. It was an ongoing process, one that was engineered, restricted, and opened up by the particular circumstances, communal concerns, expectations, and assumptions. Most of the documents that early African Americans left behind show that they proceeded by collaboration, cooperation, compromise, and creative adaptation. How and how well depended in part on external factors, such as where they landed, with whom, and in what kind of environment. But at certain times, beliefs and practices were as different among the members of some African American communities as they were between them and other African American communities. Recently compiled records, for example those of the transatlantic slave trade, help explain why a committee to create a "regular mode of procedure" for marriage rituals would have required many difficult conversations.

New scholarship shows that the slave trade was far more atuned to market preferences than previously assumed Scholars such as Michael Gomez demonstrate that until 1807 or so, when direct importation was forbidden by law, customers in Georgia and South Carolina wanting to grow rice tended to buy people from Sierra Leone and Gambia. Louisiana had a high proportion of Bambara and the Fon-Ewe-Yoruba, and as Gomez says, "the uniqueness of Bambara custom was transported to North America along with the Bambara themselves."[3] Those who came from the same general area, even though not necessarily of the same culture, were likely to share sufficient commonalities to produce fairly cohesive and consistent cultural practices—at least from sundown to sunup or whenever they were away from the eyes of their owners. Where their languages were similar, they could communicate, they could tell their stories, assign responsibilities, and work out plans. Muslims could bond with one another, Senegambians with Senegambians, or Igbo with Igbo. They could maintain some of their traditions.

Scholars don't agree on how long these cultural silos could operate, or how pervasive they were. Gomez argues that by 1830 a "translation has taken place" and the "preponderant African sociocultural matrix" was replaced by an "African American one" (Gomez 5). Claire Robertson is less sure. She says that "only in certain instances did the favorable concentration of a low sex ratio (relatively even numbers of women and men) and a high concentration on large stable plantations of persons from one African culture allow substantial retentions of particular familial forms." She complicates the arguments of scholars like Gomez by saying that "when these conditions did not prevail, there was extensive interethnic marriage and a loss of particular ethnic identity; most creole families were quite different from African families as a consequence."[4] In *The Birth of African-American Culture: An Anthropological Perspective,* Sidney Mintz and Richard Price argue that regardless of when and whence, "the Africans in the New World colony in fact became a *community* and began to share a *culture* only insofar as, and as fast as, they themselves created them" (Mintz and Price 14; italics in original).

Whatever the details, the basic plot is the same. From different regions, in different circumstances and over time, a diverse and dynamic African American culture emerged. Africans who were Muslim or who practiced tribal religions did not have the same rituals and rules as those who were Catholic or who practiced Unitarianism, spiritualism, or Shakerism. Those who accepted mainstream Protestant concepts had different politics and probably somewhat different aspirations from those who were Afro-Protestant.

The African societies of the eighteenth century were composed of people from many different areas with diverse beliefs. In the *Annals of the First African Church in the United States of America,* William Douglass writes: "this was an age of a general and searching inquiry into the equity of old and established customs" (Douglass 11). Marriage held its value quite well. Marriage had, as always, the potential of creating, from two people, a union of energy and emotional support stronger and more satisfying than the simple sum of its parts. Marriage was also a basic resource for African America as a whole. Most would agree with Orlando Patterson that "without consistent and lasting relations between men and women, and without a durable, supportive framework within which children are brought up, a group of people is in deep trouble."[5]

One thing the people of African descent had in common, as cultural heritage, survival strategy, and human propensity, was that "they put great stock in marriage."[6] The cost was tremendous, but they invested nonetheless. It was their only social security. They understood it was a case of pair up or perish. They also understood, as everyone should today, that investment is a strategical process, recognizing that future experiences might require some reallocation of resources.

African Union societies' efforts to create shared rituals and common bonds among free Africans represent numerous other efforts to defend individual and community rights for self-definitions and self-regulation. At the same time, they were efforts to make one from many—and the acceptable ways of marrying and being married were certainly many. The investments and the returns of such efforts were varied. But they shared one essential element: the idea that marriage was meaningful not just for the couple but for the entire community.

The bonds of matrimony that antebellum African Americans invested in were influenced by a number of factors. Education, wealth, leadership, political power, or access to people of power helped determine what social capital a given marriage was expected to convey. Such factors also determined when and for how long African Americans participated in a marriage. An accurate calculus of United States antebellum marital expectations must include these considerations. Certainly when trying to solve problems about African American history's impact on its present and future, the values African Americans assigned to themselves and their most personal relationships should be prime. When read in the context of their times and against other materials, early African American print culture offers narratives of love and marriage that substantially enhance our understanding of the marital endowments people expected. One of the earliest and most telling accounts of this consideration comes from the records of another African American mutual aid society—the Free African Society of Newport, Rhode Island, an affiliate of the Philadelphia group. It is a story we can extrapolate from a letter they received.

ONLY PROPER PERSONS

...it appears to be within the competency of those persons in this town to whom the said address is directed, and that they are the only proper persons to carry out the seventh article into execution, so far as it concerns themselves.

—Free African Union Society, December 1, 1796

On January 6, 1796, Theodore Foster, president of the Abolition Societies in the United States, addressed a letter on behalf of that organization to "the free Africans and other people of colour in the United States."[7] Professing only the "purest regard" for their welfare and identifying his organization as "friends and brethren," Foster wrote to notify "the free Africans and other people of color" of several resolutions concerning them that a recent convention of abolitionists in Philadelphia had passed. Apparently, Foster sent this as a form letter to several recipients. Our copy comes from the records of the Free African Union Society of Newport, Rhode Island. The response of this society to the resolutions by their "friends and brethren" shows one way less powerful people of African descent interacted with and defended themselves against cultural dominance.

This story makes more sense if we think about the social context within which it occurred. Slavery in eighteenth-century New England was a fairly fluid and a locally proscribed condition. It was not as socially acceptable as in other sections of the country, and emancipation was not infrequent. Individuals such as the poet Phillis Wheatley—were sometimes freed after becoming famous enough that public opinion demanded it. Often, like Venture Smith, they were able to purchase themselves, their land, and other slaves. Some, such as Sojourner Truth, simply self-emancipated. Most enslavers owned only a few people, and others often worked alongside them—apprentices, indentured servants, and hired help at home, on farms, in shops, on ships, and at the docks. If the enslaved people had not come via the Middle Passage from Africa, their parents and friends likely had. They knew and shared their knowledge of themselves as human beings of various cultures, religions, and classes now sharing a common situation that might or might not be permanent. The American Revolution provided freedom to many people from Africa, and it bolstered their claims to the same inalienable rights as other human beings. Life, liberty, and the pursuit of happiness were more readily achievable, as long as they stayed in their place as quasicitizens and a separate, subordinate people. African America, like the United States of America, was just emerging. What they were, then, and were to become was then and still is being imagined and negotiated.

Abolitionism was a part of this process, though not nearly the major preoccupation it was to become after the 1830s. From the beginning, however, to be antislavery didn't suggest you were pro-equality. Abolitionist societies, like most organizations in antebellum United States, were segregated by race and gender. Women formed their own separate groups, often as auxiliaries to the men's groups. Sometimes a white abolitionist group cooperated with a black abolitionist group. In some cases, a token white or three actually belonged to a black group, and vice versa. The "friends and brethren" who wrote to "free Africans and other people of colour" were white men. They were antislavery, but their knowledge of and attitudes about people of African descent were not free of prejudice. Their anxious admonition to free men of African descent to "act worthily of the rank you have acquired as free men," betray their paternalism." Their advice was mutually advantageous the white men opined. By their good behavior, "people of colour" would not only "do credit" to themselves but would also "justify the friends and advocates of your color in the eyes of the world."

To help African Americans understand what behaviors were worthy, a "convention of Deputies from the Abolition Societies in the

United states, assembled at Philadelphia" (*Proceedings*, 145) sent via Theodore Foster's letter, a list. First, free Africans should regularly attend public worship. Second, they and their children should learn reading, writing, and arithmetic. Third, they should see that their children had vocational training. The seventh resolution reads: "We wish to impress upon your minds the moral and religious necessity of having your marriages legally performed; also to have exact registers preserved of all the births and deaths which occur in your respective families."

The Newport Free African Union Society took almost a year to respond to their white "friends and brethren." On December 1, 1796, the Society decided to take the letter "into serious consideration." Their minutes report that they voted to think about the proffered advice because they believed "the members of said convention are sincere friends." The Society's members agreed with most of the resolutions. Indeed, the African group's own rules and regulations already required moral behavior and called for religious worship, enabled business and educational expertise, and advocated loyalty, honesty, frugality, and charity. Members agreed the resolutions were the kind that made life better for them and would help "generations yet to come" (*Proceedings* 147). However, they decided to form a committee to study one issue: the idea of "legally performed" and officially recorded marriages.

Three weeks later, the Society invited the African American community to a special meeting to hear the committee's report. On December 22, the marriage committee affirmed that legally performed marriages could "be a great benefit and blessing even to generations to come." But it stipulated that the marriages and the records thereof were their prerogative, that only they were "the proper persons to carry out the seventh article into execution, so far as it concerns [our]selves" (*Proceedings* 147). Having accepted the committee's report, the Free African Union Society voted to reply to the Abolitionist Societies thanking them for their kindness and forwarding to them a copy of the Free African Union Society's rules and regulations. It also decided to instruct "all free blacks and other people of colour" to bring their records of births, marriages, and deaths to the Society to be included in its records. The Society's minutes show that it purchased three books, one each for births, marriages, and deaths. However, as historian William H. Robinson notes, "for reasons unknown, there was not much done in the way of recordings these events" (*Proceedings* xi).

When this incident occurred, the Free African Union Society of Newport, Rhode Island, had been keeping written records for nearly 20 years. One wonders why, therefore, after purchasing three new books, little was done to record in them the births, marriages and deaths. Could it be that official records of vital statistics were not a priority for the Free African Union Society? Could it be that they had other reasons not to want to record such information? The records of this group indicate that it met regularly. Why, then, was it nearly a year to the day before it replied to its "friends and advocates"? Does the 11-month delay in even considering the letter suggest that the anxieties of the abolitionist who had convened in Philadelphia were not particularly important to the Free African Union Society? Did the Society delay its response because its members took that long to control their anger at the whites' presumptuousness? These are questions I cannot answer. But whatever the cause of the delay, it is clear that marriage was one cultural institution they intended to oversee for themselves.

That legal marriage was the only topic of the nine in Foster's letter that the Society sent to committee for further study suggests that in matters of religious observance, education, frugality, fairness, honesty, and faithfulness "in all the relations you bear in Society, whether as husbands, wives, fathers, children or hired servants," African Americans did not demur or differ significantly from other Americans. Taking other peoples' advice about how to conduct their marriages, however, was an issue requiring focused consultation. A group consensus emerged only after having "taken the said article into serious consideration." In its response to Foster's letter, the Free African Union Society agrees to endorse legal marriages, but it asserts that there are those in its own community who can perform legal marriages. The Society's members declare that "they *only are the proper persons* to carry out the seventh article into execution, so far as it concerns themselves" (my emphasis). Having made this declaration, the group purchased its own books, chose its own recorder, and agreed to notify "all free blacks and other people of colour to get a copy of their marriages, births, and deaths to the said clerk to be recorded in the said books." Reading literally here, we can conclude that African America already had its own decentralized system for documenting significant life events. We can also conclude that in antebellum United States, legal and social distinctions between free people of African descent and others were common, but regular interaction did occur. Both the abolitionists and the Africans included "people of colour" in their discussion. Free Africans had more and different advantages than others, but they were grouped by others with, and did not segregate themselves rigidly from, other people of color, whether enslaved, Native American, mixed, or other. The Free African Union Society records also reveal that Euro-Americans sometimes prohibited or discouraged enslaved and free people from fraternizing. But the records of the Newport group and of other African American mutual aid societies, churches, and the like show that they ignored such prohibitions when and as they pleased.

It would be helpful, of course, if we had more details, more documents, at least, another story or two that record how other African American groups reacted. But we can know, with this one, that what the members did and did not record suggests other instructive stories that are also open to interpretation. In comparison with their detailed minutes registering other Society activities, the Free African Union Society's lackadaisical employment of the official record books might mirror continued ambivalence about conforming their recording practices to the standards set by Euro-Americans. The Society's need to study the issue suggests that its members had no consensus that legal, formal, or Euro-American-style marriages were necessary. Or, maybe they kept two sets of books, one for themselves and one for others to see. The exchange between the Abolitionist Societies in the United States and the Free African Union Society shows that marriage was a site of conflict between whites and blacks. The Africans' reply to the white abolitionists shows that the Africans preferred to conduct their own rituals in their own ways. While they agreed that some compliance would increase their "happiness" and the happiness of their "generations to come," they also knew that they themselves were "the only proper persons" to officiate their marriages. Their personal affairs were not the concerns of the general public. These African Americans, like others, were determined to maintain as much independence and sovereignty as possible over their domestic lives.

In matters of love and marriage as in matters of religion and spirituality, differences were sometimes extraordinarily political. The rituals and rules created by the various African Union societies were in many respects quite similar to those espoused in Euro-America. However, they were also quite similar in both theory and in practice to many in Africa. We can read the rituals as alloys, as signifiers, as resistance, and as accommodation. The differences are often in the details.

"HAVING DECLARED THEIR INTENTIONS
OF MARRIAGE"

Back in Philadelphia, another event took place that helps us understand the later appearance of marriage announcements in *Freedom's Journal.* The Free African Society of Philadelphia adopted a "Report Concerning Marriage" that established a tripartite marriage process consisting of multiple consensus, communal witnessing, and official certification. First, multiple consensus meant that while courtship and marriage proposals were allowed to be as private as these affairs can be, when a proposal was accepted, the union became a community concern. According to the Society's dictates, when a couple decided to marry, the man was to inform the marriage committee or its representative of their intentions. The committee would then ascertain the consent of the parents and friends of both parties. If parents and friends acquiesced to the union, the committee brought the couple's proposal to the membership of the Society. If the Society approved, the committee set a wedding date convenient to the couple and to the Society.

Second and third, communal witnessing and certification, began when the committee then selected the wedding guests. It invited "men and women of sober deportment" who were not members to attend the meeting of the African Free Society during which a ceremony was to be performed. Not every detail of the ceremonies was fixed in advance, but the committee created a template for a marriage certificate that was to be subject to only "minor variations as the circumstances necessitate." The template suggests what the written record should show. It begins thus:

> *Whereas,* A. B., son of A .B., of the City of P., and State of P., and S. T., daughter of S. T., of same City and State, having declared their intentions of marriage with each other before several members of the "African Society for the Benefit of the sick," and also obtained the consent of parents and relations concerned, their said proposals were allowed of by the society... (Douglass 38)

The certificate summarizes the couple's vows as both having promised "through divine assistance to be...loving and faithful...until death should separate them." It ends with a space for the signatures of the newly married couple and notes that the bride should sign "according to the custom of marriage assuming the name of her husband." The certificate then has spaces, after the bride and groom's signatures, for the signatures of witnesses.

Certain assumptions are immediately apparent and are handled consistently throughout the recommended ritual. Marriage is a personal decision between a man and a woman. As a first step, a woman and a man mutually consent to wed one another. But marriage is not merely a private understanding between two individuals; it is a communal relationship that requires the consent of relatives, friends, and a broader community. The couple makes a private agreement, but the man makes it public by submitting their decision for approval. The committee verifies that their parents, their relatives, and their friends, as well as the members of the Society, consent to the couple's desires. The committee, not the individual couple or its families, controls the proceeding by setting the wedding date. The Society meets, invites guests of "sober deportment," and participates in the ceremony. The report does not specify who could conduct the service, though in all probability the officiator was the Society's chaplain or a religious leader from the African American community. The marriage is expected to last a lifetime, and the vows assert that "through divine assistance" each will be loving and faithful to the other until death.

In many ways, the marriage ceremonies devised by the African Union societies are identical to those used by Euro-Protestants at that time. This does not mean they were imitative. The basic elements of assent by the couple and by its community, of gifts to the couple and/or its family, of the couple exchanging of pledges and symbols thereof are also intrinsic to African and other cultures. The differences are in the manner of conducting of the ritual, who participates and who does not, and in the emphasis on expectations. As the Free African Union Society of Newport made so clear, the rituals were to be performed and its records were to be kept by people of African descent. As the documents of the African Union Society of Pennsylvania assert, the vows were exchanged *"before several members of the 'African Society for the Benefit of the sick.'"* The couple had *"also obtained the consent of parents and relations concerned."* And "their said proposals were allowed of *by the society.*" Each of these statements casts people of African descent as independent and self-governing. The couple needed the approval of their parents, which shows that family structure was assumed to be intact and was intended to remain so. The couple and the parents also needed the approval of the community.

As time passed, the various African societies divided, merged, dissolved, and reconstituted themselves into a variety of organizations, including mutual aid societies, educational institutions, and churches.

For example, the Free African Society of Philadelphia divided into two Afro-Protestant churches of different denominational affiliations. The rituals, however, continued to require and to affirm the tripartite structure of deity, community, and betrothed.

The January 1859 issue of the *Repository of Religion and Literature* contains enticing details about prenuptial rituals among a particular class in African America. This is the story it tells:

> Do you see that woman there? Her head is full of the most pleasing thoughts about the day when she will be led, leaning on the arm of her beloved to Hymen's altar, and there with faltering lips whispers her vows to love and to cherish till life itself shall cease....
>
> [S]he is shopping, buying, and also making all the articles necessary for the handsome wardrobe of a bride.
>
> Now she is consulting her dear mother, then her bride's maid, and then her mantua-maker about the color, quality, and style of her wedding dress. Nor does she forget to commune with her beloved about the house in which they shall live, the furniture that shall decorate it, and the minister, who shall have the honor to pronounce them husband and wife....
>
> Well, the day is come, and the hour also, when her maiden name is to be changed; she enters her chamber, goes to the wardrobe, and takes out her bridal dress—she goes to the casket, and takes out her bridal jewels—she is now at the toilet, oiling, combing, curling, pressing her hair—dressing herself.
>
> The last pin is stuck, the last string is tied—the handkerchief perfumed—the glove placed upon her hands.... She is now ready to be led by her espoused to the place where the sacred knot is to be tied. The groom enters the chamber, and with majestic strides leads her to the altar.
>
> Behold! While the minister of the sanctuary invokes the blessings of God upon her, she tremblingly takes the vows and becomes a wife. (20–21)

The wedding ritual described here is in many ways a scripted performance, a tale of multiple origins and roles. The bride and groom exchange vows before an altar identified with Hymen—the Greek god of marriage—that is also a Christian sanctuary. The man and the woman decide together on the minister. The woman consults with her family, friends, and fiancé on various aspects of the ceremony, but she is clearly in charge of arrangements. In this description, she even gowns and bejewels herself without needing attendants. Her costuming and preparations, which include the talismans of perfumed handkerchief and gloves, evoke those of brides in many cultures, including Africa. But the details of her toilet include a decidedly African American ritual of "oiling, curling, pressing her hair." The bride, having arranged the ceremony and prepared herself to come before the altar, then *plays the role* of the trembling bride of a majestically striding groom. Like the announcements of marriages in *Freedom's Journal* that began this chapter, articles published in the antebellum African American Press constitute a truly important part of our history. They provide the context that changes our interpretations of many prominent stories of love, marriage, and sexual morality in antebellum African America.

THE LOVE-DREAMS OF THE ENSLAVED

Most of the members of African Union societies and of the Afro-Protestant churches these societies begot were legally free. Others were not. Those who were legally "slaves" could have weddings but not legal marriages. However, African America had its own laws, its own definitions, and its own elaborate and nuanced system of social class. Personal narratives by enslaved persons verify that some of them expected to choose their own mates, have church weddings, and exchange rings and vows. In *Incidents in the Life of a Slave Girl*,[8] Harriet Jacobs writes about being a bridesmaid in friends' weddings. Her parents, Daniel and Deliah, had married in a church ceremony; upon their deaths, Jacobs inherited her mother's wedding band and her silver thimble. Being enslaved did not necessarily prohibit couples from having elaborately formal weddings complete with rings, veils, flowers, and ministers (or masters) as officiants.

In *Behind the Scenes: Thirty Years a Slave and Four Years in the White House*, a letter from Elizabeth Keckley to her mother, Agnes Hobbs, shows the wedding activity in some enslaved people's lives. Keckley was living in Hillsborough, North Carolina, when she wrote the following to her mother on April 10, 1838:

> There have been six weddings since October; the most respectable one was about a fortnight ago; I was asked to be the first attendant, but...on the wedding day I felt more like being locked up in a three-cornered box than attending a wedding. About a week before Christmas I was bridesmaid for Ann Nash; when the night came I was in quite a trouble; I did not know whether my frock was clean or dirty; I only had a week's notice and

the body and sleeves to make, and only one hour every night to work on it...I wish you would send me a pretty frock this summer.[9]

Keckley's own wedding was legally invalid, but it was a formal affair in which Hugh Garland, a prominent lawyer and Keckley's legal owner, played an important role. "The wedding," Keckley wrote, "was a great event in the family. The ceremony took place in the parlor in the presence of the family and a number of guests. Mr. Garland gave me away, and the pastor, Bishop Hawks, who had solemnized the bridals of Mr. G's own children, performed the ceremony" (Keckley 31–32).

Keckley was a "modiste": that is, she was celebrated as an exceptionally talented seamstress with acute sense of fashion and style. Undoubtedly, her wedding dress was designed and made for the occasion. Few enslaved women had that privilege; however, their descriptions of their marriages often dwelled more on what they wore than on any other aspect. Sarah Allen of El Paso, Texas, recalled that "I had a nice weddin.' My dress was [w]hite and trimmed with blue ribbon. My second day dress was white with red dots. I had a beautiful veil and a wreath and 'bout two, three waiters for table dat day."[10] Sometimes wedding dresses were recycled. One interviewer reports a former slave as saying that her mistress "give her wedding dress to my ma. Dat was de fines' dress I ever seen. It was purple and green silk....All the nigger gals wear dat dress when dy git marry. My sister Sidney wo' it, and Sary and Mary. I don't know 'bout Polly and 'Melia." Malinda Pugh Daniel recalled: "I wo' a party dress of Miss Sara's...made outen white tarleton wid a pink bow in de front. I had a pink ribbon 'roun' my haid." While John Bates' wedding clothes were not the equivalent of tarleton or silk, he seems quite proud when he recalls : "My weddin clothes was a pair of old jeans britches and shirt, made at home and a pair of shoes made by myself."

The rites and rituals of marriages among enslaved people are particularly varied. The most minimal informal weddings were known as "home weddings." Harre Quarls said "us have de home weddin' bur not any preacher. Us jus' 'greed live together as man and wife and that all they was to it. Us have one gal and one boy." Eli Davidson said "I married Sarah Keys. We had a home weddin' and 'greed to live together as man and wife. I jus' goes by her home one day and captures her like. I puts her on my saddle behind me and tells her she's my wife then. That's all they was to my weddin.' " Hal Hutson narrates a more elaborate variation on the home wedding while revealing what could happen if the parents of both couples did not consent. Hutson says: "[I] married at my mother's house 'cause my wife's mother didn't let us marry at her house, so I sent Jack Perry after her on a hoss and we had a big dinner—and jest got married."

Earlier, I mentioned that "The Old Maid's Diary" and "A Bachelor's Thermometer" both suggest that these types' failures to find a spouse began when they thought about courting before they were old enough. Historian Ann Patton Malone notes that the age at which enslaved people married varied considerably according to when, where, and how they were enslaved. However, she notes, the common attitude among enslaved people themselves was that in the antebellum period "a gal's 21 'fore she marry" (Malone 230). What Malone writes about enslaved people in Louisiana applies to antebellum African Americans generally:

> When a wedding ceremony and celebration were not permitted, the lack was sorely felt by the slave community, which made careful distinction between a marriage and a wedding....One could enter into a marriage without a wedding ceremony, just as one could be buried without a funeral, but neither was considered proper. (Malone 225)

Julia Blanks reported that hers was almost a "home wedding" or, as it was called where she lived in San Antonio, Texas, "a run-a-way marriage." She was 15—younger than Ann Malone and other historicans indicate as the average age of marriage—but her description of her wedding conforms generally to the pattern reported by others in the oral narratives of Rawick and others while providing some vivid details:

> [My] wedding dress was as wide as a wagon sheet. It was white lawn, full of tucks, and had a big ruffle at the bottom. I had a wreath and a veil, too. The veil had lace all around it. We danced and had a supper. We danced all the dances they danced; the waltz, square, quadrille, polka, and the galloped—and that's what it was, all right; you shore galloped. You'd start from one end of the hall and run clear to the other end. In those days, the women with all them long trains—the man would hold it over his arm.

Antebellum African Americans married in all manner of rituals. Some had elaborate weddings that were carefully rehearsed and staged in grand settings, including baroque Afro-Protestant churches, the luxurious parlors of prosperous African Americans, and the front porches and gardens of slaveholders. Others simply moved their belongings into the spouse's quarters. The vows they exchanged ranged from the deliberate

and carefully prescribed words of their church Disciplines or benevolent
societies to the extemporaneous, sometimes condescending or belittling,
words of ministers and masters. In some areas, especially among Catholics, weddings included signing of licenses or church registries. Ellen
Betts, an enslaved woman who was moved from Virginia to Louisiana
around 1853, suggests that the reason those in her community did not
have marriage licenses was because their owner refused to allow them to.
Betts reports:

> When a black gal marry, Marse marry her hisself in de big hous. He marry
> 'em Saturday, so dey git Sunday off, too. One time de river boat come
> bearin' de license for niggers to git marry with. Marse chase 'em off and
> say, "Don't you come truckin' no no-count papers round' my niggers. When
> I marry 'em, dey marry as good as if de Lawd God hisself marry 'em and it
> don't take no paper to bind de tie." Marse don't stand no messin' round,
> neither. A gal have to be of age and ask her pa and ma and Marse and Missy,
> and if dey 'gree, dey go ahead and git marry. Marse have de marry book to
> put de name down. (Rawick 272–76)

The following is one version of what several anthropologists and folk-
lorists report as a "slave marriage ceremony":

> Dark an' stormy may come de wedder;
> I jines dis he-male an' dis she-male togedder.
> Let none, but Him dat makes de thunder,
> Put dis he-male an' dis she-male asunder.
> I darfore 'nounce you bofe de same.
> Be good, go 'long, an' keep up yo' name.
> De broomstick's jumped, de worl's not wide.
> She's now yo' own. Salute yo' bride!

This ritual reveals several important details. The dialect in which it was
recorded suggests that this story was recorded under much the same pro-
tocol as the WPA narratives; that is, linguistic difference was important,
and while it may not be rendered accurately, it does suggest that the
described ceremony was one affected by uneducated officials for common people. Words such as "he-male" and "she-male" may be used for
humor, but they also conform to the not-so-funny and certainly significant fact that during the era of enslavement in the United States, women
and men of African descent were not recognized as women or men, and
that female and male were among the nicer nouns used in speaking of,

or to, them. The use of metaphors of "dark an' stormy…wedder" mirrors that in other folktales, suggesting and affirming the poetic and symbolic language and concepts by which even those who were enslaved lived and communicated on special occasions. "De broomstick's jumped" refers to, and confirms, present-day notions that the most common ritual by which marriages were performed included the couple jumping over a broom. The officiant's decrees that "none, but Him dat makes de thunder" should dissolve the union gives credence to the idea that marriages in the olden days were made for life. This contradicts the folkloric assertion that enslaved people vowed to be married "'til death or distance do us part" and refutes any ideas that a slaveholder can invalidate a marriage. Significant to this ceremonial blessing also is the idea that "you bofe [are] the same. Be good, go 'long, an' keep up yo' name." Good behavior or at least good reputations were important to a married couple, even if their "world's not wide." Being "de same" is a version of legal coverture, for in de facto if not in de jure, the husband is given the wife: "She's now yo' own. Salute yo' bride!" She belongs to him. He may acknowledge it with a salute, meaning with a gesture of acknowledgment and respect. Generally a marital salute is enacted by a kiss, but in the nineteenth-century vernacular, "salute" also meant to have sexual intercourse. Since procreation was a mandate for married couples, this interpretation may be as valid as any other. As noted, "jumping the broom" is so well known and imitated today that many people think that was the way all antebellum African Americans wed, but this was not so, even for enslaved people. In fact, some historians, for example Anne Patton Malone, state that enslaved people preferred a "Scripture wedding," and that by 1850 jumping the broom had become a fairly rare or old-fashioned way of marrying (Malone 224). Nonetheless, "jumping the broom" is the best known and most commonly reenacted ceremony today. As such, it merits more discussion.

JUMPING THE BROOM

My daughter had a church wedding that modified the standard ceremony prescribed in the AME Church by using African drumming, a procession that included attendants, bride and groom, libations to the ancestors, and jumping the broom. Like many African Americans today, Krishna and Kwasi wanted a ceremony that reflected their

African and African American heritages as well as their own ideas and
ideals. They concocted their special wedding from what they'd seen
others do and from books such as *The Nubian Wedding Book: Words and
Rituals to Celebrate and Plan an African-American Wedding* and *Jumping
the Broom: The African-American Wedding Planner.*[11] Still, they had more
questions than answers. For example, they had a problem deciding
exactly what the broom was to look like and how they were supposed
to jump it. Descriptions and prescriptions varied greatly. Variations
and interpretations abound as these few stories of the broom jumping
ritual demonstrate.

> Da way dey done at weddings dem days, you picks out a girl and tell your
> boss. If she was from another plantation you had to git her bosses 'mission
> and den dey tells you to come up dat night and get hitched up. They says
> to de girl, "You's love dis man?" Dey says to de man, "You loves dis girl?" If
> you say you don't know, it's all off, but if you say yes, dey brings in de broom
> and holds it 'bout a foot off de flor and say to you, to jump over. Den he
> says you's married. If either of you stumps you toe on de broom, dat mean
> you got trouble comin' 'tween you, so you sho' jumps high. (Jeff Calhoun,
> Texas; Rawick)

> After while I was taken a notion to marry, and Massa and Missy marries us
> same as all the niggers. They stands inside the house with a broom held
> crosswise of the door, and we stands outside. Missy puts a li'l wreath on my
> head they kept there, and we steps over the broom into the house. Now
> that's all they was to the marryin.' After freedom I git married and has it
> put in the Book by a preacher. (Nancy Reynolds; Rawick)

> When Slaves got married they jus' laid down the broom on the floor and
> the couple jined hands and jumped back-uds over the broomstick. I done
> seed 'em married that way many a time. Sometimes my marster would fetch
> Mistress down to the slave quarters to see a weddin.' Effen the slaves gittin
> married was house servants, sometimes they married on the back porch
> or in the back yard of the big 'ouse but plantation niggers what was field
> hands married in they own cabins. The bride and groom jus' wore plain
> clothes ka'en they didn' have no more. (James Bolton, Athens, Georgia;
> Rawick)

Occasionally we find versions with two brooms such as this one reported
by University of California professor Alan Dundes:

Dey lays de broom on the floor and de woman puts her broom front de man and he put he broom front de woman. Dey face one 'nother and step 'cross de broom at the same time to each other and takes hold of hand and dat marry dem.[12]

Ultimately, Krishna and Kwasi created their wedding ritual according to their own tastes and imaginations. Their Aunt Angie decorated a broom brought especially for the ceremony. They designed a wedding program that identified all the participants and, explained their roles and what they represented, and they wrote a short description of what jumping the broom meant to them. What Krishna and Kwasi probably didn't know is that it was less the jumping of the broom that made their public vows of their personal love a part of their ancestral tradition. It was their improvisation—their blending of several rituals as they interpreted them from various stories and as they fulfilled the expectations of their families, friends, and the government. Their synthesis of tradition and law, fashion and individual fantasy, was their ancestral legacy. They were doing exactly what African Americans have been doing for centuries.

The records and stories recounted earlier are reminders that what matters now also mattered then: the determination of African Americans to define and to enact marriage for themselves. The earliest documents of the earliest formally organized African communities in colonial America reveal that such determination was focused and fierce. While personalized and improvised, the reenactments by many African American couples today of jumping the broom demonstrate the persistence of and respect for tradition. At the same time, jumping the broom is popular because of the stories told. The worlds that are most often conjured emerge from the stories that are most promulgated.

MYTHS, MEMORY, AND SELF-REALIZATION

WHEN KRISHNA AND KWASI STOPPED TRYING TO FIGURE out exactly *how* to "jump the broom" and concentrated instead on figuring out *what* "jumping the broom" *meant* to them, they moved from confusion to confidence. They realized that the primary task of ancestral stories is not prescription but description. The multiple versions encourage flexibility and adaptation. Myths and music are kin. Music stirs the soul in wordless wonder. Myths use words to explain the wonderful. Myths and traditional stories are akin to jazz. Learning the song comes first, but to own that song and to own our cultural heritages, we need to creatively adapt ourselves to them and them to ourselves. Tis means we need to synthesize, improvise, and perform our own arrangements while always keeping the original melodyies as our standard, our boundary and our guide. To define ourselves both individually and collectively, we need to act within cultural boundaries even though by our very existence we are, at the same time, changing them. Krishna and Kwasi had learned enough about tradition to understand that their responsibility was not to resurrect a wedding ritual, but to enact it. Their wedding became a reflection of them, where they came from and what they envisioned themselves becoming.

Learning to use one's past is the necessary sequel to learning about one's past. There is a lot of mystery around which myths have developed, especially in and about marriage. The previous chapters have offered stories about courtship, love, marriage, and sexual morality from the stories told by African Americans who lived during the antebellum period, about themselves and primarily for themselves. Knowing such stories, interpreting them as accurately as possible, and deciding what they can contribute toward inspiring and healing us are difficult endeavors. It's tough in part because needs and desires are not always static, not usually synchronized, and often not even known. In this chapter, I explain why the material in the previous chapters is significant and useful, as I make three points. First, it is important that we have even more stories from the perspective of observers who tell us what antebellum African Americans did, and we need to know the stories in their context of what antebellum African Americans believed, hoped, and envisioned. Second, we need to get at least some of these stories in their own words, to interpret those words accurately, and to hear what is not being said. Third, to do this, we need to be very clear about how myth and memory work to make us who we are.

FACTS, FIGURES, METAPHORS, MYTHS, AND "THE TRUTH"

Myths are the stories that explain the inexplicable, define the natural, substitute for fact, construct memory, and dictate our perceptions of past, present, and future. Myths may be factual. They may not be. Time itself is a special kind of myth-maker. Nobel laureate William Faulkner wrote that the past is not dead, it isn't even past. Pulitzer Prize–winning biographer David McCullough says: "The past is not only a source of instruction, but it has made us what we are. All of us are the products of our parents, teachers, and friends, as well as of the writers, artists, and other public figures who have had a hand in shaping our minds and characters."[1] The ways we know who we are, why we are, what we might achieve, and what we could achieve are determined by stories we tell ourselves and the emotions these stories arouse. Our minds and characters, perceptions and memories are shaped by our stories and the values they transmit.

Growing up in African America, long before my teachers injected traditional canons of literature into my universe, I had already learned that songs, prayers, and testimonies could change the ordinary into the sacred. I knew how to provide entertainment and how to avert violence while getting my licks in with "snaps," "lies," and "stow-ries." My schoolmates and

I learned how to distinguish audaciousness from assaults and how to deal with both. Some of us were lucky enough not to get the Disney version of Brer Rabbit first, so we recognized more quickly the value of cultivating quick wit and smooth talk. By the second grade, at least, I knew how the dozens could win arguments and how a good rap could win a friend. The many sayings and stories passed down from generation to generation were ingenious and invaluable tools for survival and for success—once we learned how to interpret them. "God don't like ugly." "Take it easy, Greasy, you got a long way to slide." "Pick your battles carefully." "What goes around, comes around."

From the old folks, we young folks learned that "everything that glitters isn't gold." But we also learned that not everything our elders and friends told us applied to every situation. Almost as soon as we learned to talk, we heard that "Sticks and stones may break your bones, but words will never hurt you." Even before we knew exactly how to say so, we realized that words might not break our bones, but they could certainly break our spirits. Almost at the same time, we understood that words could be many different things. Learning to use language includes learning that a word can have multiple and sometimes conflicting definitions, learning that a word can mean both more and less than its definitions, and learning that the context within which the word is used determines a great deal about its meaning. Knowing the right words to use at the right time and to interpret how others are using words in given situations are essential for self-realization and sometimes basic to living long enough to learn anything else.

The dozens and Grandma's directives notwithstanding, as a child I came to realize that sometimes music won't charm the beast, a soft answer won't turn away wrath, and I shouldn't wait for what goes around to come around any time soon. More important, I realized that what I didn't know could hurt me, and that even if I asked them no questions, some folks would still tell me lies. I, and the wisest of my friends discovered that speaking truth to power wouldn't necessarily defeat more powerful stories, but unless we spoke up, no one would hear us at all.

The image of the ignored or unspoken truths that warp the wisdom of twenty-first century people and that proscribe our futures is sometimes represented as a "skeleton in the closet," "an elephant—or an 800-pound gorilla—in the middle of the room," or a "sleeping dog." We're sometimes advised not to look for trouble, to tread carefully, or to let things just be. But in venues that range from Alcoholics Anonymous meetings

to Sunday morning sermons, from the Def Comedy Jam to poetry readings in university lecture halls, people practice and preach the power of
truth-telling and life definition through words and narratives powerfully
conveyed. Clearly, such discoveries and such storytelling are not, by any
stretch of the imagination, limited to African Americans. Recognizing,
reciting, and reconsidering facts, figures, metaphors, myths, and "the
truth" are survival skills essential to living in any society.

For centuries, important truths have been conveyed by stories. In
every major religion, anecdotes and dramas teach shared values. According to the Bible, "Jesus told the crowds all these things in parables; without a parable he told them nothing."[2] When the disciples asked Jesus
why he spoke that way, he explained that using stories was the most effi-
cient and effective way to communicate: "The reason I speak to them in
parables is that 'Seeing they do not perceive, and hearing they do not
understand'" (Matthew 13:13).[3] Jesus used parables so often that one of
its contemporary definitions is "stories Jesus told."

Long ago, educational research proved that people learn more
quickly from narratives than from lists of data, plainly dressed research,
or charts and diagrams. This is one reason why learning so often relies
on heuristic devices that create an image or personal association of the
idea to be learned. Such memory aids work even when the device one
uses to memorize the data is more complex than the data itself. Think,
for example, of the sentence taught to learn to spell "arithmetic": A rat
in the house may eat the ice cream. When thinking about narratives used
for learning and remembering, we have to think about words and their
interpretations, stories and their histories, texts and their contexts. We
have to realize the work and worth of myth in defining ourselves and
one's relationships to others.

"STRIVING TO CAPTURE THE 'LIFE AND SOUL'"

Often, much too often, not only the narratives of our culture but also the
narratives of our schools, our arts, and our popular entertainments teach
things that are not helpful, that are, in fact, harmful to our own and others' health. Historian Robin D. G. Kelly writes about learning to deal with
"capping," "snapping," "the dozens," and other forms of verbal insult
and instruction on the streets, but, he says, reading "newspapers, mono-
graphs and textbooks" nearly destroyed him. "I realized," Kelley writes in

Yo Mama's Dysfunctional! "that many academics, journalists, policymakers and politicians had taken the 'dozens' to another level."[4] In what Kelley calls "a cruel, high-tech game of the dozens that has continued nonstop since the first slave ships embarked from West Africa to the New World" (Kelley 3), many people of African descent have been, and are still being, both mortally and morally wounded. One of Kelley's examples is the common practice of identifying African American mothers as dysfunctional, emasculating matriarchs, or as sexually promiscuous victims of domestic violence whose children continue the same cycle of deprivation and depravity. As African Americans, we read that our fathers are crack-head criminals, dope pushers, and dawgs, that our brothers prefer gangs to families, and that our sisters are hoochie mamas, gold diggers, or baby-mamas in training. Black History Month stories of Sojourner Truth (a single mother), George Washington Carver (an eccentric geek), Frederick Douglass (who married a white woman), and even Kunta Kinte (African Superman) are simply too flawed, too few, or too fantastic to counter the continual production of negative contemporary narratives. Unless, that is, African Americans, and all of us, come to understand how narratives work. Icons and celebrities are not an adequate substitute for more revealing stories about ordinary people.

Often, much too often, the narratives about African American culture that are presented as positive also teach things that are not helpful. Our textbooks and learning guides, the stories told in the schoolyard and at home, the dramas of television, videos, and music misrepresent the diversity of our history and the resilience of our ancestors. As we focus on the stories of love, marriage, and family that antebellum African Americans told about themselves, we really must think about what stories are, how fact and fiction, history and narrative, and belief and being are related, and how this has relevance to our lives.

Virtually every high school history teacher tells us that if we don't know the past, we're doomed to repeat it. And many of us have heard some version of Sankofa: "If you want to know where you're going, you have to know where you've been." By definition, nonfiction is factual, objective, and independently verifiable. By tradition, we define history textbooks as the ultimate nonfiction. We are taught to think of historians as our legacy keepers, preserving the past for the benefit of us all. Less often do we admit that we can't really *know* our past, that what the best historians do is weave narratives of facts with cultural probabilities and educated hunches. As facts are discovered or refuted and as our notions of probability and possibility change, so, too, do our historical narratives. If you don't believe me, compare American history textbooks of 1808, 1908, and 2008. As women's studies, African American studies, and other relatively recent areas of inquiry have demonstrated, until it occurs to someone to ask a question, we have no semblance of an answer. When we rediscover or reassess data to fill in the gaps, we often need to reconcile discrepancies. When we offer new narratives, we awaken sleeping dogs, trouble the waters, and generally inspire concerns, criticism, and contestation.

Eventually, some of us discover that historians are often gate keepers, preserving the status quo so that those it favors keep their privileged positions. Consider the many years during which historians denied that Thomas Jefferson had an intimate relationship with Sally Hemings. Some simply said he was too much a gentleman to have sex with a Negro, especially one of his slaves. Others said he was too racist. Most simply denied it by omitting any mention of Sally, their several children, or of the many stories, songs, and rumors that circulated about them during their lifetimes. These were not necessarily bad historians. They were human beings interpreting data according to the established criteria of their profession, the objectives of their unstated goals, and the limits of their own credulity.

Professor Ira Berlin of the University of Maryland, College Park, puts it this way: "by definition, the reconstructed past is contested terrain. It proceeds from great skepticism. Nothing is taken for granted. Everything is contingent. Everyone lied—at least as a presumption."[5] Nell Irvin Painter, Edwards Professor of American History at Princeton University and former president of both the Southern Historical Association and the Organization of American Historians, is more diplomatic when she declares: "in order to make sense of what took place, you need to select what is important." Historians, she writes,

> have to select, because if we do not pull out what is important, the past remains a confusing, meaningless morass of detail. Making sense of the past is the work of historians, who create *historical narrative*. Historical narrative endows certain people and events with historical importance and denies historical importance to other people and events.[6]

Painter's final statement has major implications for this book. It holds that history is a mystery that we interpret as truth. Underlying this understanding is the fact that as we shape our stories, our stories shape us.[7]

So if historians can't get the story right, then why should we pay attention to the past? There are many reasons, but one of the most powerful is *myth*. Too often we interpret that word to mean something "not true." But the primary definition, the one scholars use and what I mean in this book, of "myth" is "a traditional story accepted as history; [that] serves to explain the world view of a people."[8] You see, it doesn't matter really whether a myth is fact or fiction. What matters is how myths work. Myths explain the inexplicable. Myths answer the questions that are most important to a person, a community, a nation, a world. "Who am I and what is my relationship to the world?" "Who made me and the world around me?" "What is life and how should we live?" "Why is there war? "What is love?"

Myths answer these questions. Myths are what we live by. Whatever gets us up and keeps us going traffics in mythology. What we call the "American Dream," what we call "history," what we recognize as "fiction," "documentary," "biography," "autobiography," "memoir"—these are myths. They are all, in a way, "docu-fiction." Myths can motivate healthy and positive decision-making. They provide structure, interpretation, and application for things that might otherwise appear to be chaotic, random, and omnipotent. Using the primary definition of this word, our religions are "myths." One of my favorite gospel songs reveals a wonderful rationale for myth, that is, for living as if we believe a story, even if there's no available evidence.

> If heaven never was promised to me,
> Neither the promise to live eternally,
> It's been worth just having the Lord in my life.
> Living in a world of darkness,
> He brought me the light.[9]

THE WORD MADE FLESH

Their evil is mighty
but it can't stand up to our stories.
So they try to destroy the stories
let the stories be confused or forgotten.

They would like that

They would be happy

Because we would be defenseless then.

—Leslie Marmon Silko, *Ceremony* (1977)

Myths make our memories. They guide and protect, inspire hope and mental health. Leslie Marmon Silko writes about life on the Laguna Pueblo Reservation: "the chanting or telling of ancient stories to effect certain cures or protect from illness and harm have always been part of the Pueblo's curing ceremonies. I feel the power that the stories still have to bring us together, especially when there is loss and grief."[10] Stories, Silko writes, are often "all we have to fight off illness and death" (2).

Acknowledging the power of myths to heal requires acknowledging their power to harm. Philosopher Hilde Linneman Nelson's analysis stems from the same concepts as the gospel song and the novelist's testimony, but it has a more intellectual heft. Nelson explains—as does an introductory psychology course—that attitudes and actions, perceptions and psyches, our senses of ourselves and of our possibilities are created by a complex interaction of external and internal data. "The way in which others identify us," Nelson explains, "establishes what they will permit us to do....This restricts our freedom to act. How we identify ourselves establishes our own view of what we can do....This too restricts our moral agency."[11] Both external and internal influences form what Nelson calls "mandatory identities," which in turn "set up expectations about how group members are to behave, what they can know, to whom they are answerable, and what others may demand of them" (Nelson xii). When a powerful group or person oppresses a less powerful group or person, the result is unequal opportunities and damaged identities. To make it worse, the damaged persons may internalize the disrespect and believe that they are, indeed, as their oppressors define them. Their own aspirations and self-respect constrict accordingly.

The implications are serious and pervasive. Elaine Horwitz, Dolly Jesusita Young, and Cornelius C. Kubler are among those who research "language anxiety" and its relationship to learning foreign languages. Horwitz, for example, has found that "language anxiety" can account for nearly a 25 percent variance in performance. Moreover, "language anxiety," they have discovered, is not confined to low-performing students. Even language teachers sometime suffer its symptoms. Researchers consider "language anxiety" a psychological response to stories about the difficulty of learning foreign languages and to an individual's own self-confidence as a language learner. Why the anxiety? Stories! We are told that learning another language is hard, and the older we are, the more difficult language acquisition becomes. We are rarely told that "being hard" does not translate into "cannot be done" or that in some countries everyone speaks—at least—two languages.

Probably the most well-known research on the influence of narratives on performance and self-image is that of Claude Steele, who has investigated, for more than 20 years, the effects of "stereotype and social identity anxiety." Steele has shown conclusively that the academic performance of African Americans and other students of color can be manipulated by the stories they believe about themselves and about those with whom they know themselves to be identified. Steele's work is not limited to test scores and grades. His research groups include high-achieving athletes and middle-aged computer professionals. The experiments are essentially the same, and so are the results. People who are extremely intelligent, highly successful, and generally self-confident are divided into two groups and asked to perform tasks or take tests that they are perfectly capable of completing efficiently and effectively. Prior to the test, examiners give one group inaccurate or incomplete historical data that stresses the negative performance of people like themselves. This group does not do well. The control group might be told that folks like them tend to excel or they might be told nothing. Their performances correlate with what their previous achievements would suggest. For example, a group of golfers might be told that golfers tend not to do as well as basketball players on this test. These golfers would perform less well than others would in a control group who had not been given that information. Steele and other social scientists also observed middle-aged computer geniuses who performed with mediocrity in Silicon Valley businesses dominated by young and restless nerds 20 years their junior. The researchers attribute this new mediocrity to the middle-aged employees' conceptions that in these youth-oriented offices, they were perceived as out of place, less inventive, and over the hill. On the flip side, researchers have told groups whose past performances were average or below that the test they were to take was routine, the task was easy, and they had nothing to worry about. Told that others like themselves have generally done quite well, these groups tended to perform at higher levels than ordinarily expected. Such social science complements the personal testimonies cited earlier in this chapter, including that of Robin D. G. Kelley.

But there is more to the story of stories than this. Myths impact the behavior and belief systems of individuals even though they tend to be collective or cultural in nature. Memory, on the other hand, can be cultural, but it is often more individual.

MEMORY, REMEMORY, AND THE POLITICS OF THE PERSONAL

For more than a century, researchers have been trying to work out the raw ingredients for personality, the sweetness and neuroses that make Anna Anna, the sluggishness and sensitivity that make Andrew Andrew. They have largely ignored the first-person explanation—the life story that people themselves tell about who they are, and why. Stories are stories, after all.

—Benedict Carey, "This Is Your Life (and How You Tell It)"

(*New York Times*, 2007)

At a conference held at Emory University on memory, meaning, and narrative as responses to trauma, social scientists Robyn Fivush and Beth Seeling explained the workings of personal narrative this way:

Human beings seek meaning, and when experienced events cannot be understood, the human mind returns again and again to the event to try to make sense of it in a repetitive and compulsive way. For adults, this impulse seems to take the form of trying to create a coherent narrative. By structuring experience in language, and more specifically in narrative form, individuals strive for meaning. Narratives go beyond simple verbal descriptions of events. Narratives provide a coherent framework—a beginning, middle, and end to experienced events. Perhaps most important, narratives provide causal links and explanations for how and why events occurred the way they did, and they help to integrate raw emotion into an explanatory framework.[12]

Stories affect our individual common sense and our ability to process information rationally or realistically. In *How the Political Brain Works*, Dr. Drew Westen reports that our politics interfere with or distort our perceptions.[13] Working with a team of neuroscientists and others, Westen used brain scans to study the reactions of partisan Democrats and Republicans as they were presented with information that made their candidates look good. Then they were given information in which their candidate looked as if he was completely contradicting himself. The scientists discovered that this information activated the circuits in the brain that control emotions. "When [a subject is] confronted with potentially troubling political information," Westen writes,

> a network of neurons becomes active that produces distress. Whether this distress is conscious, unconscious, or some combination of the two we don't know.... The brain registers the conflict between data and desire and begins to search for ways to turn off the spigot of unpleasant emotion. We know that the brain largely succeeded in this effort, as partisans mostly denied that they had perceived any conflict between their candidate's words and deeds.... Not only did the brain manage to shut down distress through faulty reasoning, but...circuits involved in positive emotions turned *on*...activating reward circuits that give partisans a jolt of positive reinforcement for their biased reasoning. These reward circuits overlap substantially with those activated when drug addicts get their "fix." (Westen xiii–xiv)

Studies such as these teach that "our brains are vast networks of neurons (nerve cells) that work together to generate our experience of the world. Of particular importance are *networks of associations,* bundles of thoughts, feelings, images, and ideas that have become connected over time" (Westen 3).

Seventy years before Drew Westen published his scientific findings, Zora Neale Hurston began her novel *Their Eyes Were Watching God* with a similar observation:

> Ships at a distance have every man's wish on board. For some they come in with the tide. For others they sail forever on the horizon, never out of sight, never landing until the Watcher turns his eyes away in resignation, his dreams mocked to death by Time. That is the life of men. Now, women, forget all those things they don't want to remember, and remember everything they don't want to forget. The dream is the truth. Then they act and do things accordingly.[14]

Hurston was an anthropologist as well as a poet. Her classification by gender may have been based on her research, or may have been the poetic license necessary to frame her story of a woman's quest for meaning. Nonetheless, in science and in the humanities, we have reasons to understand a narrative as a result of physical as well as emotional "networks of associations." When we reconcile contradiction, when we identify something as cause and something else as effect, when we form random data into a pattern from start to finish; when we recall, interpret, and communicate, we are creating stories.

Rationality and emotion. Expectation and fulfillment. Stereotypes and exceptions. Reality and illusion. Myth and historical narrative. These are factors we all face in trying to influence the future, or reconstruct what has been, and from whom we come. A first step in taking charge of this calculus is to realize that something is missing. As Toni Morrison has written, "somebody forgot to tell somebody something" or, at least, we've been "playing in the dark."[15] Then we must remember that memories are made, we are made by memories, and history is a reconstruction of the past. If we can live with the fact that the truth, the whole truth, and nothing but the truth about anything will probably never be known, we're on our way.

RABBIT TALES AND CABIN STORIES

Understanding how stories work and how our brains incorporate stories brings us a long way toward understanding how important the past is to the present. Ultimately, to understand and to benefit from the past we have to know how to read its narratives. Folktales and children's stories are our earliest lessons in literary interpretation. One of the first characters we encounter is the trickster. Two of the most well-known tricksters are Brer Rabbit and Bugs Bunny. Since Bugs Bunny is the polycultured descendant of Brer Rabbit, and not quite as relevant to antebellum African America, I'll take Brer Rabbit as the prime example. Brer Rabbit is among the smallest and most vulnerable members of the animal world, but he inevitably overcomes the bigger, badder bear, fox, and alligator. Consider the "Tar Baby" story. Brer Rabbit got caught in the Tar Baby because he got mad when she didn't return his greeting. He let his anger override his good sense. He lashed out and found his paw stuck. He hit with the other paw. The same thing happened. Brer Rabbit continued to lash out until he had no free appendages. When his nemesis Brer

Fox discovered him in this predicament, it seemed that Brer Rabbit was doomed. But Brer Rabbit convinced Brer Fox that being thrown into the briar patch was worse than being trapped with the Tar Baby. Eager to add insult to injury, Brer Fox pulled Brer Rabbit loose and flung him into the briar patch. But, as the rabbit gleefully informed the fox, he had been "born and bred in the briar patch." Brer Rabbit was home free.

Antebellum African America, people were exposed early to the power and the glory of words. From stories of tricksters such as Brer Rabbit and John de High Conqueror or from the imaginative sermons of preachers from the ceremonial songs of the ancestors to the ballads of their contemporaries, they absorbed important lessons about the power of words woven into truthful, though not necessarily factual, narratives. As we confront these ancestral stories of love and marriage, we need to read closely what is said and how it is said. We need, also, to consider what is not said.

Let me demonstrate what I mean with a brief description of the life and letters of Paul Laurence Dunbar, a late-nineteenth-century poet whose stories of antebellum African America were popular with white readers and with black readers at a time when their expectations and realities were quite different. With the assistance of wily editors such as James Newton Mathews and William Dean Howells, Dunbar's poetry was published in such mainstream literary journals as the *Atlantic Monthly* and *Saturday Evening Post*. We could consider Dunbar's story an inversion of Brer Rabbit's Tar Baby experience. Brer Rabbit made the fox believe that he greatly feared the briar patch when it really was his home. Dunbar made white readers believe he had a native's knowledge of the antebellum South, but he was born and reared in the postbellum North. The antebellum narratives in prose and in poetry that Dunbar recited and sold were constructions of his imagination or translations of tales he had learned from others. They were neither accurate nor actual. But Dunbar made a good living from his writings and public readings. Americans of all ethnic backgrounds loved his quaint and funny sketches of life in the slave quarters.

His poetry appealed to people of different cultures and realities. Like Brer Rabbit, he was a trickster. Dunbar excelled in a rhetorical device that did, in fact, exemplify antebellum African American literature. He signified; that is, he communicated with a deliberate ambiguity that said more than one thing simultaneously. Like Brer Rabbit, Paul Laurence Dunbar didn't actually lie. In fact, in the writings in which he uses standard English and traditional Western literary forms, he is pretty clear about his politics and his practices. For example, "We Wear the Mask" begins with this statement:

> We wear the mask that grins and lies,
> It hides our face and shades our eyes,
> This debt we pay to human guile;
> With torn and bleeding hearts we smile,
> And mouth with myriad subtleties.[16]

The mask, Dunbar says, pays a "debt" to "human guile." It is worn to keep the world from knowing a person too well. The mask keeps private the thoughts and feelings that would anger or frighten the dominant society. Under a cloak of humor, wearing a mask of good cheer, Dunbar wrote about things that were neither.

Dunbar's poem "A Cabin Tale" gives us a chance to practice our interpretative skills while seeing at the same time how signifying works. "A Cabin Tale" is subtitled "The Young Master Asks for a Story" and begins this way:

> Whut you say, dah! Huh, uh! chile,
> You's enough to dribe me wile.
> Want a sto'y; jes' hyeah dat!
> Whah' 'll I git a sto'y at?
> Di'n' I tell you th'ee las' night?
> Go 'way, honey, you ain't right.
> I got somep'n else to do.
> 'Cides jes' tellin' tales to you. (Gates and McKay 919)

The narrator could be male or female, Mammy, Aunt Jemima, Uncle Remus, or Uncle Ben. I'll assume here the narrator is male. The narrator speaks in a literary dialect that signals to the general public that the teller lacks sophistication, education, and probably intelligence. But the narrator's words are our only source for the story. He controls what we know and how we know it. And from these words we also understand immediately that the boy may be the "young master," but the narrator is in control. He has something the boy wants, he can censor or condense or distort what he tells the boy, and, if we thought about it, we'd realize that he can do the same to us. The narrator calls the boy "chile" and "honey," but that simply sweetens the rebuff that says the boy's desires are not his priorities. He seems disinterested in, indeed tired of, such requests. The dialect and its connotations along with the singsong rhyme give a lilt that seems light and harmless to the gruff, even hostile, response to the request for a story. The slippage between what is being said and how it is being said is one way of signifying.

Another is the story itself. The speaker responds to the boy's pleas for a story with a tale about a weasel. The little animal has two problems. An ax-toting farmer interferes with the weasel's efforts to carry off the farmer's chickens. A big bear not only takes the chickens the weasel wants but also ridicules him for being so small. The wily weasel makes up a story that gets the farmer to kill the bear, and turns the farmer into an ally who actually gives him a fat chicken. The weasel does this by telling each one a different set of selected facts fashioned into a plausible narrative. When the internal story ends, the child asks for another story but the narrator refuses saying, "Want some mo, you rascal, you? / No, suh! No, suh! dat'll do" (Gatesand McKay 921).

The weasel's cunning, the poem's rhythm, the dialect's inherent positioning of the speaker as unschooled and naïve all make it easy to read this piece as a harmless, humorous story. But it doesn't take much to see the somber tones coloring this scene. The poem's title is "A Cabin Tale." "A" suggests it is one of many situations or many tales. "Cabin" carries connotations of less complicated, more pastoral lives. But such lives and those who live them are also construed as lowly, simple, and humble. People of lower classes and lesser economic means live in cabins. In the postbellum period of Dunbar's publications "cabin" also would have evoked slave quarters. A really significant signifying sign is the subtitle "The Young Master Asks for a Story." The weasel tale establishes the importance of discerning between what is said and what is meant, what sounds truthful and what is true. The story that frames the weasel tale is also about appearance and reality. The "Young Master" is asking for a story, but should his request be denied directly or abruptly, he does have the power to force a recitation. A "master," young or mature, represents power, if not outright ownership. The young master asks for a story. But the request cannot be directly or abruptly refused. The storyteller can grumble and can invoke a series of requirements for the young listener, however. Over the course of events, he orders the master to be quiet, to sit up straight, and to stifle his questions. When the master interrupts to check the facts, asking whether the teller had actually witnessed the events, the narrator threatens to send him to bed without a conclusion to the tale.

The tale of the weasel, the farmer, and the bear and the tale of the telling of the tale are essentially the same. In each case, the less powerful exercises some control over the more powerful. The teller chooses what to tell and how much. Words work to negotiate power. People who were aware of signifying would quickly realize similarities with their situations. Readers familiar with the range of Dunbar's writings generally, and specifically with signifying, would expect Dunbar's poems to be both humorous and serious, entertaining and instructive. They would immediately recognize the tale within the tale. Those who were predisposed to hear a particular story might have an inkling that more was being said than they knew. But they generally would have accepted the story at face value. They would not have heard all that was said. Or, if they did, they would be hard pressed to articulate their discomfort.

Much of what we know today as antebellum history was learned by young masters who failed to hear the stories in context. They could not see beyond their informants' masks. When we realize this, we can recognize several things. Some of the stories that have been passed down to us were responses to requests that were really requirements. They may not be what the teller would have volunteered as much as what the teller said to accommodate others. Much of what has been passed down to us comes from those who selected witnesses whose testimonies they expected to please them, and who only half heard or simply didn't hear the parts with which they disagreed or were uncomfortable. Some stories that have been passed down to us are told not by participants but by others who are speaking for or about them.

Distanced as we are by time and circumstance, we need to listen and read with eyes and ears tuned to what we can know about the speaker and the speaker's circumstances. Academics offer their narrative versions of skeptical dispassionate interest by referring to this as "discursive contexts" and "hermeneutics of suspicion." As is the case with "A Cabin Tale," if we employ these techniques, we can see more than ordinarily meets the eye. Or, as our grandparents would likely say, if we just "consider the source" and "take it with a grain of salt," we can get close to what is real.

THE REAL, THE TRUTH, AND THE
AFRO-PROTESTANT PRESS

"What is real?" asked the rabbit.

—*Margery Williams,* The Velveteen Rabbit (1922)

*"Words are real," said Ole Time Religion, "and you'd best figure
out not just their source and what they mean. You need to know that
in the beginning was the word and you need to know that words can
become flesh and blood. You need to believe that you can help make
reality by being 'Doers of the Word.'"*

One of the reasons why we must consider as many stories as possible and
interpret them correctly is because they are our models and they model
us. Much of what we can know about love and marriage in antebellum
African America comes from the publications they created and lived
by. In these publications, ranging from the privately printed sermons,
broadsides, poems, stories, and memoirs of the eighteenth century to the
earliest known African American newspaper, *Freedom's Journal*, published
in 1827, love and marriage are frequent topics. From whom to marry
to how to marry, to who married whom, to how to live married until
death or beyond, we have pages and pages of such discussion. Given that
these documents were created by African Americans for African Americans, we could rightly expect more candor, more revealing writing. But
lest we forget—not only can paper fall into hostile hands, but African
America was diverse. Being united is not the same as being unanimous.
Most of the publications were produced and distributed by a small group
of people with similar religious beliefs and political goals. Everything
they wrote was not fact. A lot of it was what they wanted to become fact,
or Word made flesh.

John 1:1 says: "in the beginning was the Word." In some West African religions, Nommo is "the Word," and Nommo is transmitted from
one's senses into one's mind. In Christianity and in such African tribal
religions, "the Word," like Nommo, comes from God and is God. Many
religions affirm the interconnectedness of word and creation, of omnip-
otence and communication. Both the tribal religions and Christianity
rely upon stories to convey seeds of truth. The seeds must be planted and
nurtured within the minds and hearts of a recipient, who then must nur-
ture a rightful interpretation and use. "The Word" must become flesh.
Afro-Protestantism melds theologies and cosmologies from African tribal
heritage and from Judeo-Christian heritage. Afro-Protestantism stresses
hearing "the Word" and becoming "Doers of the Word." A favorite
twentieth-century gospel song that captures ancestral desires proclaims

"I have to live the life I sing about in my song." The lyrics elaborate with details such as needing to consistently behave as instructed. "I can't go to church on Sunday and run around all day Monday." But living "the Word," especially under antebellum slavery and racism, was difficult enough without adding the task of trying to convince others to live similarly. This required more than just faith. Ideals had to become ideas. Ideas had to be translated into actions. Enter African American print culture. Enter the Afro-Protestant press. By "Afro-Protestant" I mean the AME Church and the African Episcopal Church, which grew out of the African Union Society of Philadelphia under the visions of Richard Allen and Absalom Jones. I mean the Colored Episcopal Church, the African Methodist Episcopal Zion Church, the African Union Methodist Protestant Church, and the many congregations and congresses of Presbyterians, Congregationalists, Episcopalians, Baptists and other denominations governed and predominately populated by African Americans. By "Afro-Protestant press" I also mean the publications and publishing presses, the distribution centers, and the writers and readers that were intentionally developed under the auspices of Afro-Protestant denominations and congregations. I mean the publications by writers whose Afro-Protestant affiliations were publicly and prominently known, even when they published independently or as autonomously as was possible in antebellum African America.

We can recognize some of the Afro-Protestant publications because their denominational affiliation was clear. The *Christian Recorder's* masthead announced that it was "published by the AME Church in the United States, for the Dissemination of Religion, Morality, Literature and Science."[17] However, we should not assume that the auspices determined the paper's audience or its impact. The *Recorder* included some denominational business, but it was an international newspaper, and its purview extended beyond the religion, morality, literature, or science its masthead proclaimed. The *Christian Recorder's* parent publication was Martin Delany's paper the *Mystery,* founded in Pittsburgh in 1843. Delany sold the *Mystery* to the AME Church when he joined Frederick Douglass in founding the antislavery newspaper the *North Star.* Though some contributors were ordained ministers and some of the news related to Afro-Protestant church business, neither the *Mystery* nor the *North Star* was a church organ. The *Mystery* became the *Christian Herald,* was moved to Philadelphia, and in 1852 was renamed the *Christian Recorder.* It printed news from around the world and enjoyed an international readership. How much attention it gave to AME concerns varied with its editorship.

Whether sponsored by a particular denomination or not, virtually every antebellum African American periodical carried subtitles or printed mission statements that declared moral, material, and civic progress to be its purpose. The integration of secular and spiritual goals began with the first known Afro-Protestant paper, *Freedom's Journal.* Among the founders and editors of that paper were prominent ministers such as Richard Allen and Samuel E. Cornish. Its founders and contributors were also men who were known more for their radical politics than for any theological interests or activities, for example David Walker and John Russwurm. *Freedom's Journal* identified itself as a paper "devoted to the dissemination of useful knowledge among our brethren, and to their moral and religious improvement." It identified its motto as "Righteousness exalthed a Nation." The *Weekly Advocate* was "Established for and Dedicated to the Moral, Mental and Political Improvement of the People of Color" in 1837. The *Repository of Religion and Literature and Science and Art* began publication in Indianapolis in 1858. It operated as a consortium of literary societies in Missouri, Indiana, and Baltimore. The San Francisco *Mirror of the Times* in 1856 was "a weekly newspaper devoted to Freedom, Morality, Industry & Intelligence." San Francisco's *Lunar Visitor* was "devoted to the Moral, Intellectual and Social Improvement of the Colored Race." Its editor signed himself "J. J. Moore, V.D.M."[18] John Jamison Moore was an AME Zion minister who not long afterward was appointed a bishop.

Contributors to the Afro-Protestant press were not necessarily baptized true believers. Before the Civil War and the politics of Reconstruction added other avenues, the Afro-Protestant church was the vehicle by which words might become deeds. Afro-Protestant churches were the community centers. They were communications headquarters. They were the sites of communal wealth and economic development. The earliest publications were printed with their support. The Afro-Protestant church wielded whatever political power African America had. Politicians and spokespersons such as Frederick Douglass, Henry Highland Garnet, and Frances E. W. Harper held their rallies and gave their lectures in their churches. Regardless of their personal beliefs and usually without significant alteration, virtually all African American writers and spokespersons found it expedient to shape their words so they could be published in Afro-Protestant newspapers, periodicals, and other media outlets.

There was genuine conflict of course. Some held rigid beliefs that resisted alternatives or compromises. Institutions and individuals competed for power and priority. But in general, the Afro-Protestant press was the voice of antebellum African America. It tried to create a unified culture from many differing ones. The press admonished against thinking of oneself as independent of the group. It repeatedly reminded its readers that the actions of one reflected on the reputations of all, and warned of the perils of anomalous behaviors. African Americans knew well the distance between the cup and the lip, between theory and practice, and between literary depictions and actual behavior. They appreciated the necessity of a rhetoric of righteousness. They knew that theory and proclamation were not necessarily congruent with the ways the authors and speakers themselves lived, let alone the audiences they were trying to convince.

The press regularly played on class differences and class aspirations to promote particular behaviors and to contain others. It frequently printed satirical or humorous pieces that showed what ought not be done. The objects of satire tended to speak in dialect in order to emphasize their behavior as lower class, uneducated, or unsophisticated. They were identified as "rustics" or foreigners. Articles reporting the most egregious violations of moral consensus or rectitude were usually identified as being reprinted from European or Euro-American sources. This practice was clearly one worthy of Brer Rabbit. The sources of these articles imply—but do not say—that the perpetrators were not African American. This allows the publishers to use the foibles of whites to instruct blacks. It allows them to ridicule and judge inappropriate behavior by the dominant society under the guise of innocently repeating what is already public knowledge. Afro-Protestant writings were almost always designed to affirm particular behaviors in correspondence with the social and political philosophies favored by Afro-Protestantism, which tolerated a surprising amount of theological and pragmatic diversity. Still, it was not an equal opportunity employer. Most of the extant African American documents published before the end of slavery were created and distributed by a relatively privileged and homogenous segment of the African American population. Those who preached and lectured were not always the elite and literate class, but those who were published and who were quoted generally were. They were denominational leaders and ministers of the more influential and wealthy churches. They were the teachers, fraternal or sororal officers, community spokespersons, and successfully self-employed barbers, caterers, and other skilled workers. Some were self-educated, but all had leisure to write or access to amanuenses. They had the money or influence to have their writings published and their words heard, if not heeded. We must read the wealth of information and opinions about dreams, aspirations, and marriage ideals with this in mind. We should read the stories, essays, songs, sermons, and poems as if their authors say, like Elizabeth Keckley, "everything I have written is strictly true; much has been omitted."

The absence of the voices and viewpoints of those who did not publicly adhere to Afro-Protestantism is a major omission in early African American print culture; yet enough documents remain to remind us that there were many people of African descent who were not Afro-Protestant.[19] We must therefore remember that there were regions in African America that were dominated by Afro-Muslim or Afro-Catholic theologies and that many, possibly the majority, of the antebellum people of African ancestry embraced cosmologies that enjoined behaviors antithetical or anathema to Afro-Protestants. A few such as Sojourner Truth and Rebecca Jackson were closely associated with spiritualists, Shakers, Quakers, and other Eurocentric cults and religions. Nonetheless, in antebellum African America, Afro-Protestantism and African American print culture were so integrally and inextricably connected that they were virtually one and the same.

All print culture is to some extent already encoded. Early African American print culture was especially so. Satire and irony were popular rhetorical devices in the antebellum United States. But signifying that is colored and contoured by the experiences of slavery and racism carries additional connotations and conditions. One key to decoding or reading antebellum African American literature correctly is to remember West African predilections for teaching indirectly by allusion, metaphor, and signifying. Another key is remembering the context of communication. What is whispered is often more revealing than what is put in writing. Publication did just that: it made matters public. Antebellum African Americans had many reasons to protect their privacy. Especially with family matters and concerning issues of love and marriage, people of African descent did what was necessary to be as autonomous and real as possible. An African American ancestral aphorisms expresses the situation this way: "De black snake keeps up wid de fam'ly secrets ob de settin' hens." Deciding who the snake is, who the setting hens are, or what is masked and what is straightforward, is not always simple. It is important

to remember that the more enemies know about you, the more dangerous they are, even when it isn't quite clear who the enemies are.

Culture is always a work in progress. Conditions are always changing.
Behavioral adjustments are negotiated sometimes voluntarily, sometimes
by coercion. Action and attitude are not necessarily the same. In reconstructing African American history and culture, as with reconstructive
history generally, we must always remember that what we see is not necessarily what we get. Every shut eye ain't sleep. Every good-bye ain't gone.

Much of the African American print culture with which we are most
familiar was written and published for an interracial audience. Racial
etiquette, common sense, and untranslatable language influenced what,
how, and how much was written. Harriet Jacobs wrote, "I have not exag-
gerated the wrongs inflicted by Slavery; on the contrary, my descriptions
fall far short of the facts"—and signs that attestation with the pseudonym
"Linda Brent."[20] James Mars begins his narrative by saying that in his
story, "there were a great many things that I did not mention."[21] William Craft writes: "this book is not intended as a full history of my wife,
nor of myself; but merely an account of our escape; together with other
matter."[22]

The fact that incidents have been omitted, names were sometimes
changed, and descriptions regularly "fall short of the facts" does not
mean the truth is not being told. Testimonies by African Americans are
as legitimate as those from witnesses of other geographic and cultural
origins. What they wrote is historical evidence. All stories are essential if
we hope to come closer to knowing the whole truth. We must not interpret any single writer, article, or source at face value. We should not mis-
take half a truth for the whole. People do not write in a vacuum. Time,
place, intention, and perception vary. Our ancestral scribes knew, maybe
better than many e-mailers do today, that discretion is the best part of
valor. Printed material can fall into the wrong hands or can be used for
purposes for which it was not intended. Our ancestors donned verbal
masks. In writing, as in conversation, they often employed ambiguity and
signifying. Granny would call this hitting a straight lick with a crooked
stick.

SIX

GETTING STORIES
STRAIGHT, KEEPING
THEM REAL

"HITTING A STRAIGHT LICK WITH A CROOKED STICK"
is a wonderfully precise way of saying that we don't always need the perfect tool to do a good job. Sometimes improvisation and imagination are
as useful—and more satisfying to use. But in order to know how to hit
a straight lick with a crooked stick, we have to know the stick is crooked
and how to compensate for its deficiency. Scholars advocate that we
interpret stories knowing the context within which a story originates and
how it compares with others of its kind. African American folk advise the
same thing when they remind us to "Consider the source," that "Every
good-bye ain't gone," or as a popular calypso song says:

> You have to live doubting,
>   and yet believing.
> That's the way we get by.[1]

However the idea is worded, the moral is that we need to know how to
decide what, when, and how much to believe. We need to decide which
ancestral stories and historical accounts to pass on, and how best to do
so. We have to know which to disavow or how to supplement. This takes
skill and practice, but we can take a lesson from rock hounds. Before
searching for gemstones, they learn where the rocks they seek are most

likely to be found and how to distinguish among precious stones, semi-precious stones, and leave-em-lies. They learn to distinguish between gold and fool's gold. However, even the most experienced prospectors must still assay their findings before they know the value. But search and analyze we must. If we do not, we risk forgetting what must not be forgotten, losing the knowledge of how we can survive and what we need to transcend. And if that happens, then as in Toni Morrison's *Beloved*, "By and by all trace is gone, and what is forgotten is not only the footprints but the water too and what it is down there."[2]

THE HALF-LIFE OF HALF TRUTHS

Dr. Martin Luther King, Jr., an African American griot and a true Doer of the Word, told a familiar story:

> On the plantation the institution of legal marriage did not exist.... There were polygamous relationships, fragile, monogamous relations, illegitimacies, abandonment, and most of all, the tearing apart of families as children, husbands or wives were sold to other plantations.... Masters and their sons used Negro women to satisfy their spontaneous lust or, as concubines.[3]

In *Families and Freedom: A Documentary History of African-American Kinship in the Civil War Era*, historians Ira Berlin and Leslie Rowland record this variation:

> The conjugal relationships of slaves had no legal standing, no formal protections against intrusions by the owner. Husbands and wives could reside together or visit across plantation lines only with their owners' consent. They had no recourse against sexual abuse. Their unions could be permanently shattered at any time by the sale of a spouse or other forced separation.[4]

Both accounts are factual. Both are narratives that have gone on to acquire the power of myth. That is, these and similar narratives have unknown or multiple authorship and explain institutions, situations, customs, rites, and rituals that are otherwise seemingly inexplicable phenomena. They are stories that contain at least some truth. They are stories we believe, or at least act as if we do.

Since we all need something to believe in and to direct our behaviors, it would appear that we should pass this story on to others. But the stories we tell shape the lives we live. It is necessary then to evaluate each story's worth. Would this story help or would it hurt? Would it enhance our self-esteem or motivate strong and healthy relationships? If not, then maybe the story is, as Toni Morrison puts it in the novel *Beloved*, "not a story to pass on." But if we were to stop telling this story, would we be avoiding the truth of our past? Would we be guilty of whitewashing history? Do we have the right to select the stories, both personal and public, that we pass on to others and the stories that we pass over? By omitting the bad and the ugly, would we be making propaganda, reconstructing history, forgetting our Beloved? When and how ought *re*memory replace memory? I don't intend these questions to be merely rhetorical, but I don't have cut-and-dried answers either. What I do have are admonitions about making sure we have as much information, and as many versions as possible, before we pass on what we think we know.

I began this section with a myth based on half truth. First of all, I quoted only part of the story Dr. Martin Luther King, Jr., told that day. After stating that plantation slavery tore families apart, Dr. King continues:

> Through the ante-bellum era, the Negro family struggled against the odds to survive, and miraculously many did. In all this psychological and physical horror many slaves managed to hold on to their children and developed warmth and affection and family loyalties against the smashing tides of emotional corruption and destruction. (King 405)

After reporting that slaves could not marry and that slaveholders could and did disregard their wishes, Berlin and Rowland continue:

> In the face of these circumstances, slaves forged their own understandings of marriage, the proper regulations of sexuality, the obligations of husbands to wives and wives to husbands, and the role of the wider slave community in sanctioning and enforcing such expectations. With the long-awaited end of slavery, they adapted these understandings to the new world of freedom. (Berlin and Rowland 154)

If you did not notice that the first versions were incomplete, you are probably in the majority. The first half of the story is better known and many shape their lives knowing only that half truth. Others use only the second half. Combined, the two halves make stories, but still neither nor both tell the whole story. Myths and histories are passed on both by those who wish us harm, and those, such as King, Berlin, and Rowland, who would give their lives to protect us from harm. Like the radioactivity from X-rays and nuclear spills, the half-lives of half truths continue long into the future. If I can stretch this metaphor a bit farther, I will say also that some of the people who extend the half-lives of half truths have destructive motives: for example, those who seek to prevent African Americans from surviving and thriving, artists who are primarily concerned about producing what promises the most profit, and others who are so intent on getting what they want for themselves that they don't care who they hurt or help. Having noted that not all myths are created for good, I turn my attention now to myths created with good intentions.

In this chapter, I use stories told by our friends and families, our scholars, teachers, and preachers, and other allies who want to help make us well. I am offering stories on which they and we build our therapies, our palliative public policies and laws, stories of stories that are being passed on to us, stories that shape our ideas of others and of ourselves. I am passing on stories that are potentially more helpful and concurrently more harmful because they are passed to us by our leaders and heroes. These stories are myths that we believe and by which we live. They are words made flesh. They are, therefore, stories that we should not pass on as if they were the truth and nothing but. They are, at this time, what we have and we must make do with for now. We can hit fairly straight licks with these crooked sticks if we analyze the defects and use them to our purposes.

OUR KIN AND OUR KIND

Kinship is an excellent example. For generations, people of African descent in the United States have spoken of themselves as kinfolk, as extended family. We African Americans use *aunt* and *uncle, brother, sister, mother, father, cousin,* and other relative terms in churches, fraternities, sororities, lodges, and clubs. Thus, when the February 2005 issue of *Essence* had a Valentine's Day focus on restorative love, we readers readily understood the obvious implications of the article title "[Our Legacy]: Breaking the Chains." I offer my version of the story of this article and the stories that underlie it as an example of stories told with all good intentions that are inappropriate or incomplete.

The question *Essence* posed to a social worker, a psychologist, and a psychiatrist was how "can we set ourselves free" from the "bonds of slavery [that] continue to hold Black folks captive?" Nearly a century and a half has passed since enslavement of black people was legal in the United States. A substantial percentage of people of African descent in the nation are not descendants of those enslaved in this country. African immigration did not end with the slave trade. In the second half of the twentieth century, especially, the United States has been a destination for millions seeking asylum or the American Dream. Those whose ancestors did witness slavery in the United States are about seven generations removed from that experience. However, *Essence* rightfully reports that many people see the roots of present-day misery in the trauma of slavery in the United States.

How to "set ourselves free" from the "bonds of slavery" assumes that "Black folks" are enchained by slavery's legacy and that freedom is something "Black folks" can achieve for themselves. Since Africans were enslaved not merely on the North American continent or in the Western world but also in South America, Europe, Asia, and Africa, the slavery of the past that may bind "Black folks" today was global. The panelists accepted the assumption of a past-defined present, but the slavery that they referenced was that made in the USA. Moreover, the restored love on which they focused is that desired by heterosexual couples. Their answers focused on romantic or marital relationships between women and men. The history that underlies the *Essence* article is summed up in one panelist's statement:

> So even when people were able to form relationships and create family, it was all tenuous, because at any moment the slave owner could say, "I'm going to sell you." I believe that created a sense of tentativeness and impermanence in relationships that we sometimes see today. Combined with the trust issues, this may help explain the divorce rate in our community—which is estimated to be 20 percent to 30 percent higher than for White couples.[5]

This statement is problematic. It suggests that the panelists and the reporter, like most of us, forget, ignore, or don't know stories about people such as Isaac Forman. Forman was enslaved in Norfolk, Virginia. His wife lived in Richmond. They were allowed to visit only once or twice a year. So when in December 1854 Isaac Forman got the chance to escape to Canada, he took it. Almost immediately he wrote to William Still, a famous African American "conductor" on the Underground Railroad, asking if someone could rescue his wife. A few months later, he was frantic and almost ready to return to enslavement. "What is freedom to me, when I know that my wife is in slavery?" he wrote. His letter of May 7, 1854, reveals the strong, deep love he had for the wife with whom he had not lived for more than a few days a couple of times a year:

My soul is vexed, my troubles are inexpressible. I often feel as if I were willing to die. I must see my wife in short, if not, I will die. What would I not give no tongue can utter. Just to gaze on her sweet lips one moment I would be willing to die the next. I am determined to see her some time or other....If I had known as much before I left, as I do now, I would never have left until I could have found means to have brought her with me....You must oblige me by seeing Mr. Brown and ask [*sic*] him if he would oblige me by going to Richmond and see my wife and see what arrangements he could make with her, and I would be willing to pay all his expenses there and back....I am determined to see her, if I die the next moment. I can say I was once happy, but never will be again, until I see her; because what is freedom to me, when I know that my wife is in slavery?[6]

We learn Isaac Forman's story from two letters William Still includes in *The Underground Railroad*. Forman's story is incomplete. We don't know if he and his wife were reunited. We don't even know his wife's name. But what we do know is that this story, like many others related in this book, contradicts the dominant historical narratives that say that for enslaved people, love and marriage were too fragile to withstand separation. Isaac Forman's story reminds us of why we need to "live doubting and yet believing" when we hear that the "sense of tentativeness and impermanence in relationships that we sometimes see today" is the legacy of African Americans before the Great Emancipator freed them during the Civil War.

The myth of the Great Emancipator is in itself a wonderful example of a half truth with a remarkably long half-life. Abraham Lincoln's "Emancipation Proclamation" freed slaves only in the "rebel" states that had seceded from the Union. Another part of that story is that the secessionists had formed a separate government. They considered themselves part of the Confederate States of the Union. Lincoln was not their president. Jefferson Davis was. For enslaved people, Lincoln's words were rhetoric, not relief. His edict had no legitimacy in the rebel states to which it was directed, and it did not address the conditions of the enslaved in Union states. Nonetheless, the myth that prevails today is that President Lincoln's Emancipation Proclamation "freed the slaves," after which they were able to marry. But by then, so the story goes, the damage had been done.

Details differ, but the conclusion that prevails is always the same: after the Emancipation Proclamation, after the Civil War, and after a couple of constitutional amendments, people of African descent still could not love and cherish one another. Black women and black men were at odds. The men, overpowered by the combined assaults of white people outside and black women inside their communities, simply could not survive by being loyal and tender. The women, traumatized by regular rape but empowered by greater access to money and work, could not or would not accept masculine authority or protection; thereby not allowing black men to behave like *real* men. Our knowledge of cause and effect informs us that slavery coupled with postemancipation racial discrimination brought forth the poverty, despair, anger, hurt, shame, and suspicion that characterize too much of African America today. We conclude then that multiple marriage malfunctions or lifetimes without ever marrying are our legacy from slavery.

Such conclusions completely ignore some obvious realities. First of all, they do not recognize the multiple and changing realities of class, caste, creed, or condition of servitude in antebellum African America. Second, rape is a violent imposition of power, a tool of control. White men certainly raped black women. They probably raped enslaved women most often, but they preyed on women of every ethnicity, free or not. Common sense should tell us that white males were not the only sexual predators. Adults assaulted children. Men assaulted women. Women assaulted men. Men assaulted men, and women assaulted women. Then, as now, the strong exploited the weak with every variety of sexual congress imaginable.

On the other hand, antebellum sexual relationships cannot be summarized by the stories of nonconsensual or exploitative attachments. Family stories, published fiction, memoirs, and court cases bear witness to love, seduction, infatuation, or mutual attractions that defied race and class. In the mid–nineteenth century, William G. Allen, an African American, and Mary King, a Euro-American, loved one another. In *The American Prejudice against Color,* Allen writes that they thought they knew all of the "difficulties, embarrassments, trials, insults, and persecutions" that their "diversity of complexion" would cause. As Allen's account indicates, their imaginations were not enough to forewarn them of the incredible uproar that their engagement incited. Nonetheless, the couple persisted. Allen also tells a version of a story many of have heard. A Louisiana law prohibited marriage between "white" men and even those women who appeared white but were known to have African ancestry. The only exception was for those "white" men who could prove they, too, had "African blood." The besmitten couple pricked their fingers, mingled their blood, and married legally.[7] Whether it fits our personal politics or not, we ought not ignore the fact that despite law and custom, even during the slave era, interracial love and marriage was a fact.

Furthermore, romantic relationships were not then and are not now exclusive to heterosexuals. To ignore same-sex relationships is to ignore our own history, a history relevant not just to homosexuals but also to all of us. It obscures ways in which definitions and enactments of heterosexuality are based on and intertwined with those of homosexuality. It oversimplifies and distorts social constructions, identities, and challenges in antebellum America. When we tell stories of the past, when we repeat stories of the past, when we ponder them, we should privilege the stories that are like prisms revealing the complexity and multiple hues of light. The stories that reveal the multiplicity of conditions and experiences, and the beliefs and behaviors of people of African and other descents, will be most helpful to us.

In antebellum times, as now, people of African descent lived in a world increasingly smaller and increasingly confounded by racism and ethnocentricity. And it is a fact that myths can help. One of the first things to get straight, however, is that slavery was not the same reality for all African Americans. Not all enslaved African Americans worked on cotton or rice plantations. Not all were chained, whipped, and physically abused. Some antebellum African Americans, even in the places where slavery existed, were not and never had been enslaved. Some descended from generations of free people. Some free African Americans did not know anyone who was enslaved. Some owned slaves themselves.

We need to know and to reconcile stories such as the *Narrative of the Life and Adventures of Venture, A Native of Africa*. In various confrontations with his "owners," Venture Smith defended himself with a pitchfork, threw their whip into the fire, and used fists and feet to "stomp" them. When he was handcuffed, he thanked his mistress for his "gold rings." When his master hit him with a club, Venture "snatched the club out of his hands and dragged him out of the door" (Gates and McKay 178). Eventually Venture Smith purchased himself, his sons, a daughter, his wife, and others. It is not clear whether Venture freed those he bought or even intended to free them. It is clear, though, that when one man escaped and when his son died at sea, Smith was greatly distressed that this depleted his capital by 135 pounds in colonial cash. It may have been, as it was with some other slaveholding people of African descent, that he could not afford to free them legally. There were often huge "free taxes" or restrictions on freed people that made freedom an unnecessary expense or disruption of family life. We can also consider the fact that at particular times and in some places, the differences, especially for women, between being enslaved, apprenticed, indentured, and married were slight. In Venture Smith's case, owning his wife did not interfere with his love for her. In the conclusion of his narrative, he writes, "Amidst all my griefs and pains, I have many consolations; Meg, the wife of my youth, whom I married for love, and bought with my money, is still alive" (Gates and McKay 185).

Other half-truth myths that we should resist passing on are those that use African Americans to represent the entire African Diaspora. The stories of people of African descent in the United States are part of a larger history. The British, French, Portuguese, Spanish, Dutch, and Danish were not the only purveyors of human flesh, and even they did not ship their captives only via the Middle Passage. The African slave trade was international, transnational, and global. People from one nation, culture, or tribe of Africa were scattered across other parts of the African continent. Africans were sent—or went—to the places we now know as Asia, the Middle East, Australia, and India, as well as other smaller and lesser known islands and land masses everywhere on the planet Earth. African Americans are similar to, and different from, their African diasporic kin in other parts of the world. We are certainly different today. "Black folks" were and are a diverse and continually evolving group. When we speak of ourselves as "family," when we assume a common slave heritage, we create stories that are simplistic, disorienting, and often damaging to family unity. To define our legacy as "chains" that must be broken is to assert our ignorance or our disregard for what our heritage includes.

As with many stories, there is another side we should acknowledge. Despite our many descriptions of African America as marginal, a nation within a nation, or more African than *American*, the global power of the United States of America is and has long been "a black thang" also. Cassandra Pybus's study *Epic Journeys of Freedom: Runaway Slaves of the American Revolution and their Global Quest for* Liberty[8] includes many stories of wives and husbands, mothers and fathers, and children who went to Nova Scotia, Germany, Australia, England, Guyana, Belize, and other places. Some sank into abject poverty. Some prospered. Some assimilated into the indigenous culture. Some remained separate or, like those in the United States, created hybrid cultures. Many in the diaspora espoused cultural values of Africans in the United States. Often antebellum African Americans voluntarily went to Africa, Haiti, Jamaica, Russia, and other diaspora sites to spread the gospels of Euro-Christianity and of capitalism as practiced in the United States.

Even today, African America has a good amount of cultural capital. Jacqueline Nassy Brown and other anthropologists verify "the formative influence that Black America, in many forms, has had on racial and cultural identity" worldwide, and that for African diasporic people, generally, African America is a "mythical place." But some of that myth is solely the creation of a media that is not African American and whose stories have little or no bearing on the realities of African American culture. We must remember this, and we must offer alternative stories to counter the fact-laced fictions, exaggerations, and fantasies of dominant narratives that misshape our past and mislead us in the present. One reason why "[Our Legacy]: Breaking the Chains" is a problem is that the slanted fictions on which the discussion rests are not the best way for truth to be told. Indeed, this article is a fine illustration of why, as the calypso song says, we "have to live doubting, and yet believing." Because the storytellers here are professionals whose words are authoritative and whose services are directed by their interpretations of social and personal narratives, the stories that shape their minds and ministrations are especially important.

Representing the global with the parochial is a common occurrence nowadays, largely because technological advances have redefined and reinvigorated cultural imperialism. The prevalence of such misrepresentation has significant consequences. For better or for worse, rightly or wrongly, many African Americans—if and when they actually think beyond the United States at all—tend to consider themselves the original or archetypal people of the African Diaspora. So it's not surprising at all that though the question is about "Black folks," the *Essence* article focuses exclusively on declining marriage rates, routine distinctions between love and sex, and increasingly casual and careless sexual relationships in present-day African America.

Half-truths about Americans of African descent radiate misunderstandings beyond the boundaries of African America. Manning Marable has written that "ignorance of our shared history sustains our parallel racial universes."[9] Ignorance and misinformation beget many kinds of prejudice, bigotry, and racism. But knowledge and analysis, doubting and believing individually and collectively, can make parallel universes intersect or even integrate. Marable says:

> The state of being critically self-aware prefigures both a sense of power and a capacity for action. For the oppressed in racially stratified societies, self-awareness involves a fundamental recognition that many common practices of daily life retard one's development. As racialized populations reflect upon the accumulated concrete experiences of their own lives, the lives of others who share their situation, and even those who had died long ago, a process of discovery unfolds that begins to restructure how they understand the world and their place within it. That journey of discovery can produce a desire to join with others to build initiatives that create space, permitting the renewal or survival of a group, or a celebration of its continued existence despite the forces arrayed against it. (Marable 36)

We all need to speak truth to power and to tell at least some of our stories to people who are not necessarily "family" but with whom we coexist.

To do so is to begin to give due respect to slavery and enslaved people and their roles in our lives. To do so is to begin to create a foundation for a future in which we might actually become the best that we can be. Now, as never before, all of us in the United States or in places where the United States has influence are shaped and informed by stories of the antebellum past. Slavery fundamentally shaped public and social policies and practices in the United States of America. Though slavery was not the lived experience of everyone who arrived in the United States before 1865, slavery determined the economic conditions and social customs of all Americans then, and slave profits and failures are a legacy for all of us now. Slavery and racial prejudices like sexism and religious intolerance were increasingly significant presences in politics. Much more than we acknowledge, today's conflicts with fundamentalist religion, oppressive and tyrannical governments, and exclusive and abusive concepts of love, marriage, and sexual morality are part of our heritage. While we are unlikely to ever get all the pieces to fit into one inclusive and totally true history, we can at least learn and try to reconcile the multiple histories that compose our personal and cultural narratives today. Knowing what has been, and from what we have been shaped, we can figure out how to make what we have works for us. Once we know we have a crooked stick, we can, with practice and imagination, learn to hit a straight lick anyway.

When Dr. King said "on the plantation," he was not talking about those on farms and the frontier, in the villages and the cities. He was not talking about people who were not enslaved "on the plantation." To say "There were polygamous relationships, fragile, monogamous relations...[and] the tearing apart of families" is not to say how prevalent or how affective these situations were. We must contemplate what is said, what is not said, who is saying it, when, and with what authority. The story told by Dr. Martin Luther King, Jr., also helps us understand that negative narratives do not always come from those who mean to harm. Dr. King was a drum major for freedom. He wanted his words to lead us straight to the Promised Land. The staff he used was the strongest he had. E. Franklin Frazier is another example of friendly fire in our battle to be a free people in a free country. Frazier was an African American sociologist whose work informed much of that tragic chapter known as "The Moynihan Report." Like W. E. B. Du Bois, Carter G. Woodson, and other twentieth-century African American social scientists, E. Franklin Frazier gathered data and interpreted it in light of the history that he knew. Unfortunately, most of the history he knew, like the theories and methods he employed to make sense of it, was created by people who had not witnessed slavery. It relied heavily on accounts woven from legal documents, official statements, and the testimony of the enslavers, accounts that gave scant attention to what enslaved and free African Americans reported. These stories were distorted because they ignored, or were ignorant of, stories told from other perspectives and experiences, for other purposes and intents.

In *Black Rage*, mental health experts William Grier and Price Cobb foreshadowed *Essence*'s version of how to break our chains. Grier and Cobb told of a "cultural paranoia" that stemmed directly from destructive legacies of slavery and racial oppression. In the 1970s, many (mostly African American) mental health experts developed strategies and techniques based on stories in which slavery and the racism it engendered were the catalysts for increasingly dysfunctional behaviors of the day. While some looked across the Middle Passage back to Africa for insights into origins of African American customs and concepts, too few turned the same intensity of intentions to our own African American culture. Too many forgot what our forebears warned us about. We forgot to consider the source. Consequently, today's educational curricula, social welfare programs, and mental health therapies still overwhelmingly interpret our legacy as chains, victimhood, and martyrdom.

To "break the chains" of slavery's legacy, we need a fuller understanding of what that legacy is, who left it, and what it is worth. We need to see enough of what we have been bequeathed to compare, select, and use what is most valuable to achieve our aspirations. To know that slaves were forbidden by law to marry is to know a fact. That such proscriptions did not stop enslaved people from marrying is another fact, one that is essential to interpreting the former fact accurately.

Marable and others suggest that our immediate need is for "authentic history"; that is,

> a historical narrative in which blacks themselves are the principal actors, and . . . the story is told and explained largely from their own vantage point. The authentic narrative rejects out of hand the inferiority—biological, genetic, or cultural—of people of African descent to any other branches of the human family. (Marable 21)

He—as do I and others—calls for a juxtapositioning of "master narratives" and "counter narratives." When we consider, for example, the personal narratives of people who had been enslaved or who witnessed life among the enslaved, we probably won't believe the notion that enslavement "created a sense of tentativeness and impermanence in relationships that we sometimes see today." Why? Because accounts from antebellum African America reveal that marriages were common, long lasting, and highly valued. Some suggest that loving and stable relationships among African Americans were even more prevalent then than they are today.

But again, I emphasize that rather than substitute for the narratives of others the counter-narratives of antebellum African Americans who wrote about love, marriage, and sexual morality, we should think carefully about the circumstances of their publication and preservation, about what they say, how they say it, and what they do not say at all. We should think about their mythos; that is, the complex of attitudes and beliefs that characterize a particular group. And consider how these stories make us—and others—feel right now. Then we should accept the stories that are closest to the truths that create a healthy society. The myths of early African America tend to make us feel bad, sad, or mad. References to slavery days are generally embarrassing and disheartening. The stories of antebellum African America that we most readily recognize make us feel vulnerable, guilty, angry, and depressed. They provide few models for making today better, and they give little hope for the future. We should question this constellation of stories that defines and evaluates people of

African descent. Where did the most prevalent African American mythos originate? What or whose interests does it serve? Do we have or need alternatives? There are some stories we need to do more than think about. These are the stories that have come to form our mythos.[10]

MYTHS AND MIRRORING THE PRESENT PAST

Myths are powerful in part because they offer answers to present-day concerns. Our myths tell us that faith the size of a mustard seed, or a little ole ant, can move mountains. We rightly interpret them to mean that big changes can come from small beginnings. Why do we believe that one individual can change the course of the world? Perhaps because we pass on stories about Moses, Jesus, and Mohammed, and about Eve, Mary, and Kadijah. About Abraham Lincoln, Martin Luther King, Jr., Mahatma Gandhi, Mother Theresa, Rosa Parks, and Joan of Arc. About Adolph Hitler, Idi Amin Dada, Osama bin Laden, Mata Hari, Delilah, and Jezebel. We interpret the David and Goliath story to mean that despite apparent or actual power, a mighty foe can be defeated by a small boy with a slingshot— provided the boy has practiced using it. To harness mythic power, we need to remember, first of all, that myths are made and they can be unmade.

There is, however, more to myth-making or myth-remaking than just concocting or resurrecting stories. The stories must be told, believed, and ingrained into our minds and hearts. We can start with facts. Most myth-makers do. To be useful, facts about the historical past must be carefully chosen and recounted. It is a fact that by law and constitutional declaration, slaves were three-fifths human. It is also a fact that poetry and petitions, sermons, songs, stories, and other official documents show that "slaves" were 100 percent human. Facts change. Our Supreme Court affirmed in 1857 that people of African descent could not be United States citizens. People of African descent (and others) defied the United States Supreme Court edict and continued to define themselves as citizens who agitated for civil rights until the law changed. Laws are more helpful for knowing what was or might be occurring that legislators wished to curb than about what people were actually doing or trying to do. We can understand facts as verifiable, but we cannot assume that stories composed from facts alone will do the work of myths.

It may be less well known or it may not be remembered, but generally for every fact there is an equal and opposite one. For example, while defined as chattel or moveable property, enslaved African Americans regularly defined themselves otherwise. They knew themselves to be enslaved, but they knew they were not "slaves." African Americans, both enslaved and free, defied law and custom by forming churches and other organizations, owning property, and making contracts and covenants. It is a fact that African Americans who were not enslaved continually agitated for and articulated their determination to be more than second-class citizens. The idea that laws and circumstances stopped African Americans from developing intimate, loving, and marital and family relationships is naïve if not simply absurd.

Myths that mislead or are too readily misused need to be revised or replaced by more factual narratives that offer better evidence for the unexplained and the ignored. Antebellum African Americans remembered, passed on, preserved, and replicated cultural histories, rites, and regulations that resisted, countered, and ultimately withstood the inhuman and inhumane designs of slavery and racism. They adopted and adapted, from memories of their old culture and from imperatives of their present situations, soul-sustaining myths that not only helped them survive but helped them grow. Despite laws, customs, and fervent declarations to the contrary, many African Americans promoted a mythos that validated their humanity. They chose words that would make them more than flesh, and they defined themselves as human beings who were being denied rights and privileges to which their humanity entitled them. Knowing this makes it easier for us to do likewise.

Common sense, logic, and experience support stories that illustrate how the law and its enforcers could influence African American domestic practices. But it is also true that law and enforcement could neither constrain African Americans' personal desires nor hinder their romantic imaginings. The legal definition of "slave" greatly affected the rights and privileges an enslaved married couple might expect. However, neither the law nor the lawful owners of slaves could prevent two people from loving one another, and pledging their troths.

WHICH SLAVERY IS REALLY TO BLAME?

A Google search on August 13, 2009, gave 265,000 hits for "posttraumatic slavery disorder" and 113,000 for "posttraumatic slavery syndrome." These two concepts are contemporary myths that seek to answer questions about how and why love and marriage seem so fragile in present-day African America. The Google citations included BBC television shows, conferences involving Africans and people of African ancestry, and many books by prominent mental health practitioners and media pundits. I am inclined to believe that people of African descent may have more obvious trouble with gendered relationships than some other people. I tend to believe that men of African descent have particular problems defining and enacting masculinity. So, too, do women of African descent have peculiar investments in being respectable and respected. But I resist the part of the myth that makes slavery its genesis. I am troubled by narratives such as this one written by Dr. Jeffery Gardere:

> It started with slavery.... During slavery it was nearly impossible for us [African Americans] to form lasting and healthy relationships. The problem is that, when it comes to getting together for the long term these days, too many of us still act as if the slave master were standing over us with a whip. These carryover mental and behavioral patterns and all the other lingering after-effects of slavery can be described as Post-Traumatic Slavery Disorder, or our PTSD.... Our PTSD affects virtually every person of color whose history was blighted by slavery and colonialism. The danger is that if we do not acknowledge and then exorcise the trauma of our PTSD so that it no longer contaminates our hearts, minds, and souls, we are doomed to act out our buried anger and pain through repetitive negative and dysfunctional relationships, especially with each other. Without question, our Post-Traumatic Slavery Disorder is at the root of the current battling between black men and women.[11]

I'm troubled first because whenever I hear the words "without question," I tend to question. Gardere is a clinical psychologist with a Ph.D. who operates several clinics designed to help African Americans cope with, or overcome, a variety of stresses and diseases. He has hosted a show on the American Health Network and has participated in syndicated television confabs on *Oprah!* and *The Sally Jessie Raphael Show*. Without question, "Dr. Jeff" is an authority with a large and responsive audience. Moreover, Gardere's theory that "posttraumatic slavery disorder" is the root cause of today's "war between black men and women" is supported by other well-known professionals.

What Gardere calls "post-traumatic slavery disorder" Dr. Alvin F. Poussaint and others call "posttraumatic slavery syndrome." The symptoms include extreme sensitivity about masculinity and femininity and the inability to make commitments such as marriage and monogamy. Being called "boy" or being called "girl" can be fighting words. Whether a health professional uses "disorder" or "syndrome" is basically a technicality. Either way, "posttraumatic slavery syndrome/disorder" is used to explain everything from a rising suicide rate among black males to increasingly hostile My Baby Daddy relationships and the growth of HIV-AIDS-related deaths in African America. It makes homosexuality unspeakable but being "on the down low" a problem to be cured. Slavery's legacy becomes a justification for why interracial friendships must always be suspect, why reactionary assaults on gays and lesbians are understandable, and why marriage in the United States is an endangered institution moving swiftly toward extinction.

Those who advocate the usefulness of the concept of posttraumatic slavery disorder/syndrome are right in saying that successful treatment must "include an understanding of how American history continues to influence the lives of blacks. The hopelessness and cynicism currently felt by many African-Americans more than a century after the end of slavery did not develop in a vacuum."[12] I agree with bell hooks, that "the telling of our stories enables us to name our pain, our suffering, and to seek healing," hooks and those is on the right track.[13] But any story that defines slavery as the source of our social diseases and individual illnesses is not only a half truth; it is the half of the truth that does us the most harm.

In life and in thought, in word and in deed, our memories of the past shape our perceptions of the present and of ourselves. Popular media, especially the cinema, shape our cultural concepts and form much of what we believe to be our memories. Present-day personal relationships, gender expectations, and marriage performance are affected by our perceptions of our ancestral heritages. The posttraumatic slavery disorder that Gardere describes and much of what the *Essence* article articulates are real. The problem is that what they present as the historical legacy of African America is not all that was bequeathed. The "slavery" that might be at the root of weak and worrisome relationships is based more on myth than on truth. The "slavery" they cite is a post-emancipation phenomena made possible by the omission of testimony by those who were actually enslaved. When the voices and visions of antebellum African Americans are heard more clearly and interpreted more carefully, we can recognize that our legacy is more than we've believed. We can understand more clearly what antebellum African Americans wanted to leave us. We can decide what aspects of the historical narratives that shape the ways we view ourselves and our ancestral pasts, and which parts of the myths that influence our analyses and applications, we should pass on.

Linked to myths related to posttraumatic slave disorder/syndrome is what I call the myth of missing manhood (a.k.a. failure of fatherhood). This story asserts that an unmanning of African American males in antebellum America is a root cause of infrequent marriages, frequent divorces, and rampant paternal irresponsibility in the twentieth and twenty-first centuries. It forms facts into narratives like this one, offered by Harvard professor Orlando Patterson:

> The status and role of husband could not exist under slavery, since it meant having independent rights in another person and, in both the U. S. South and West Africa, some authority over her. Fatherhood could also not exist, since this meant owning one's children, having parental authority over them. Both infringed upon the power of the master and were therefore denied in law and made meaningless in practice.[14]

Patterson elaborates by listing the "minimum requirements of the roles of husband and father as found in all human societies except for a couple of museum-piece polyandrous communities of concern only to anthropological theorists" in a series of questions:

> Could he [an enslaved man] monopolize his partner's sexual services and guarantee that her progeny were in fact his own? Could he protect her from the sexual predation of other men? Could he at least partly provide for her materially? Could he prevent her from being brutalized and physically punished by other men? Could he prevent her from being torn from the place where she was brought up, bundled like cargo, and sold away from him, her children, her kinsmen, and her friends? If the answer to any of these questions is "No," the role of husband did not exist. If the slave could do none of these things, then the role of husband had been devastated. (Patterson 32)

The myth of missing manhood rests on present-day expectations and assumptions, beginning with the definitions of the two words most important to its interpretation: "husband" and "fatherhood." This myth also confuses "fatherhood" with "patriarchy."

The idea that "the status and role of husband could not exist under slavery" makes sense within a patriarchal rubric. However, patriarchy is itself a myth based on several contested assumptions. Patriarchy declares that a husband's role is to protect his wife from predatory men and to "provide at least partly for her materially." It assumes that a husband must have exclusive sexual access to his wife and that a husband must be able to prevent his wife from being sold and separated from her children, friends, and family. Slaves could not do any of these things. Ergo, slaves could not be husbands. This concept of "husband" makes being a husband almost the same as being a father. "Could he...guarantee that her progeny were in fact his own" assumes that fatherhood was based on "owning one's children, having parental authority over them." The reasoning seems to be that a "real" husband is a "real" man, and "real" manhood is defined as holding property and wielding power.

Perhaps it is the patriarchal base that does not consider the roles of females or motherhood relevant to its conclusions. Patriarchal perspectives ignore the impact of slavery on women and imply that womanhood did not suffer similar assaults or that women's oppression is less important to today's problems. But enslaved women were not considered "true women" either. They had no more inherent "parental power and authority" over their children than enslaved men did. Women may have had greater responsibilities for taking care of the children, but they had no greater authority. Slave owners could supersede women's desires or orders as quickly, if not more so, than they could override the authority of enslaved men. If missing fatherhood impacts today's family and gender patterns, then so must "missing motherhood." If such standards were applied to both sexes, then, "slaves" could not be "fathers" or "mothers."

Mythic power includes words, deeds, and memory thereof. However, we must remember that definitions have inconsistent consensus, and both denotation and connotations continually change. Today's definitions of sex and gender, marriage and family, husband and wife, come from those that operated in the past (though they are not the same). The myth of missing manhood assumes that since the laws forbade marriage between enslaved people, "the status and role of husband could not exist." This is based on a definition of manhood that may be more particular to the postbellum than the antebellum period. It does not give sufficient attention to differences between act and interpretation. For example, distinguishing between a physical or sexual experience and the psychological or gendered interpretations it engenders is crucial. Believing oneself a "victim" or a "survivor" makes a lot of difference. It is not a stretch of the imagination to believe that people then viewed rape and even seduction as regrettable but uncontrollable circumstances and that the *why* might be more important than the *what*. Whether "manhood" means being able to create a family, to protect it, and to provide for it may not have been the most important determinant, either. Stories that say slavery denied African American men opportunities to develop personal attachments with women and children need to be reconsidered. Assertions that relationships between African American men and African American women are fraught today because African Americans have no history, and no models of positive, supportive, trusting, and trustworthy gender relationships don't just distort history, they create dangerous myths based on half truths.

"MY FATHER WAS A MAN . . ."

The most often cited narratives by antebellum African American men seem to support posttraumatic slavery disorder/syndrome and the myth of missing manhood/fatherhood. But careful reading of more narratives than simply those by Frederick Douglass and William Wells Brown, or when we read more carefully what Douglass and Brown wrote, how they wrote it, and what they intended us to understand from their words, our understandings of what African Americans valued in marriages and how they defined fatherhood and motherhood change. When we interpret these writings in the context of their own times and circumstances, some of our definitions prove inappropriate. We realize that what we expect antebellum African Americans to have valued may be based not on *their* perceptions of life's possibilities but on *our* ideas about what they might have imagined or desired.

One example of the many personal narratives offering profiles of fathers and mothers whose enslaved status did not prevent their active parenting and sometimes their assertions of prime authority is *Life of James Mars, a Slave Born and Sold in Connecticut*.[15] When his owner decided to take his human property to the South, Mars's father, Jupiter, refused to go. "My father was a man of considerable muscular strength, and was not easily frightened into obedience," James Mars writes (Mars 38). Jupiter Mars hid his family and made things so difficult that a compromise had to be negotiated. The owner agreed to free Jupiter, his wife, and his daughter. Jupiter agreed to let his sons be indentured. That is, the owner could collect lease the boys to a third party for a specified amount of time, after which they, too, would be freed. Even then, Jupiter Mars did not trust blindly. When the boys were apprenticed in a nearby town, Jupiter Mars moved there to monitor their treatment. As James Mars tells it, "on my way to my new home I saw my father; I will not attempt to describe my feelings when he told me he had taken rooms in the same neighborhood, and should be near me. That made the rough way smooth. I went on then cheerful and happy" (Mars 47). Jupiter Mars was enslaved, but he was also a "husband" and a "father"—even according to present prevailing notions of masculinity,

James Mars grew up to be a chip off the old block. When he was 20 years old, James Mars asked when his indenture would end. Indentured servitude for boys generally ended at age 21; however, Munger, the man Mars served, said he would release James and give him a cow when he reached his twenty-fifth birthday. James asserted what many today would call his "manhood" this way:

> I asked him if that was all that I was to have if I stayed until I was twenty-five. He said he would see. I asked when he would see. He said when the time came. I then told him I had been told that Warren (that was the name of his nephew) had told him not to give me what he had agreed to, and I wanted to know if he would do as he had agreed to or not. He said I belonged to him, and I could not help myself. I told him I would stay with him as I had said if he would give me a writing obligating himself to give the sum we had agreed upon. After hesitating a short time, he said he would not give a writing; he would not be bound. I told him I had got that impression, "and if you say you will not give me what you said you would, I will not work another day...." The next day I picked up what few duds I had, left his house, and went to my father's. (Mars 51)

Munger took James Mars to court. Mars served as his own lawyer and won his freedom (though he had to pay $90 for it). Mars married and fathered eight children. One son enlisted in the navy, another fought in the Civil War. His oldest daughter became a teacher and went to Africa. Clearly, Jupiter and James Mars were both "husbands" and "fathers." They had both been enslaved, but neither had ever been a slave.

Another antebellum African American who contradicts the myth that enslaved mothers and fathers routinely relinquished parental prerogatives is Harriet Jacobs, who describes this telling incident between her father and her brother:

One day, when his father and his mistress both happened to call him [her brother] at the same time, he hesitated between the two; being perplexed to know which had the strongest claim upon his obedience. He finally concluded to go to his mistress. When my father reproved him for it, he said, "You both called me, and I didn't know which I ought to go to first." "You are *my* child," replied our father, "and when I call you, you should come immediately, if you have to pass through fire and water."[16]

Reading beyond slave narratives gives helpful corroboration. The periodical press of the time helps us understand that "fatherhood" was more than "patriarchy" and that "patriarchy" may have been practiced differently than we imagine. Most newspapers and magazines show that African American men behaved as husbands and fathers, although they may have defined their roles differently than we do today. James Reed's description of gender relationships is fairly representative of those published in mid-nineteenth-century African America. His "Essay on the Importance of Family Duty," delivered to Israel Church's Literary Society in Washington, D.C., and published in an 1859 issue of *Repository of Religion and Literature,* a periodical distributed out of Indianapolis, begins by asserting that "family duty…is essentially necessary for the happiness of mankind." A family, Reed writes, includes more than the parents: "all the household, over whom he or she may be the guardian." Reed's model family is one in which the father is "king," the mother is "queen," and the children are "the subjects over whom they are to rule." Reed explicitly ties his model to the historical "government first originated in the houses of the Patriarchs." The king-father's first duty is "to make suitable laws and regulations for the government" of his family. The father is also to provide for the family. The queen-mother is to assist the father. This rendition of patriarchy differs from many we might know because it emphasizes cooperation and interdependence over power and authority. It does not focus exclusively on restricted masculinity and the limitations of husbands and fathers. It defines manhood within a family context. The first duty of family "is the duty which the husband owes to his wife." The husband and the wife share the duties of training their children and praying for their children. They both "stand equal as teachers and instructors of their children." Reed concludes that "God, our Creator, when he made man gave him the woman to help him." Then it is true, "united we stand, divided we fall."[17]

Another example of an African American whose story can recast current mainstream understanding of patriarchy comes an 1862 article published in San Francisco's *Pacific Appeal.* The writer, identified as "M.E.R." from Petaluma, California, argues that husbands should not try to assume absolute authority over and responsibility for their wives and children. "Tell Your Wives"; M.E.R. advises, judicious consultation will increase cooperation and make men's lives easier. For example, financial burdens will be made lighter if wives and children do not think money supplies are inexhaustible. If the wife knows more about family finances, the author wrote, she will help relieve the husband's economic burden and make him a happier man. If husbands bring their wives "into partnership," they will "never regret it." M.E.R. assumes the man will be the breadwinner and does not advocate absolute equality within the marriage. He sounds a bit sexist; he warns husbands that when they explain economic realities to their wives, they should expect "a slight shower at first, but that is natural." However, M.E.R. says that once the wife is over her tears and has absorbed the news, she will adjust, spend less, and actually point out ways to save more:

> You will find a wonderful change in her tastes and appetites.... Before you have thought much about it, you will find yourself spending evenings at home...so full of domestic enjoyment and fireside pleasure, that you will look with wonder on the record of last year's expenses.... My friends, if your outgoes threaten to exceed your incomes, be sure and tell your wife of it—not in a tone and manner that will lead her to think you do not want her to buy furs this winter—but just as if you wanted a counselor in the day of your trouble; and if she does not come up, heart and soul, and most successfully, to your relief, put me down for no judge. (*Pacific Appeal,* November 1, 1862, 3)

Articles such as these were probably not primarily addressed to "slaves." But California and the Northwest Territories, like the District of Columbia and the Midwest, were heavily populated with fugitives and formally enslaved people. Possibly M.E.R. herself or himself was legally a "slave." But more important than status are attitudes and ideals, and the likelihood that such attitudes were held or proffered to enslaved people as well as free ones is high. True, too, that Afro-California culture in 1862 may not have been typical of other parts of African America or the times just before and after it. But that is part of my point. The stories that we choose to pass on should be more diverse. They should reflect the strengths and resistance of our ancestors as well as their dysfunctions and vulnerability. At least some of our stories should give equal opportunity to the fact that not all people of African descent were enslaved and that among those enslaved, many did not comply physically or emotionally with the rules made by slaveholders. The early press is less likely to offer articles that lament the loss of authority as fathers or husbands than it is to remind men that authority should be shared and cooperation desired.

MYTHIC RECONSTRUCTIONS FOR MODERN TIMES

I cited Gardere, Poussaint, and Patterson, as I did King, Berlin, and Rowland earlier, as examples of half truths used by those who wholeheartedly work for greater harmony in these United States. I, like many others, find value in their contributions, and I learn much from their interpretations. Patterson, especially, one of our most respected twentieth-century social scientists, has contributed an enormous amount of scholarship that has significantly enriched our understanding of our past. I agree with his conclusion that present-day African Americans suffer from internal and external isolation and that while external isolation may be declining, internal isolation is getting worse. The story is more complicated than he suggests, but I am inclined also to accept Patterson's idea that internal isolation is related to what he calls "the sorry state of relations between men and women." Clearly, we agree that any understanding of our current situation "requires an analysis of the underlying gender roles and relations that make them up and the broader socioeconomic and historical context in which they are situated" (Patterson x).

Our stories diverge on the uses of "autobiographical and anecdotal" sources. Patterson argues that "a great deal of the non-sociological writings on Afro-American gender and family relations rely heavily on autobiographical or anecdotal sources, which is perhaps the main reason why the crisis in these [domestic] relations has been either misinterpreted, underestimated, swept under the rug, or denied altogether" (Patterson xix). He prefers the use of quantitative data such as the national census and surveys to produce broad institutional views. Yet in *Rituals of Blood: Consequences of Slavery in Two American Centuries,* he "unapologetically" interprets some of his data by using Greek myth. As a humanities scholar, I believe that personal testimony, stories, and folklore, but most of all the written history of antebellum African Americans, are major sources for reconstructing our past. I find the Afro-Protestant press an especially useful trove of stories, deliberately and carefully constructed to allow people of African heritage to understand themselves and their past, present, and future. I consider statistics, official records, and other external data, but I do not take them any more seriously than I do the personal experiences and observations of African Americans who lived during and commented on the antebellum period.

For me, the nonsociological data are exactly what society and those who comprise it need to balance, complete, or compete with the quantitative sociological information. Ours is not an irreparable division between the humanities and qualitative research and the sciences and quantitative. In the sciences, one can find exquisite examples of poetry and creative analysis. In the humanities, one can find countless theoretical and methodological schemata hardly distinguishable from those used in mathematical laboratories. From one view we get forests. From another we see the trees.

Myths that privilege law and the intentions of racists and enslavers over the resistance and cultural mores of the enslaved fail because they do not help us learn to live as humans of equal worth. They perpetuate the work of racists and enslavers who enlisted law and literature, stories and sermons, science and art to convince human beings that they were not human. They conjure forced ignorance, false narratives, and physical abuse into poison for the souls of all folk. In the antebellum United States, the poison sometimes—too often—worked. It murdered souls and enchained bodies. People became chattel, property, inferior beings created or cursed to become servants of others. But slavery and racism worked imperfectly on others and not at all on some. To keep these people enslaved required excessive and incessant physical punishment, and often capricious abuse, as well as a continuous repetition of lies and half truths. To keep their minds and their hearts free, enslaved people had their own antidotes. They countered with their own myths.

People experienced enslavement in a multitude of ways. Experiences varied considerably on the basis of the jobs they were given, the places they lived, and whether and how they regularly interacted with other African Americans. The opportunities for developing African American culture were greater on large plantations. The opportunities for interaction among free and enslaved African Americans were greater in urban areas. Either way, it's more than likely that not all, maybe not most, enslaved African Americans were actually "slaves." From folktales, music, and early African American print culture, it appears that most enslaved people never bought the hype. They simply could not believe they were innately inferior or that their bondage was natural and inevitable. Even if they did have times of internalized inferiority, they also had times of knowing they were equal in the eyes of God, Allah, or other gods. In one of her most often quoted poems, the eighteenth-century writer Phillis Wheatley wrote that she believed it was mercy that removed her from a "*Pagan* land" to the New England colony where she could live as a Christian. But her conversion had also made her equal. Her religion taught her that she was a "joint heir" in a congregation wherein there were no privileged people. Wheatley concludes her testimony with this assertion: "Remember, *Christians, Negros* [*sic*], black as *Cain*,/ May be refin'd, and join th' angelic train."

The dominant myths are not necessarily the best ones to pass on. We can choose to emphasize the half-full or the half-empty glass. We can recognize that there are at least two ways to describe a situation. This, in itself, would be a decided improvement over accepting myths that make us feel what mental health professionals nicely encapsulate in the very simple words "bad, sad, or mad." Acknowledging that despite its best efforts, slavery ultimately failed to fully impose its myths of identity and destiny on people of African descent frees us from its mythic power. It restores to antebellum African Americans some of the rightful and hard-won respect they claimed. It also increases the power of the positive stories we do claim. Antebellum African Americans such as Crispus Atticks, Benjamin Banneker, Jarena Lee, Richard Allen, Nat Turner, Frances E. W. Harper, Martin Delaney, Charlotte Forten, Elizabeth Keckley, and Francis Grimke remain heroes and sheroes of liberty and justice. But they are no longer the lone exceptions that prove the rule. Slavery's influence was pervasive. Its legacy remains an incredibly haunting presence. The impact of free minds, even when they were in bound bodies, must not be underestimated or ignored.

Using slavery as the defining factor in antebellum African American lives obscures the many ways enslaved and free people interacted. It suggests boundaries that did not always exist. It assumes that legal restrictions were not circumvented or ignored. The law books engender such conclusions as "the status and role of husband could not exist under slavery." Our most popular histories say that divisions between free and enslaved people were worse than those between field and house slaves. However, stories passed down to us give countless counter-examples. Frederick Douglass worked in the fields, in the house, and on the docks. Venture Smith was a free African American married to an enslaved woman. Dilly was a free woman in Virginia married to an enslaved man. William and Ellen Craft were an enslaved couple who, as their narrative's title proclaims, ran "a thousand miles to freedom" together. It is not a fallacy to believe that the status and roles of men of African descent, whether under slavery or not, were not the same as the status and roles of men of European descent, or of men of Mexican, Chinese, or Native American descent either. Their situations differ socially, economically, and politically. But important aspects of African heritage led African Americans to resist adopting the priorities concerning property and inheritances that people of other cultural and spiritual legacies embraced. Claire Robertson, among other historians, argues that African women and men traditionally practiced more economic independence than Euro-Americans: "most spouses in Africa did not and do not practice community of property. In many societies, women have historically had the right to own and convey property without male permission."[18] Consequently, even if enslaved people could not help one another materially, this would not necessarily have been a reason to reject marriage. For African Americans, "possession, protection, and provision" were not the inevitable advantages or responsibilities of marriage. Those who were free could contract formal or legal marriages, and many did; but pervasive poverty, coupled with the practical impotence of their civil rights, made "to have and to hold" more applicable to forming companionate marriages based on mutual affection and emotional sustenance. Despite all that, marriage vows were made. Material and legal restrictions did not succeed in destroying the desire for, and the existence of, marriages for antebellum African Americans.

SEVEN

ALCHEMY OF PERSONAL POLITICS

There is a mystery in matrimony, which none can read but the initiated.
—Daniel Payne, "Matrimony" (*Repository of Religion and Literature and Science and Art,* 1859)

Marriage is like the sphinx—a conspicuous and recognizable monument on the landscape, full of secrets.
—Nancy F. Cott, *Public Vows* (2000)

FIRST COMES LOVE, THEN COMES MARRIAGE, THEN comes Mama with the baby carriage. Children learn very early the trinity of adulthood and the right sequence for achieving the American Dream. However, as they mature, children start to realize that what they call love and who they think are potential mates often clash with what their families and communities declare. They discover that the sequence is often altered or incomplete. And, eventually they understand, even if they object or protest, that their definitions of love and marriage are not, and have not been, universally accepted.

Nineteenth-century theologian Daniel Payne speaks for some who an understanding of marriage is generally different for those who marry from those who do not. Like twenty-first century historian Nancy F. Cott, many conclude that while almost everyone knows something about marriage, almost no one totally understands it. Marriage is a mystery. Marriages have secrets. This is not to say that folks don't try to define these things for themselves and for others. The Knights of Columbus, National Organization for Marriage California, and Focus on the Family, all of which backed California's Proposition 8, the movement "restoring and protecting marriage," assert that "the meaning of marriage is written in the very nature of man and woman....Its unique place in civilization is both derived from God and inherently natural to man."[1] Maggie Gallagher, president of the Institute for Marriage and Public Policy acknowledges the difficulty of defining marriage, but she knows that it is both religious and secular. In a talk entitled "If Marriage Is Natural, Why Is Defending It So Hard? Taking up the Challenge to Marriage in the Pews and the Public Square,"[2] Gallagher asserts that "The essence of marriage is unity and indissolubility."

Perhaps the difficulty of clearly defining "marriage" is the reason why the United States government has invested in a particular model of marriage that regularizes property rights and inheritances, and that enables social contracts and control. Like many European nations, laws of the United States make marriage a matter of possession, protection, and provision. But, truth be told, in the United States, many people insist that marriage is, and has always been, a personal commitment between individuals. Thus, today as yesterday, we have multiple versions of marriage enacted by individuals and recognized, if not always encouraged, by the communities they live in. Since the personal or particular is also the public and the prescribed, conflict and contradictions abound. The personal is political, and politics becomes personal. This has particular implications for African Americans, and it has implications for others as well. I cannot conclude this discussion of love, marriage, and sexual morality in antebellum African America without discussing what these things mean to people in the United States and, others as well.

THE BONDS OF MATRIMONY

Marriage is a mysterious concoction of ideal and real, sacred and secular, personal and political. Most people in the United States believe that February 14 separates the casual boyfriends from the committed. We know that June is the wedding month. Many of us think that "old maids" are failures and "lifelong bachelors" are suspect. We affirm that the decision to marry is personal and voluntary, but we also withhold respect and authority from politicians or business people who are not married to partners we deem appropriate and who behave according to our expectations of married people. Our country has laws to protect individuals from involuntary marriages and from voluntary unions based on fraudulent or incomplete information. Our laws also decide who can marry and how. To be officially married, a couple must have a license from the appropriate governmental office. By law in all but a few states, unions are only allowed between one man and one woman, both of whom must have reached a specified age. Ipso facto, not everyone who wants to marry can do so. The law distinguishes between a marriage and a wedding, but it regulates both. A wedding can be performed in many ways, but the marital vows can be administered only by someone duly authorized by the government. And once duly married, two individuals have legally become one entity, with certain obligations regardless of whether either or both persons want them. Once married, a couple cannot dissolve its union without government permission. In short, while we aren't really sure just what marriage is or whether it is actually a divine mandate, we tend to define it as a moral and civic responsibility, which just happens to model good government as well.

Probably the greatest story ever told is the myth of the golden age of marriage, when "once upon a time" a "man" took a "wife" and they lived happily ever after. In the golden age of marriage, each spouse performed her or his role responsibly. The couple, once married, had sexual intercourse that resulted in children. The children had little or no legal identity, and social security numbers were unnecessary until they began to work for someone other than their parents. Whether the children were seen and not heard, whether they were center of their parents' lives, in a proper family children were clean and well behaved. At the appropriate time, the children fell in love with appropriate members of the opposite sex. They reenacted the coupling conventions, and families, communities, and cultures flourished. But, we are told, that golden age has passed. Somehow, someway, something went wrong. Children began to improvise on the marriage plot. They began to marry people of different cultures and religions. They divorced capriciously. And sometimes they refused to become parents. In other words, marriage became corrupted, and Western civilization, having been built upon the foundations of the golden age of marriage, became endangered.

Eventually, things degenerated so that for an increasing number of people, the golden values did not even have nostalgic value. "Middle America" seemed to be holding fast, but in the outlying geographic areas, in states traditionally wayward, things were changing drastically. More people were proclaiming marriage as a private relationship between consenting adults. They were saying that historically marriage had privileged some citizens over others and violated constitutional freedoms. Legislators in California, Vermont, Hawaii, and other such places were saying that same-sex couples had, should have, or soon would have the same legal status and civil rights as heterosexual couples. Boston, the bastion of Puritanism, the benchmark for banning immorality, had become our ground zero for "gender neutral" marriages. The Supreme Judicial Court of Massachusetts had heard arguments that limiting marriage to heterosexual couples violated the state constitution.

Perhaps they couldn't define marriage, but opponents believed they knew marriage when they saw it and these new-fangled versions were definitely not what it was. They needed help and they needed it fast. This was not a job for Superman—or Batman. They both wore tights and had dubious relationships with Lois Lane and Robin. What the keepers of the myth of the golden age of marriage needed was a knight in shining armor, a Promise Keeper, or a G.I. Joe. On February 24, 2004, the president came to the rescue. Standing regally in the Roosevelt Room of the White House, George W. Bush recited his version of the past saying that eight years ago, he said, "Congress passed and President Clinton signed the Defense of Marriage Act, which defined marriage for purposes of federal law as the legal union between one man and one woman as husband and wife."

This story surprised some listeners. They had believed that the nation's laws defining marriage as a heterosexual union that magically transformed a man and a woman into a husband and a wife had always existed and were certainly written as such into the U.S. Constitution. But according to Bush's statement, this was not true, and that definition was actually less than 10 years old. This may have been one of Bush's many bloopers, and it certainly was not his point. What Bush wanted us to understand was that some within the judicial branch of the government were interpreting the law differently from some in the legislative branch. And neither branch was clearly unanimously agreeing with him, the head of the executive branch. This was good news to some who understood his story as verifying that the system of checks and balances on which our tripartite government was founded was working. Some people considered his comments and understood that the "Contract with America" promised during his campaign was not working. The Contract with America had promised less federal governmental interference, more state and local rights, and as much privatization as possible. But some people were taking privatization too far. They were saying that marriage was private and anyone who wanted to accept the responsibilities of marriage had the right to do so. Some states and some individuals were testing legal mandates and customary assumptions about marriage in the courts. The results were, Bush declared, "arbitrary court decisions, more litigation, more defiance of the law by local officials, all of which adds to uncertainty." Uncertainty about marriage was certainly not tolerable. Marriage was about more than individuals. Marriages defined legitimate families, and our government required legitimate family units for many of its operations. Tax incentives, passport rules, and responsibility for indigent elderly and wayward youth would have to be revised. Employers and businesses would have to redo their benefits and create new ways of collecting on debts. In times like these, we did not have time for judges to carefully consider points of law or, even worse, to interpret recent definitions of marriage as unconstitutional. In times like these, we could not afford debate. If the Constitution did not clearly define marriage the way the newly created Marriage Act stated it, if the Constitution could be so open to different interpretations, then the Constitution had to be amended.

Thus, Bush reasoned that the Constitution needed to be changed so that the Contract with America was more enforceable. Since the nation's forebears did not clearly define the characteristics of husband and wife, it was high time that their descendants did. Bush ordered others to fix the problem, saying: "Today, I call upon the Congress to promptly pass and to send to the states for ratification an amendment to our Constitution defining and protecting marriage as a union of a man and woman as husband and wife."

Bush, whom the media described as the moral opposite of Clinton, coupled his proposal for a constitutional amendment with a reiteration of the import of the Defense of Marriage Act, which Bill Clinton had signed into law in 1996. Bush, whose election engendered a partisan Congress, reminded us that Congress had approved this Act by an overwhelmingly bipartisan vote. The Senate vote had been 85 to 14, the House of Representatives vote 342 to 67. By placing his story within a bipartisan setting, Bush was recharacterizing its protagonists as more than fundamentalist Christians or morality police who covered nude statues in public places.

In his story, the Defense of Marriage Act was the will of the people. "Activist" judges (and a few others) were insurgents. This was a national emergency with a threat level worse than red—it was lavender. The morality tales of the politically dominant were under attack. And so to arms!

Since 1996, various states had been refusing to recognize marriages made in other states as legal. They had been granted that license by the Defense of Marriage Act. But both federal and state judges were challenging the restrictions laid out in the Act by suggesting that they violated the U.S. Constitution. The judicial branch of the government was not interpreting the executive legislative branches' actions the way they wanted or intended them to be interpreted. To President George W. Bush, this meant that "Activist judges and local officials" were trying to "redefine marriage," and unless preemptive strikes were made immediately, the Defense of Marriage Act might "be struck down by activist courts." Moreover, our president warned us, the dangerous judges might be just getting started. Bush predicted: "even if the Defense of Marriage Act is upheld, the law does not protect marriage within any state or city." Such uncertainty, to Bush, must not be tolerated in these perilous terrorist times. If one state could force another state to accept its standards for marital behaviors, what was called, during the Vietnam era, the "domino effect" might happen. In 2004, President Bush said: "decisive and democratic action is needed because attempts to redefine marriage in a single state or city could have serious consequences throughout the country." Nothing less than a constitutional amendment was needed to shock and awe the nation back into civilized conformity.

When George W. Bush issued his call for Congress to protect marriage, it was a decidedly ahistorical and idiosyncratic moment. He seemed to envision the federal government as a table where the legislative and judicial branches were the support for the executive top. "After more than two centuries of American jurisprudence and millennia of human experience," Bush said, "a few judges and local authorities are presuming to change the most fundamental institution of civilization. Their actions have created confusion on an issue that requires clarity."

Not only was President Bush's version of the United States government skewed, but his history was way off. The definition of marriage he asserted is not shared worldwide; it is a relatively new notion even within Western civilization. I doubt that Bush actually knew (or cared) that his historical narrative was not the most factual. I do not think that Bush even knew that marriage, like any human social construction, is, and has been, a work in progress, a process of negotiation and compromise as well as stability and unity. But I do know that his story is one that is believed, told, and retold by many people. It is a commonplace modern marriage myth. There are others.

In *Public Vows: A History of Marriage and the Nation,* Nancy F. Cott, who has spent a bit more time studying the marriage and its myths than has George W. Bush, offers a counter-narrative. In Cott's analysis, marriage is a conspicuous monument that everyone recognizes, but about which no one knows everything. Its meanings multiply according to the imaginations and assumptions of those contemplating it. Like one of the Wonders of the World, marriage looms large and provides foundation and inspiration for some of our most profound hopes, dreams, and myths. Depending on the person, marriage may appear more religious, more secular, more stable, or more unpredictable.

Bush said marriage has been the same for "two centuries of American jurisprudence and millennia of human experience." Cott's research reveals that in 1944, U.S. jurisprudence agreed that although marriage had public consequences, it was essentially a private affair. "The U.S. Supreme Court," Cott writes, "portended a momentous line of interpretation by finding that the U.S. Constitution protected a 'private realm of family life which the state cannot enter.' "[3] Employing Cott's narrative, we could interpret the Defense of Marriage Act of 1996 as a twentieth-century home invasion.

Assumptions about, and practices of, marriage change. The issue is whether and how they could change to the best advantage of all concerned. In the United States, perhaps more so than in many countries, marriage has been a sphinx-like combination of private and public definitions. It's the head of religion on the body of government. At the same time, the ways we define marriage influence our basic ideas of gender, of what a man and what a woman are. Again, to use Cott's words, "turning men and women into husbands and wives, marriage has designated the ways both sexes act in the world and the reciprocal relations between them. It has done so probably more emphatically than any other single institution or social force" (Cott 3).

ID-ING THE SPHINX

Careful scrutiny of the matrimonial monument that dominates our current political and religious landscapes illustrates why we need to think some more about many of our common definitions and assumptions.

Prudent interrogation of narratives that describe how marriage is and has been practiced could alleviate many of the anxieties and embarrassments about the present-day health and probable longevity of marriage in African America. It would challenge some diagnoses, should revise some negative prognoses, and could rewrite prophylactic prescriptions. To begin, all we need to do is to embrace the idea that much of what we know and believe about marriage ain't necessarily so. Examination of popular images using a clear eye and an assortment of instruments shows that some of what we see as natural or biological is not. Some of what we believe about history is not accurate, either.

We are heirs to marital myths that are neither inevitable nor universal. Jewish law, Muslim law, the laws of Eastern cultures, including India and Africa, and the laws of the indigenous people of what is now the United States derive from various and diverse myths, yet all to some extent provide the basis for different marital concepts that prescribe different behaviors. The statement "Marriage as a union of a man and woman as husband and wife," ignores certain facts. In Judaism, Christianity, and Islam, the "religions of the Book," as well as in the oral traditions of other religions, polygamy and sometimes polyandry were practiced by some of our most revered ancestors. Abraham, Jacob, Esau, David, Solomon, and Mohammad had wives and concubines. In the nineteenth-century United States, despite our uneasiness, we did accommodate the early Mormons and other utopian groups who had multiple spouses or complex marriages. Today, we are allowed to marry more than one person, but only one at a time. Serial monogamy is legal and socially acceptable, as long as each time we expect the union to be permanent. Islamic law recognizes temporary marriages (*muwagat* and *muta'a*), mainly with prostitutes, to avoid the sin of adultery. Other cultures are flexible on the one man, one woman rule also. Some require a man to marry the widows of his relatives whether or not he already has a wife.

In a contemporary version of Roman mythology, Cupid's arrows strike love into our hearts. But in Roman mythology, Cupid was a sex god. He stimulated lust and erotic love. Some theographies say Cupid and Chaos are siblings. Cupid has two sides, one mischievous and the other debauched. In Hindu mythology, Kama is kin to Cupid. While the Kama Sutra does devote a good amount of discussion to marriage and respectable behavior, Kama himself is most often identified with sexual desire and passion.

The proof is lacking for two truths we often hold self-evident: that marriage has usually meant one man and one woman and that love and marriage should be inextricable. Stephanie Coontz, the director of research and public education at the Council on Contemporary Families, provides an alternative narrative that argues: "marriage had nothing to do with the relationship between a man and a woman. It was invented to get in-laws."[4] This statement is a short and simplistic summary of a central thesis in her 313-page *Marriage, a History: From Obedience to Intimacy or How Love Conquered Marriage.* In this book, Coontz explains that until approximately two centuries ago, marriage was a means of uniting political or economic interests between families, tribes, or nations. Rather than putting the blame on "activist judges," Coontz identifies "love" as the most imminent threat to traditional marriages in many Western cultures. Love, Coontz argues, may have enhanced the quality of life for the spouses, but it threatened the "stability of marriage as an institution." In other words, when love enters the matrimonial mix, the government is forced out of the home and into the street. With the Defense of Marriage Act and subsequent federal program interventions, the government is trying to march itself back inside.

To understand how our recent history derives from, and compares with, a complicated and contradictory past, we should go back a bit farther. John Witte, Jr., a specialist in the legal history of marriage and family, gives a thorough chronology of the emergence of the marital expectations and requirements that now prevail in our society. Witte reminds us that Western marriage myths basically originated from Greek and Roman society and that these myths did not reflect a consensus, and do not provide a complete depiction, of all who practiced and preached at that time.[5] The classical Greco-Roman formulation, upon which foundation, the Western Christian world concocted many of its political and religious mores, identifies both the *goods* and the *goals* of marriage. The *goods* of marriage are, as Witte explains, "its virtue, its reason for being, its intrinsic worth." The *goals* of marriage are "its purposes, its expected consequences, and its instrumental value" (Witte 1022). The Roman Catholic tradition, especially as shaped by Augustine and Aquinas, built on the Greco-Roman concept of the "end (*finis*) of marriage" by defining

> three inherent goods: (1) *fides*—a faithfulness and friendship between husband and wife that goes beyond that demanded of any other temporal relationship; (2) *proles*—children, who are to be nurtured and educated to perpetuate the human species and to transmit and live out the proper norms and habits of spiritual and temporal life; and (3) *sacramentum*—an enduring expression of Christ's love for his Church, an indissoluble chan-

nel of God's grace to sanctify the couple, their children, and the broader community. (Witte 1068)

Emerging Anglican Protestant traditions modified the Roman Catholic concepts, Witte reports, by emphasizing both the "intrinsic goods" and the "instrumental goals" of marriage. Protestant theology maintained that "marriage was created by God to foster love, to deter sin, and to produce children," but it was not a sacrament to be held inviolate. Under early Protestant rules, "if one or more of these created marital goals were permanently frustrated, those parties who could not reconcile themselves to this condition could seek divorce and remarry" (Witte 1068–69).

In the New World of North America, colonial, pioneer, frontier, and other conditions of living made certain Old World rituals and regulations impossible to perform, or at least easy to disregard. In the days before the War of Independence, the collection of colonies in North America was inhabited by people from a variety of ethnic, national, and religious origins. Mixed marriages often created a mixture of marital assumptions and behaviors. In frontier settlements, marriage, like slavery, could be a more flexible, more individualized, and more fluid institution than it might be in more established antebellum cities. Circumstances often changed marriage customs and laws. For example, under Euro-Protestant laws of coverture, usually the rights of wives were subsumed under the rights of their husbands. Wives did not own property, and children belonged to husbands. But some wives, especially the wealthy, were at least partially exempt and retained control over their assets. During times of war, or when husbands went off to seek fortunes or find work, wives exercised a good deal of independence and authority. Often they would not resume subordinate positions when husbands returned.

John and Abigail Adams apparently had a compatible marriage, but they did not think alike. During the Revolutionary War, Abigail Adams, like many wives, had to provide for and protect their family while John Adams, like many husbands, went off to create a new country. Abigail Adams wrote to her husband, "in the new Code of Laws which I suppose it will be necessary for you to make I desire you would Remember the Ladies....Do not put such unlimited power into the hands of the Husbands."[6] Despite Abigail's personal political activism, the new code of laws did not extend civil rights to women or to men of color.

Abigail Adams was not unique in knowing that leaving "the Ladies" out of the "new Code of Laws" would leave them without recourse in their pursuit of happiness and their liberty to live their lives as they might wish. Government and church officials understood the family unit as the micro version of their institutions. They promoted compatible myths that gave cosmic answers to mundane questions such as: Who could and who could not marry? How ought women to behave in this newly created nation? Who was responsible for the health, education, and welfare of children? A conscious creation of the United States of America out of multiple colonies of peoples was the movement toward a unified theory, if not practice, of matrimonial obligations. Public representations and legal mandates about marriage morphed into more uniform ideas of wifely and husbandly behaviors. But the cultures of the Catholics in Maryland and the Congregationalists in Massachusetts, the Anglican arguments of Virginia and the Baptist beliefs in North Carolina, the Spanish Catholic and French Catholic influences of Florida and the Louisiana Territory—all these and more—dictated other standards. Their legacies, diffused as they were to become, lasted through generations. As the United States moved from its revolutionary and developing stages toward a more organized and urbanized capitalistic culture, the distinct diversities in attitudes, secular and sacred, became more apparent.

Though religion's grasp on the nation's reins gave way to a more secular society, its myths of divinely mandated behaviors in marriage were still useful. Had Abigail Adams's idea worked, the dominant myth might have become what Gail Collins calls the "race of Amazons in America" (Collins 80). Instead, the public image of wives in civic society was that of the "angel in the house." The New World version of the Old World European house angel ideal had to vary her form just a bit. Rural life was more wilderness than pastoral and like Abigail Adams, wives sometimes found themselves managing if not working the family farm. An antebellum urban middle-class wife's life might be fairly well contained within the domestic sphere, but because the men of her family were increasingly involved in the economics and politics of an emerging industrialized nation, Mrs. U.S.A. not only ran run her own household, but expanded her domestic duties to include the households and personal affairs of her social inferiors. Like her European foremothers, she was often represented in print as "an ideal, a model of selflessness and of purity of heart."[7]

Our all-American antebellum woman may have even aspired to become a wife whose "only resources were spiritual" and who kept her husband's love "by increased anxiety to please" (Collins 88). But ideals are not real. Aspirations are not achievements. Words are not deeds.

Even those whose writings seemed to promote the true woman as a loving but lowly wife to the man who protected, provided, and presided over her home and his children did not necessarily live the lives they wrote about. Some, for example Harriet Beecher Stowe, Clara Barton, and Lydia Maria Child, were not characterized by an "increased anxiety to please" their husbands or, in fact, anyone else. Sarah Josepha Hale, Fanny Fern, and E. D. E. N. Southworth were professional writers and single mothers. Like the archetypal angel in the house, Emily Dickinson did live a life of "considerable isolation," but hers was hardly a "model of selflessness and of purity of heart." Many nineteenth-century women, like Dickinson, chose not to marry. Others delayed matrimonial ties until after they had worked, traveled, or contributed to religious, social, or political organizations or reform. And, maybe most interesting, becoming a wife did not automatically make angels into mothers. Condoms were officially introduced at the Philadelphia World Exposition in 1876, but researchers have noted that in the antebellum United States, birth control methods already included condoms, as well as douches, sponges, and abortion.[8]

In the early nineteenth century, the honeymoon of the newly united states gave way to the clouded compromises occasioned by the difficulties of day-to-day living, the changes in technology, the rise of urban centers, and the kinds of sectional, cultural, and other differences that led ultimately to dissolution and the Civil War. Debate over divorce and spousal prerogatives became more frequent as that war became imminent. Redefinitions of marriage and of proper gender roles did not necessarily change the behaviors or attitudes of most Americans. For those who aspired to social or economic upward mobility, laws of coverture, separate sphere teachings, and prescriptions for proper marriages formed the templates for public avowals. Yet even those who desired to practice the approved theory of marriage found it did not always work within their private realities.[9]

Over the years, the questions of definitions and intentions, of what constituted the social and religious mandates of matrimony, waxed and waned in importance. Discussions and decisions about divorce and spousal prerogatives came and went. Legislation and denominational creeds convey much of the public stories as authored by those in power, who by then were generally white, Anglo-Saxon, and Protestant men. More revealing conversations went on among diverse peoples in every part of the United States and its territories.

WEDDINGS AND WEDLOCK

Considering love and marriage in early African America within the context in which it existed can impact more general interpretations of American culture. It's true that inalienable rights to life, liberty, and the pursuit of happiness are founding principles of the nation—but not for everyone. The nation's pride in evading Old World problems arising from a unified church and state is justified, but as Mark D. Jordan and other scholars argue, "marriage remains the great testimony to the inseparability of church and state, to their ancient commingling."[10] Theologians and philosophers fulsomely document how marriage myths in the United States were constructed from various beliefs and practices in Christianity and British common law, which had been founded on stories created by careful selection of specific segments of Greco-Roman and Jewish traditions.

When someone cites millennia of practice that underlie current ideas about marriage, the stories left untold are Greek and Roman customs that included easy divorce, same-sex intercourse, and religious practices in which sexual orgies were fundamental. To understand marriage as one man and one woman, we must ignore or interpret *sotto voce* the Christian Bible stories of men in good social and religious standing having several wives and having sex with women who were not their wives.

Theologians, legal theorists, social scientists, and observant members of the general public do acknowledge that theory and praxis, theology and practice, intent and habit routinely differ. When we remember to separate rhetoric from reality, we acknowledge that definitions and ideals of marriage are more extreme and inflexible than are its actual practices. We find it easier to understand that in the antebellum United States, as today, people might have privileged one version, but they practiced or tolerated marriage in many forms. The antebellum legal system had rules for both officiated marriages and self-marriages. Depending on the particulars, it enforced laws about marriage more or less rigidly. A lot had to do with who was breaking what law, when, where, and why. Routinely, federal and state governments effectively abdicated some of their powers of definition and discipline to various religious and community groups, though not always.

Just as pragmatic considerations helped create marriage, practical concerns also helped change it. Sometimes a couple did not marry legally because marriage licenses were too expensive. Especially for rural and frontier residents, sometimes there were no local officials or clergy authorized to perform marriages. Rather than wait to legitimize or sanctify unions, people performed the roles of husband and wife, and their communities recognized them as such. It was not uncommon that when circuit judges or itinerant preachers, priests, or missionaries arrived, the couple was married and their children baptized in the same visit. Nancy F. Cott summarizes historical practices as follows:

> local community preferences...produced a varied scene of marital coupling....White and nominally Christian Americans engaged in informal marriages, self-divorces, premarital unchastities, and bigamy, without suffering much for their sins despite the existence of prohibitory laws. Informal marriage, in which couples lived together as husband and wife without the requisite official license and ceremony—"self-marriage" or "common-law" marriage as it came to be called—was the most frequent irregularity. (Cott 30)

Informal marriages probably represented the majority of unions formed among the working class and poor. Sometimes they distinguished these arrangements as "married but not churched." It was simply a much easier, more realistic way to live.

Common law or unchurched weddings were also practical because as the colonies transformed into states, divorce generally became difficult, if not impossible. The bonds of matrimony forged by formal or legal marriages were practically indestructible. Divorce laws in most states and in federal court allowed divorce only for specific reasons, and often this required a specific act of legislation. This made things more difficult for the ordinary citizen. When a couple, or half of it, suspected that the impending union would not or should not last until death, eschewing a legal marriage made good sense.

Our common stories of living happily ever after in a golden age of marriage exist alongside lesser known narratives that disavow such notions. In the antebellum United States, unequally yoked couples suffered, often silently, without satisfactory legal redress. Married women had little or no recourse against physical abuse. As late as the mid–twentieth century, some state laws prohibited married women from making legal contracts and managing finances. They could not protect themselves or their children from their husbands' whims or wastage. At the same time, in some states or jurisdictions, married persons could sue for separation of bed and board and if successful could legally live apart. A woman could be declared *feme sole*, which allowed her to take care of her own business.

Under this limited form of divorce, unless the husband was clearly shown to be the injured party, he remained responsible for his wife's debts and behaviors. Court cases in the slave South show that even flagrant adultery, or an obviously mixed-race child born to a white, middle-class wife of a white, middle-class man, did not automatically dissolve a husband's obligation to support wife and child. This does not mean that formally married couples stayed married. As Cott puts it, "desertion was another name for self-divorce" (Cott 38).

In antebellum America, middle-class people seemed to value legally sanctioned and formally ceremonialized marriages. But even they often practiced marriage differently than the golden age myth implies. For example, cohabitation was expected but not required. Especially among seafarers, miners, or military people, but often, too, with the poor or restless, wives could expect long or frequent separations. Among immigrants, spouses were sometimes separated for many years. This was especially true for Asian men, who for many years could not bring their wives legally into the United States. Antebellum judges were often pragmatic about defining a marriage. Generally, if folks behaved as if they were married and their local community accepted them as married, courts did not require proof of authorized ceremony or a marriage license. Many jurists agreed with the chief justice of Pennsylvania, who in 1833 estimated that "if legal requirements for valid marriage were strictly enforced, the 'vast majority' of children born in the state over the past fifty years would be rendered illegitimate" (quoted in Cott 39).

Legal enforcement, whether lax or aggressive, was guided, however, by a particular model of morality. Our founding fathers, in Cott's words,

> endorsed and aimed to perpetuate nationally a *particular* marriage model: lifelong, faithful monogamy, formed by the mutual consent of a man and a woman, bearing the impress of the Christian religion and the English common law in its expectations for the husband to be the family head and economic provider, his wife the dependent partner. (Cott 3)

In this morality tale, the question of whether a female was inherently inferior to a male was of less importance. Wives simply could not be allowed to have the same civil rights as husbands or unmarried women. How could a husband be the undisputed "family head and economic provider" if the wife were financially or politically independent?

This is some of the context within which we might examine our understanding of slavery's impact on marriage. If enslaved husbands were to claim authority over their wives and children, slavery would have had to revert to feudalism. Scientific and social theories of race would be harder to defend. Legal marriage was one way of telling the difference between white and black. Whether they chose to avail themselves of it or not, free people, the vast majority of whom were white, had the right to a legal marriage. Slaves, the vast majority of whom were black, could not make such a contract. Legal marriage was also a way of keeping the "races" separate. Few states recognized the legitimacy of a marital relationship between a person legally identified as white and another person not so identified. This ensured that neither spouse nor any children could inherit property or claim political access on the basis of that relationship. The United States government had ample reason to promote particular models of marriage and to deny the possibility of interracial love. Slavery and sexism both benefited by insisting on a single model of marriage in theory, if not in practice. It is within this historical context that present-day declamations about a utopian golden age should be interpreted. And, it is within the context of antebellum values that myths about African American legacies of love and marriage should be appraised.

Today, our science and our common sense enhance our understanding of memory and its relationship to present and future behavior. We have increased archival evidence and better modes of communicating information far and wide. But instant expertise is dangerous. Integration of new knowledge is essential. Reading the documents that were written by African Americans, for African Americans, about African Americans, we can understand that their concepts of love, marriage, and sexual morality were flexible enough to accommodate situations beyond their control. They were visionary and idealistic, yet pragmatic and attainable. African Americans were never in consensus about every aspect, but there was unanimity enough that everyone knew the expectations, whether or not they lived by them. Cursory examinations can conclude that African Americans held the same moral standards as, and defined marriages much like, Euro-Americans. But it's not that simple. Myths, narratives, and stories remain the most effective means of conceptualizing and controlling ideas and ideals, ethics and actions. Now, more than ever, we need our stories.

EIGHT

Me, Mende, and Sankofa: An Epilogue

On a clear day, I can drive from Atlanta to Greensboro, North Carolina, in five and a half hours. But December 1, 2007, was a rainy day in Georgia, complete with thunder, lightning, swaying pine trees, and some small thing that hit and cracked my windshield. This day I drove more than nine hours, plenty of time to reconsider my reasons for making the journey. I am fascinated by ideas of love and marriage, ritual and change; but I rarely attend weddings, and I usually skip the reception all together. So why was I driving in through wind and rain to attend a reception for a bride I had met only twice in my life and a groom I'd never heard of before the invitation? Well, friendship had something to do with it. Despite our brief visits, I felt a strong kinship with the bride. Altruism played a small role. I knew she had few friends and no family in the United States. A bride should have well-wishers. But, truth be told, curiosity was a major motivation. I had no illusions that this marriage was a storybook ending for a woman who had experienced so much trauma, so little happiness in her life. But, from the moment I clicked on the email inviting me "to join us when we celebrate our wedding," I knew I would go. It was, I understood, a rare chance to see the themes of this book manifested. It would allow me to test my theory of how traditions change yet endure and how Africans of the diaspora become African Americans. It would be a Sankofa experience.

The bride, Mende Nazer, and I had bonded over our intense inter-est in slavery. As a direct descendant of Africans enslaved in the United States, I have been trying all my life to understand that institution and what it means, or ought to mean, to me. I was born long after the fact, but I was driving through land where my ancestors had died. My father had been born a few miles from an exit I passed en route. Mende is an African who was, until very recently, enslaved. She has spent these past years trying to understand that experience without letting it determine her future. Because of words written almost two centuries before either of us were born, Mende and I had met. Our present relationship was defined and motivated by stories we told and stories told to us about slavery.

For almost 40 years, my scholarly life had been shaped by my research in early African American culture. With my friend Nellie Y. McKay, I edited an edition of Harriet Jacobs's *Incidents in the Life of a Slave Girl* originally published in 1861. Someone, I think it was Bernadette Brooten at Brandeis University, gave that book to Mende Nazer, who read it and exclaimed, "This is *my* story!" I met Mende because she was desperate to learn more about Jacobs and about the fugitive slave narratives that *Incidents* represents. Harriet Jacobs—and my friend Nellie—were both dead. I am still around, and Bernadette Brooten, knowing I was participating in a conference honoring the nearly two-hundredth anniversary of *Incidents* and the forthcoming publication of Jacobs's papers, arranged for Mende to participate and for us to meet.

Mende is Muslim, and we met during Ramadan. So we waited not just until sundown but until the precise minute of an official sundown before we shared our first meal in a small Mediterranean restaurant in Manhat-tan. Mende was eager to know all about Harriet Jacobs, slave narratives, me, and my family. I, too, wanted to know more about her. But, I was especially interested in knowing about her experiences as a slave and I was torn between asking a million and one questions and trying not to invade her privacy. I was determined not to act like an antebellum aboli-tionist and subordinate to my own agenda her right to self-definition and to self-disclosure. I greatly feared overstepping boundaries in order to assuage my ignorance. I had read accounts by Harriet Jacobs, Frederick Douglass, and others about the many ways in which their humanity had been trampled by eager do-gooders and gawkers for whom their value was as a specimen, a spokesperson for a category. I had watched from the sidelines Mende regularly and routinely being introduced as "a former slave" and asked intrusive or cruel questions. She had been enslaved, but that was in the past. Yet to hear the story of enslavement from the lips of an actual escaped slave was an opportunity I never dreamed I would have. So, as we ate, talked, laughed, and occasionally sighed, I tried to control my curiosity and ignorance and let her direct the conversation. I was conflicted, intense, and intent, but we took to one another, and we agreed to meet again in a few weeks at the Beyond Slavery conference at Brandeis. I went home and read her book, *Slave: My True Story*.[1]

Mende Nazer was about 12 years old when she was captured during a nighttime raid on her village in the south of Sudan. She and several other children were taken to Khartoum and sold. The woman who bought Mende was Muslim, but felt no alliance with Mende. "Islam isn't for Black people," her mistress told her. Harriet Jacobs wrote that she was often hungry. Mende could eat only what was left on the plates after the meals were served. Jacobs wrote about walking through snow barefoot because her mistress had objected to the clunking of her heavy shoes. For a long time, Mende slept in a locked shed. This was not very different from Harriet Jacobs's attic abode. When she was about 18, Mende was sent to London to serve her owners' sister. Jacobs was about that age when she was sent to work on an isolated plantation. Like Jacobs, Mende eventually was able to escape. Antislavery activists helped both women find a relatively safe place to live. And antislavery activists persuaded both women to publish their stories, even though publication would make them and their loved ones vulnerable to retaliation, if not reenslavement.

Reading her book, I compared the stories of Mende Nazer and Harriet Jacobs. Like Jacobs, Nazer had strong family ties, clear religious and moral values, and high aspirations. Though enslaved, neither Jacobs nor Nazer was forced to work in the fields, and neither had been used as a breeder to increase the owner's property. Both had been physically abused, but neither had been tied to a whipping post or groped and exposed on an auction block. Both were subjected to verbal abuse and sexual harassment. They were held in bondage by people who were to all appearances upright and admirable members of their communities, people with wealth and political power, religious people for whom slavery might be an ethical issue best left unexamined or undiscussed. Words were employed as tools to break their spirits. Mende said that one of the most painful aspects of her enslavement was being called "Yebit," which means "girl worthy of no name" and is an Arabic equivalent of the "N-word" in English.

I could see some of what in Jacobs's story resonated with Nazer's, but if truth be told, I didn't understand why Mende Nazer reacted so emotionally to Harriet Jacobs's story, why she exclaimed that Jacobs's story was *her* story. Mende explained to me that escaping from one's enslavers does not mean that one automatically becomes a free person. Slavery is not just working 24/7 without pay, having no say in what you do, when you do it, or even how. Slavery tries to take one's identity. Whether the enslaved is meek or defiant, slavery still damages emotions and influences perspectives. Reading Jacobs's narrative showed her that her experiences were not entirely unique to her or to others in her village. Slavery is illegal in the Sudan, but Nazer's status was an open secret, and she knew others who were also enslaved. Jacobs's story helped Nazer understand that the institution of slavery was larger and older than she had imagined. She had not known there were books about the experiences of enslavement, narratives by former slaves who had endured and transcended similar trials and tribulations. Despite, or maybe because of, differences in time and place, reading how they had built new lives in borrowed countries, she had a better idea of how she, too, could shape her future. Nazer intimately understood what Jacobs meant when she wrote "My master had power and law on his side; I had a determined will. There is might in each." And I imagine Nazer nodded in agreement when she read Harriet Jacobs's reason for exposing her private pain by adding, as Jacobs wrote, her "testimony to that of abler pens to convince the people of the Free States what Slavery really is." Mende told her story, she says, "to speak for the thousands who are still being raped, slaughtered or forced into slavery....Allah wants me to lift my voice for vulnerable children all over this world."

My words about Harriet Jacobs and other slave narrators helped Mende see her life in the context of time and space. Mende then realized that her story and Jacobs's story fit the structure of other slave narratives: a relatively happy childhood abruptly ends when the narrator is given the new and demeaning identity of "slave"; to survive, the narrator appears to accept this definition and endures capricious and painful experiences designed to humiliate and subjugate until she can escape. Like antebellum fugitive slave narratives, Mende Nazer's memoir details dreadful experiences and describes how she sought and achieved freedom. The book then ends on the happy note of freedom. But in the nineteenth century, as in the twenty-first, the lives of the narrators continue. Their futures are shaped by their past experiences, but the next chapters of their lives will be determined by differences in time, place, and personal attitudes and actions.

Mende's stories made me know my own history in new ways. They reminded me again that Sankofa is a process, not a product. We look back to see ahead, but what was future tense soon becomes past. Reading Mende's book and talking with her filled in details that my empirical personality desired, but my academic research could not satisfy. Having studied slave narratives and antebellum African America for almost 40 years, I knew a lot of facts and, as this book shows, I have some strong opinions about how these facts should be narrated and why. I knew, too, that slavery is no longer legal in most countries but that thousands of people are literally enslaved in many countries, including the United States. Even as I write these words, children, women, and men are being bought and sold, and many of the same questions that plagued antebellum abolitionists continue to haunt the less visible but no less determined abolitionist groups of the twenty-first century. Slavery is not past, but until meeting Mende it had not been in my present, except as a historical topic of interest and personal curiosity. This isn't to belittle my scholarship. My efforts to provide context, to learn and teach complexities, alternatives, and exceptions to common wisdom are worthwhile. I know that showing how it is that we *are* the stories we tell can help us define ourselves. I've seen that providing counter-narratives, that helping to reconstruct or reform myths, that questioning history texts can make us all more healthy, more self-defined, more humane human beings. This is how we overcome ignorance, and how we grow.

In fiction, Mende and I would become fast friends and close confidants. In life, we did not keep in touch. She returned to England. I kept writing my book. Occasionally, I read about her in magazine articles or book reviews. And then came the e-mail inviting me to her wedding reception in Greensboro. It was quite an opportunity.

MENDE: BUT IT MUST BE LIVED FORWARD

I had asked my friend Ken, who lived in Greensboro, to accompany me to the reception. It was no longer a stormy night, but it was dark. The neighborhood had many deserted buildings and few street signs. When we arrived at what appeared to have been a hotel, we were at least half an hour late. The full parking lot increased my anxiety, but what really confused me were the groups of men and boys outside the open doors and the gym-sized room filled with dancers of various sizes, shapes, and ages at the back of the building. The music was mariachi, and the celebrants spoke in Spanish. Clearly, Greensboro, home of the sit-ins, was now part of the New South. "We're looking for Mende's wedding reception," we told an African American security guard in the lobby. "Don't recognize the name," he said, "but it's probably that other room on the left." Entering the dimly lit room, we saw middle-aged African Americans dancing to rhythm and blues. It was a celebration of some kind, but it was not the one to which we were invited. When we informed the guard that was not our party, he arched his eyebrows in surprise and asked, "Are *you* looking for the *Africans'* party?" Our "Yes" sounded a bit too smug, especially since the one name we knew was obviously not the one under which the room had been reserved.

I had felt more comfortable walking into the Motown party than I did entering the "Africans'" party. Since junior high school, I had elbowed my way into blue-lighted rooms of folk dancing to Marvin Gaye, The Shirelles, The Impressions, and Carla Thomas. I was used to folks carefully appraising strangers before actually speaking to them. Mende's party room was a large, brightly lit hall where people were chatting in clusters and dozens of children were running to, through, from, and around them. Standing felt conspicuous, and we quickly sat—in chairs that turned out to be too near the door. Every person who entered after us stopped, introduced themselves, and shook hands. I couldn't decide whether this was a ritual friendliness or whether we had inadvertently sat in the welcoming seat reserved for hosts. Individuals came over and made small talk, generally in accented English that required all my energies of concentration. They seemed to be taking turns making us feel welcome while determining who we were and why we were there. Between greeting entering guests and sociable conversationalists, I people-watched. Some guests were robed in what to my eyes was festive finery from a variety of African cultures. Others wore the European-style clothing I had seen worn by visitors from the Netherlands, Spain, Italy, or Japan. Something about the cut, fabric, or fit that was subtly different from that made in the U.S.A. Many seemed a bit too-American: young men swaggered about in baseball caps, oversized T-shirts, and freshly ironed jeans hanging off their butts, and children in Mary Jane–style Stride-Rites or overpriced, brightly swooshed Nikes walked among the groups of chatting adults. Women, some in Western styles and some in African ones, were colorfully but modestly dressed. Some, but not all, maybe not even the majority, of the women wore scarves, *geles* or other head coverings.

People arrived alone, in couples, in families and in what looked like van loads. About two hours after we arrived, the room was pretty full—we counted about a half dozen white people and two other blacks who seemed "not African." One of those was Nancy Rawls, a writer from Seattle; the other was her partner. The whites included Bernadette Brooten, who had introduced Mende to me; she had flown down alone from Cambridge, Massachusetts. The others, I later learned, were people with whom Mende had lived after she escaped from slavery. They had flown over from Europe for this occasion. Talking with the "African" guests, we learned they were emigrants or the children of emigrants from many parts of the African continent. They lived not only in Greensboro but in surrounding cities and states. We met a Christian woman refugee from West Africa who explained that in the old country she would not attend such a party, but in the United States being from Africa trumped religion, tribe, and other identities. We listened to people grumble about the poor manners of the children who darted about, laughing and yelling and ignoring everyone but themselves. Their consensus was "They've become like Americans."

Here was history being made before my eyes. In *Africans in America,* I had read:

> as the slaves communicated and sometimes married across tribal and regional lines, their culture became an intriguing mixture of African traditions and those developed in the Americas.... Blacks from different parts of Africa combined their beliefs, their music, and their language while borrowing from the European culture to create a commonality.[2]

As the three separate parties and the assumptions of the security guard suggest, we were not—yet—coming together in one great cultural room, but we were now partying in the same building. We were in a city central to the demise of the Old South, but not yet a part of the American Dream.

Conversations waxed and waned. People wandered about. Groups formed and dispersed. The night wore on—men came in and set up tables. Women began to load them with food. But two hours after we'd rushed in thinking we were late, still no bride and groom. Folks muttered about the delay, and various rumors about why and how long floated about. But no one seemed upset. It's "AP Time," I was told. Well now, this was new. I grew up observing "CP Time." I knew that "colored people's time" did not correlate with the clocks that dictated the beginning of school or work. But, I thought to myself, this African people's time is carrying things a little too far! Had I not driven such a long distance and had I not wanted Mende to know that I made it, I would have left. I had wanted to participate in an African Muslim marriage celebration. I hoped to verify cultural continuities and differences, and I expected to learn, but I assumed my African American self would be unaffected. But I was getting tired. Then I realized that my tiredness was worth noting. Time is a continuum, I realized, and not only is there AP time and CP time, there are many other versions as well: European people's time, Jewish people's time, Baptists' time, and Buddhist time. I was startled to discover that I live more comfortably in EP or CP time. I settled in to wait a bit longer.

Just before midnight, there came a flurry in the lobby along with whispers that "they" had arrived. A line quickly formed on each side of the door. Through the door walked five or six little flower girls, wearing fluffy dresses held out with starched crinolines. Their legs were as shiny as their patent leather shoes. Their hair was oiled and plaited, straightened and curled, even braided with extensions. The major difference between them and other flower girls of my experience is that their dresses were red. Following them were six or seven young women dressed in those you-paid-a-lot-for-something-you'll-never-wear-again dresses. (Those dresses I knew.) Finally, on the arm of a tall, slim young man, dressed in a green military-style suit, came Mende, the bride, whose smile was not at all hidden by her white bridal veil. She looked, as most brides do, beautiful—a bit tired around the eyes—but very happy. The procession circled the room as the guests cheered, applauded, whistled, and ululated. The couple mounted a small decorated platform and seated themselves on red, throne-like chairs. Bridesmaids arranged the voluminous skirt and train of Mende's white gown. Guests lined up before the platform to present themselves and their good wishes. The first ones were mainly men—but not entirely. The men acknowledged the bride but spoke mostly to the groom. The women had the most to say to the bride.

The throne threw me at first, but I quickly recognized this was a version of the reception rituals to which I was accustomed. When my daughter married, I stood in a line with the other parents and relatives for far too long, shaking hands and speaking briefly to the guests, equally aware of my aching back and of the increasingly impatient people yet to be greeted. When my son married, we opted to circulate among the tables, trying to greet each and every guest, receive their congratulations and thank them personally for coming. The platform and throne seemed a better option. The celebrated were comfortable, and the celebrators came and went at their convenience. Meanwhile the guests were free to dance and to feast.

And dance and feast, we all did! The music was from Africa but the DJ was a familiar figure. Men, sometimes with arms entwined, stepped and stomped together in circles. Women, with arms upraised, swayed in women's circles. Women joined men in their circles—not touching or dancing coupled but nonetheless demonstrating new rituals for a new situation. I saw no man join the women. Nor did men join the fluid group of women who serenaded the couple in a language I didn't know and ululated in ways I'd seen in movies but not real life. The lines that formed for the food were less segregated. And the food! Ah, the food. I recognized fried chicken and curried lamb, samosas, hummus, rice, and various breads, but I tried almost everything. Maybe it was the atmosphere, the relief that the reception had begun, or just that it was after midnight and hours since dinner, but everything tasted especially wonderful. I was so moved to see Mende's marriage commencing in this large community of support and optimism. I was full, and happy, and glad I had come.

I don't know how long the party lasted. When we left at about 1:30 A.M., the festivities seemed to be moving into high gear. Later, I learned that Mende had changed from her ceremonial white gown into a more comfortable outfit joined the festivities. The costume change and the shift from ritual to more informal rejoicing has its African American equivalent also. However, her second bridal costume, like the dresses of the flower girls, was red. In many Asian and African cultures, red symbolizes good luck. But, red in African American weddings is rarely worn. For me, Mende's marriage celebration was a mixture of the strange and the familiar. I felt at home and I felt foreign. I believe, however, that my experience was a micro-version of the continued making of African America I imagine this twenty-first century experience was much like many antebellum ones—an alchemy of Christian, Muslim, and other religious rituals. It included familiar cultural conventions performed and improvised in a new geography, and it had traits of local tradition. It was a community-making event.

Mende's marriage had made me aware that the past is not past in a new way as well. Like my antebellum African American ancestors, this couple was making a life-long commitment. However, they knew they would soon be parted by distance—at least for a while. Mende and Yassin are both refugees. They met because he heard her story and he fell in love with its teller. But Mende has asylum in England, while his asylum is in the United States. And asylum is not transferable. They can only live together as husband and wife if they can convince one of the governments to accept a spouse or a third government to accept them both. Their situation is not the same as those of antebellum African Americans. Their marriage expands the meaning of the antebellum notion of "abroad marriages," but like their diasporic ancestors, this couple has vowed to love and honor one another, despite legal technicalities and the challenges of time and distance, until parted one day by death.

SANKOFA: GO BACK AND DISCOVER WHO YOU MAY BE

Throughout this book I have argued that we are shaped by the stories we tell and we must look backward if we are to know where we can go. As I have found and learned, through stories, songs, folklore, sermons, personal memoirs, and histories, especially those that African Americans created about themselves for themselves, I have come to appreciate even more how dangerous half truths can be, how carefully we must watch, listen, and learn. My and Mende's stories put into sharper perspective the words of Ruby Dee and Ossie Davis, another couple of African descent whose marriage lasted despite spells of separation by miles and difficulties. In their jointly authored memoir *With Ossie and Ruby*, they wrote words that encapsulate the challenge:

> Looking back is tricky business. It is seeing through time, people, events; it's remembering subtleties and attitudes. It's getting the facts straight, even though the facts may have little to do with "telling the truth." So much depends on who does the looking back and why. What is the condition of the vision mechanism—one-eyed, shortsighted, farsighted, or no-sighted, blind?[3]

So much depends also on how we communicate what we see. Because Mende allowed her story to be published, I have seen my life and my culture through new lenses. Because Bernadette gave her our edition of Harriet Jacobs's work, Mende sees her life from a wider historical and global perspective. We both envision more fathomable futures. I know that we both realize more fully that we must work assiduously to see beyond the surface, to read between the lines, and to make the connections between what we are told and who is doing the telling. Our long-distance relationship reinforces my belief that telling our stories helps us become the change we envision. This book is about love and marriage in African America—the African America that was, that is, and that is becoming.

This book is about the Making of African America, then and now. I believe that my Mende story and my Sankofa book will help you understand how the past can impact your present. Whether you identify as African American or not, my wish is that you'll see both global and personal implications from the past. I want to provoke you to rethink and research what it is you know or what you'd like to understand better. And most of all, I hope that this process will empower you, will help you to form more valid opinions, and will show you new ways to enact those ideas with sagacity and satisfaction. In *Fathering Words: The Making of an African American Writer*,[4] E. Ethelbert Miller quotes Soren Kierkegaard's statement "Life can only be understood backwards, but it must be lived forwards." This twenty-first century African American man from the South Bronx found in the words of a nineteenth century Danish philosopher an idea that helped encapsulate his life Miller did not fantasize that Kierkegaard wrote those words knowing that a century later, they would help an aspiring poet. But they did. I am neither a poet nor a philosopher, but learning from both, and believing in Sankofa, I am offering of this volume with hopes it too will help friends and stangers both.

Ma'a salama. Amen.

NOTES

PREFACE

1. Stephanie Coontz, "The New Fragility of Marriage," *Chronicle of Higher Education,* May 6, 2005, B7.
2. Harriet Jacobs, *Incidents in the Life of a Slave Girl, Written by Herself,* ed. Nellie Y. McKay and Frances Smith Foster (1861; reprint, New York: Norton, 2001), 31.
3. Haile Gerima's film *Sankofa* reintroduced the concept to most modern-day African Americans. The most common Sankofa symbol is a bird's body directed forward with its head looking back. The translation I use comes from the Sankofa website: http://sankofastore.com/catalog/homepage.php (accessed November 20, 2007).

CHAPTER I

1. New Revised Standard Version (Nashville: Thomas Nelson, 1989).
2. *Before the Mayflower: A History of Black America* (Chicago: Johnson, 2007), 29.
3. Martha W. McCartney, *A Study of the Africans and African Americans on Jamestown Island and at Green Springs, 1619–1803* (Williamsburg, Va.: National Park Service and Colonial Williamsburg Foundation, 2003), 35.
4. Charles Johnson et al. *Africans in America: America's Journey through Slavery* (New York: Harcourt Brace, 1998), 38.
5. The epigraph to this chapter is from Alex Haley, *Roots: The Saga of an American Family* (Garden City, N.Y.: Doubleday, 1976), viii.
6. At www.boodrags.com/Roots, accessed October 29, 2007.
7. At www.teachwithmovies.org/guides/roots-vol-iv.html, accessed August 12, 2009.
8. Justine Labinjoh, "The Sexual Life of the Oppressed: An Examination of the Family Life of Ante-bellum Slaves," *Phylon* 35 (1974): 375–97.
9. Henry Bibb, *Narrative of the Life and Adventures of Henry Bibb, An American Slave, Written by Himself* (1849; reprint, Madison: University of Wisconsin Press, 2001).
10. Josiah Henson, *Father Henson's Story of His Own Life* (1858; reprint, New York: Corinth Books, 1962), 3–7.

11. William and Ellen Craft, *Running a Thousand Miles for Freedom; Or, the Escape of William and Ellen Craft from Slavery* (1860) in Arna Bontemps, ed., *Great Slave Narratives* (Boston: Beacon, 1969).

12. Lunsford Lane, *The Narrative of Lunsford Lane* (1842) in William L. Andrews, ed., *North Carolina Slave Narratives* (Chapel Hill: University of North Carolina Press), 104.

13. *Life of William Grimes* (1825), in Arna Bontemps, ed., *Five Black Lives* (Middletown, Conn.: Wesleyan University Press, 1971).

14. Elizabeth Keckley, *Behind the Scenes; Or, Thirty Years a Slave and Four Years in the White House,* ed. Frances Smith Foster (1868; reprint, Urbana: University of Illinois Press, 2001), 14–15.

15. Reprinted in Ira Berlin and Leslie S. Rowland, ed., *Families and Freedom: A Documentary History of African American Kinship in the Civil War Era* (New York: New Press, 1997), 22–23.

16. Sidney Kaplan and Emma Nogrady Kaplan, *The Black Presence in the Era of the American Revolution* (Amherst: University of Massachusetts Press, 1989), 238–41.

17. Biographer William S. McFeely summarizes the rumors by saying: "no self-respecting reform movement is complete without a scandal. Frederick Douglass and Julia Griffiths, earnest and devoted, supplied that ingredient for the antislavery cause." *Frederick Douglass* (New York: Norton, 1991), 163. Maria Diedrich, *Love across the Color Lines: Ottilie Assing and Frederick Douglass* (New York: Hill and Wang, 1999), is the most prominent example of current researchers' interest in such details.

Chapter 2

1. In Bruce Jackson, *The Negro and His Folklore in Nineteenth-century Periodicals* (Austin: University of Texas Press, 1967), 208–10: "Aurore Pradère, belle 'ti fille, (ter) / C'est li mo 'oulè, c'est li ma pren. / Li pas mandè robe mousseline, / Li pas mandè des bas brodès, / Li pas mandè souliers prinelle; / C'est li mo 'oulè, c'est li ma pren."

2. In Betty DeRamus, *Forbidden Fruit: Love Stories from the Underground Railroad* (New York: Atria Books, 2005), 3. DeRamus provides a bibliography for each chapter; however, she does not provide distinct sources for each story. Some are pieced together from fragments such as court cases and letters. Thus far, I have been unable to validate completely the story of Joseph Antoine. But the story, as DeRamus writes, "doesn't stand alone": African American history has many similar happenings.

3. Genesis 29.

4. E.R.J., "A Marriage of Affection," *Pacific Appeal*, September 27, 1862, 3. While the author is anonymous and the story includes no obvious racial markers, the story is introduced as "For the Pacific Appeal." As this paper was for, by, and about African Americans, we can assume the author, characters, and audience are African American.

5. Edward P. Wimberly, *African American Pastoral Care and Counseling: The Politics of Oppression and Empowerment* (Cleveland: Pilgrim Press, 2006).

6. Emma Jones Lapsanky, "Friends, Wives, and Strivings: Networks and Community Values among Nineteenth-century Philadelphia Afroamerican Elites," *Pennsylvania Magazine of History and Biography* 108(1984): 15.

7. Frederick Douglass, *Narrative of the Life of Frederick Douglass, An American Slave. Written by Himself* (1845; reprint, Cambridge, Mass.: Harvard University Press, 1973), 29–30.

8. Harriet Jacobs, *Incidents in the Life of a Slave Girl, Written by Herself*, ed. Nellie Y. McKay and Frances Smith Foster (1861; reprint, New York: Norton, 2001), 34–35.

9. *Narrative of William Wells Brown, a Fugitive Slave, Written by Himself* (1847), in William L. Andrews, ed., *Slave Narratives* (New York: Library of America, 2002), 412.

10. *A Narrative of the Life of Rev. Noah Davis, A Colored Man* (Baltimore: John F. Weishampel, Jr., 1859), 26–27.

11. Carroll Smith-Rosenberg. *Signs* 1 (Autumn 1975):1–29.

12. Carolyn Sorisio, *Fleshing Out America: Race, Gender, and the Politics of the Body in American Literature, 1833–1879* (Athens: University of Georgia Press, 2002), 41.

13. James Oliver Horton, *Free People of Color: Inside the African American Community* (Washington, D.C.: Smithsonian Institution Press, 1993), 111–12.

14. A. Leon Higgenbotham, Jr., *In the Matter of Color: The Colonial Period* (New York: Oxford University Press, 1978).

15. Jonathan Ned Katz, *Gay/Lesbian Almanac: A New Documentary* (New York: Harper and Row, 1996), 60–61. In this book and in *Gay American History: Lesbians and Gay Men in the U.S.A.* (New York: Meridian, 1983).

16. Farah Griffith, ed., *Beloved Sisters and Loving Friends: Letters from Rebecca Primus of Royal Oak, Maryland, and Addie Brown of Hartford, Connecticut, 1854–1868* (New York: Knopf, 1999). 16.

17. *Black Women, Identity, and Cultural Theory: (Un)becoming the Subject* (New Brunswick, N.J.: Rutgers University Press, 2004), 1.

18. Ira Berlin, *Many Thousands Gone: The First Two Centuries of Slavery in North America* (New York: Harvard University Press, 1998), 189.

19. *The Doctrines and Discipline of the African Methodist Episcopal Zion Church* (1848; reprint, Charlotte, N.C.: A.M.E. Zion Publication House, 1925), 36–37.

20. Herbert G. Gutman, *The Black Family in Slavery and Freedom, 1750–1925* (New York: Pantheon Books, 1976), makes an unusually extended argument in this regard. Gutman quotes an analysis of 1860 federal census that noted whites were "most amazingly interwed" and that it seemed more the rule than the exception that cousins married (89).

21. John Hope Franklin, *From Slavery to Freedom: A History of Negro Americans,* 4th ed. (New York: Knopf, 1974), 139. Franklin writes that in 1860, 88 percent of all slaveholders owned fewer than twenty slaves. Nearly two-thirds of that 88 percent had fewer than five.

22. Joseph Smith announced his revelation about polygamy, or "celestial marriage," in 1843. Though his views apparently led to his death, Brigham Young's Utah colony had at least eleven thousand members in 1850. By 1890,

when the federal government outlawed their practice, the group had about two hundred thousand members. Carole Shammas, *A History of Household Government in America* (Charlottesville: University of Virginia Press, 2002), 128.

23. My summary comes from Shammas, *A History of Household Government,* the website of the New York History Net, www.nyhistory.com/central/oneida. htm, and the Religious Movements Homepage, http://religiousmovements.lib .virginia.edu/nrms.Oneida.html.

24. Nell Irwin Painter, *Creating Black Americans: African American History and Its Meanings* (New York: Oxford University Press, 2007), 57.

25. W. D. W. Schurman. *Christian Recorder.* February 9, 1861.

26. Frances Ellen Watkins [Harper], "Advice to Girls" (1854), in *A Brighter Coming Day: A Frances Ellen Watkins Harper Reader,* ed. Frances Smith Foster (New York: Feminist Press, 1990), 68.

27. Basically, "signifying" is communication by indirect means, or goading that is sometimes good-natured, sometimes not. For example, see Claudia Mitchell-Kernan, *Language Behavior in a Black Urban Community* (Berkeley: University of California Language-behavior Research Laboratory 1971); Geneva Smitherman, *Talking and Testifying* (Boston: Houghton Mifflin, 1977); or Henry Louis Gates, Jr., *The Signifying Monkey: A Theory of Afro-American Literary Criticism* (New York: Oxford University Press, 1988).

CHAPTER 3

1. D[aniel] A. P[ayne], "Matrimony," *Repository of Religion and Literature and Science and Art,* April 1859, 21.

2. Payne's narrative is an amalgamation of the two Genesis stories. The mandate to "be fruitful and multiply and replenish the earth" comes from Genesis 1:28, which follows the joint creation of "male and female." And Payne ignores the rest of that mandate to "subdue" the earth and "have dominion" over every living thing." He notes that the female was made from the male's rib, which comes from Genesis 2:21–25. This version notes that they were unashamed of their nakedness but does not have the command to go forth and multiply.

3. In the nineteenth century—and even now—Afro-Protestants have preferred the King James translation of the Bible. Payne's quotations suggest that is the version he used.

4. Theophus H. Smith, *Conjuring Culture: Biblical Formations of Black America* (New York: Oxford University Press, 1994), 3.

5. Gayraud S. Wilmore, *Black Religion and Black Radicalism: An Interpretation of the Religious History of African Americans* (1973; reprint, Maryknoll, N.Y.: Orbis Books, 1998), 34. In this instance, Wilmore is referring specifically to what he calls "slave religion." However, it is no misrepresentation of Wilmore's work to include the other 10 percent of African Americans in this statement.

6. George Moses Horton, *Naked Genius* (1865). In Joan R. Sherman, ed., *The Black Bard of North Carolina: George Moses Horton and his Poetry* (Chapel Hill: University of North Carolina Press, 1997), 128–29.

7. Quoted in James D. Hart, *The Popular Book: A History of America's Literary Taste* (Berkeley: University of California Press, 1963), 106.

8. Samuel Ringgold Ward, *Autobiography of a Fugitive Negro* (1855; reprint, Chicago: Johnson, 1970), 23.

9. Elizabeth Keckley, *Behind the Scenes: Thirty Years a Slave and Four Years in the White House*, ed. Frances Smith Foster (1868; reprint, Urbana: University of Illinois Press, 2001).

10. William Craft, *Running a Thousand Miles for Freedom* (1860) in Arna Bontemps, ed., *Great Slave Narratives* (Boston: Beacon, 1969), 285.

11. Thomas W. Henry, *From Slavery to Salvation* (1872, Jackson: University Press of Mississippi, 1994).

12. *Christian Recorder,* December 22, 1855:1.

13. Ann Patton Malone. *Sweet Chariot: Slave Family Structure in Nineteenth-Century Louisiana* (Chapel Hill: University of North Carolina Press, 1992), 225.

Chapter 4

1. My title alludes to a fine book by anthropologists Sidney W. Mintz and Richard Price that in concise, accessible language explains this very complex concept: *The Birth of African America: An Anthropological Perspective* (1976; reprint, Boston: Beacon Press, 1992).

2. Rev. William Douglass, *Annals of the First African Church of the United States of America, Now Styled the African Episcopal Church of St. Thomas, Philadelphia* (Philadelphia: King and Baird, 1862), 15. The copy of the founding document published in *Annals of the First African Church* in 1862 dates the preamble of the Free African Society April 12, 1778; but the "Articles of the Association, with the names of the First Signers" is dated June 17, 1787. I am assuming the earlier date is a typographical error.

3. Michael A. Gomez, *Exchanging Our Country Marks: The Transformation of African Identities in the Colonial and Antebellum South* (Chapel Hill: University of North Carolina Press, 1998), 38–40.

4. Claire Robertson, "Africa into the Americas? Slavery and Women, the Family, and the Gender Divisions of Labor, in David Barry Gaspar and Darlene Clark Hine, ed., *More than Chattel: Black Women and Slavery in the Americas* (Bloomington: Indiana University Press, 1996), 19.

5. Orlando Patterson, *Rituals of Blood: Consequences of Slavery in Two American Centuries* (New York: Civitas/Counterpoint, 1998), 3.

6. Ann Patton Malone, *Sweet Chariot: Slave Family and Household Structure in Nineteenth-century Louisiana* (Chapel Hill: North Carolina University Press, 1992), 224.

7. *The Proceedings of the Free African Union Society and the African Benevolent Society, Newport, Rhode Island 1780–1824,* ed. William H. Robinson (Providence, R.I.: Urban League of Rhode Island, 1976 (1), 145.

8. Harriet Jacobs, *Incidents in the Life of a Slave Girl, Written by Herself*, ed. Nellie Y. McKay and Frances Smith Foster (1861; reprint, New York: Norton, 2001).

9. Elizabeth Keckley, *Behind the Scenes: Thirty Years a Slave and Four Years in the White House*, ed. Frances Smith Foster (1868; reprint, Urbana: University of Illinois Press, 2001), 25–26.

10. George P. Rawick, *The American Slave: A Composite Autobiography* (Westport, Conn.: Greenwood, 1972). Rawick used the same title for two series of volumes and supplements. The collection is available on the internet as *American Slavery: A Composite Autobiography*. The internet version is searchable by name; the names of the informants quoted hereafter may be used to find the original interview in that version.

11. Ingrid Sturgis, *The Nubian Wedding Book: Words and Rituals to Celebrate and Plan an African-American Wedding* (New York: Three Rivers Press, 1997). Harriet Cole, *Jump the Broom: The African-American Wedding Planner* (New York: Holt, 1993). Wedding planning books and websites are lucrative and abundant; the two I cite here are merely examples.

12. Quoted in Alan Dundes, "'Jumping the Broom': On the Origin and Meaning of an African American Wedding Custom," *Journal of American Folklore* 109, 433 (summer 1996):324–29.

CHAPTER 5

1. Ken Gewertz, "David McCullough Delivers 2002 Theodore H. White Lecture,"*Harvard University Gazette,* October 31, 2002, 11, a report on a lecture by David McCullough.

2. *The Holy Bible,* New Revised Standard Version, Matthew 13: 34 (Nashville: Thomas Nelson, 1989). Subsequent references are from this version.

3. Jesus used parables so often that one dictionary definition is "any of the stories told by Jesus to convey his religious message." Synonyms for "parable" include "fable," "allegory," and "apologue."

4. Robin D. G. Kelley, *Yo' Mama's Dysfunctional! Fighting the Cultural Wars in Urban America* (Boston: Beacon Press, 1997), 2.

5. Ira Berlin, "American Slavery in History and Memory," in *Slavery, Resistance and Freedom,* ed. Gabor Boritt and Scott Hancock (New York: Oxford University Press, 2007), 68.

6. Nell Irwin Painter, *Creating Black Americans: African-American History and Its Meanings, 1619 to the Present* (New York: Oxford University Press, 2006), xv.

7. Ann Banks, "Jim Crow's Last War," *New York Times Book Review,* February 16, 2003, 6.

8. From www.websters-online-dictionary.org/definition/myth.

9. Gospel songs become a form of folklore, whose origins are forgotten. In this case, there may be an author but I have not yet identified her or him. I quote this from memory.

10. *Ceremony* (New York: Viking Press, 1977), book jacket.

11. *Damaged Identities, Narrative Repair* (Ithaca, N.Y.: Cornell University Press, 2001), xi.

12. The conference took place April 29–May 1, 2005. The quotation comes from the published proceedings: *Interdisciplinary Response to Trauma: Memory, Meaning, and Narrative* (Atlanta: Academic Exchange, 2005), 5.

13. *How the Political Brain Works: The Role of Emotion in Deciding the Fate of the Nation* (New York: Public Affairs, 2007). Available at www.publicaffairs-books.com.

14. Zora Neale Hurston, *Their Eyes Were Watching God* (1937; reprint, Urbana: University of Illinois Press, 1978), 9.

15. Barbara Christian uses "Somebody Forgot To Tell Somebody Something" as the title of her article in *Wild Women in the Whirlwind,* Joanne Braxton and Andree McLaughlin, ed. (New Brunswick, NJ: Rutgers University Press, 1990), 326–341. Christian attributes this quote to a Morrison interview with Ntozake Shange on Steve Cannon's show "It's Magic," WBAI, New York, 1978. "Playing in the Dark" is the title of Toni Morrison's *Playing in the Dark: Whiteness and the Literary Imagination* (New York: Vintage, 1993).

16. In Henry Louis Gates, Jr., and Nellie Y. McKay, eds., *The Norton Anthology of African American Literature,* 2nd ed. (New York: Norton, 2004), 918.

17. *Christian Recorder,* April 27, 1861.

18. Penelope L. Bullock. *The Afro-American Periodical Press, 1838–1909* (Baton Rouge: Louisiana State University Press, 1982), 22.

19. For example, see *The Autobiography of Nicholas Said: A Native of Bornou, Eastern Soudan, Central Africa* (1873), ed. Precious Rasheeda Muhammad (Cambridge, Mass.: Journal of Islam in America Press, 2000).

20. Harriet Jacobs, *Incidents in the Life of a Slave Girl, Written by Herself,* ed. Nellie Y. McKay and Frances Smith Foster (1861; reprint, New York: Norton, 2001), 2.

21. *Life of James Mars, a Slave Born and Sold in Connecticut. Written by Himself* (1864), in Arna Bontemps, ed., *Five Black Lives* (Middletown, Conn.: Wesleyan University Press, 1971), 37.

22. William and Ellen Craft, *Running a Thousand Miles for Freedom; Or, the Escape of William and Ellen Craft from Slavery* (1860) in Arna Bontemps, ed. *Great Slave Narratives* (Boston: Beacon, 1969), 270.

CHAPTER 6

1. John "Rabbit" Bundrick, comp., "That's the Way We Get By," rec. 1972, Johnny Nash, *I Can See Clearly Now.*

2. Toni Morrison, *Beloved* (New York: Knopf, 1987), 274–275. These words appear in various configurations (e.g. "It was not a story to pass on." " This is not a story to pass on.") in the concluding paragraphs of the novel. What they mean depends on the emphasis we give to "pass" and "on." Emphasize "pass," and we understand that we should repeat this story to others. Emphasize "on" (in the sense of "over") and we know we should not repeat the tale.

3. "An Address by Dr. Martin Luther King, Jr.," in *The Moynihan Report and the Politics of Controversy,* ed. Lee Rainwater and William L. Yancey (Cambridge, Mass.: M.I.T. Press, 1965), 404–5.

4. Ira Berlin and Leslie Rowland, *Families and Freedom: A Documentary History of African-American Kinship in the Civil War Era* (New York: New Press, 1997), 155.

5. Gail E. Wyatt, psychiatry professor, University of California, Los Angeles, quoted in Anastasia Vasilakis, "Breaking the Chains," *Essence,* February 2005, 152.

6. Isaac Forman, *The Underground Rail Road,* ed.William Still (1871; reprint, Chicago: Johnson, 1970), 49–50.

7. William G. Allen, *The American Prejudice against Color* (1853) in Sarah Elbert, ed., *The American Prejudice Against Color: William G. Allen, Mary King, Lousia May Alcott* (Boston: Northeastern University Press, 2002).

(1798) in Henry Louis Gates, Jr. and Nellie Y. McKay, ed., *Norton Anthology of African American Literature,* 2nd ed. (New York: Norton, 2004), 168–85.

8. Cassandra Pybus, *Epic Journeys of Freedom: Runaway Slaves of the American Revolution and Their Global Quest for Liberty* (Boston: Beacon Press, 2006).

9. Manning Marable, *Living Black History: How Reimagining the African-American Past Can Remake America's Racial Future* (New York: Basic Books, 2006), 3.

10. Closely paraphrased from *Webster's New World College Dictionary,* 3rd ed. New York: Macmillan, 1988.

11. Jeffery Gardere, *Love Prescription: Ending the War between Black Men and Women* (New York: Kensington, 2002).

12. Alvin F. Poussaint, M.D., and Amy Alexander, *Lay My Burden Down: Unraveling Suicide and the Mental Health Crisis among African-American* (Boston: Beacon Press, 2000), 14.

13. bell hooks, *Sisters of the Yam* (Boston: South End Press, 1993), 16.

14. Orlando Patterson, *Rituals of Blood: Consequences of Slavery on Two American Centuries* (Washington, D.C.: Civitas/CounterPoint, 1998), 27.

15. *Life of James Mars, a Slave Born and Sold in Connecticut. Written by Himself* (1864), in Arna Bontemps, ed., *Five Black Lives* (Middletown, Conn.: Wesleyan University Press, 1971), 37.

16. Harriet Jacobs, *Incidents in the Life of a Slave Girl, Written by Herself,* ed. Nellie Y. McKay and Frances Smith Foster (1861; reprint, New York: Norton, 2001), 12; italics in original.

17. James Reed, "An Essay on the Importance of Family Duty," *Repository of Religion and Literature* (April 1859): 86.

18. Claire Robertson, "Africa into the Americas? Slavery and Women, the Family, and the Gender Divisions of Labor, in David Barry Gaspar and Darlene Clark Hine, ed., *More than Chattel: Black Women and Slavery in the Americas* (Bloomington: Indiana University Press, 1996), 9.

CHAPTER 7

1. Pasadena/San Gabriel Valley Journal News, October 16–22, 2008, 19.

2. "If Marriage Is Natural, Why Is Defending It So Hard? Taking Up the Challenge to Marriage in the Pews and the Public Square," *Ave Maria Law Review* 4, 2 (summer 2006): 409–33.

3. Nancy F. Cott, *Public Vows: A History of Marriage and the Nation* (Cambridge, Mass.: Harvard University Press, 2000), 1.

4. "Fall of Marriage: Love Has a Lot to Do with It," *Atlanta Journal-Constitution* (February 25, 2007): E1, E4.

5. Witte reminds us that "to be sure, these classical reflections were only very small fragments within a vast Greco-Roman literature, which sometimes also condoned sexual norms and habits the Christian tradition would later condemn—prostitution, concubinage, pedophilia, homosexuality, polygamy,

mixed bathing, communal propagation, anonymous parentage, casual consortium with slaves, and more" (Witte 1029).

6. Quoted in Gail Collins, *America's Women: Four Hundred Years of Dolls, Drudges, Helpmates, and Heroines* (New York: Perennial, 2003), 82.

7. See the discussion in Sandra M. Gilbert and Susan Gubar, *The Madwoman in the Attic: The Woman Writer and the Nineteenth-century Literary Imagination* (New Haven: Yale University Press, 1979), 16–27.

8. See, for example, Thomas P. Lowry, M.D., *The Story The Soldiers Wouldn't Tell: Sex in the Civil War* (Mechanicsburg, Pa., 1994), 92. James C. Mohr, *Abortion in America: The Origins and Evolutions of National Policy, 1800–1900* (New York: Oxford University Press, 1978), 48.

9. I find most useful the definition of marriage advanced by Robert W. Slenes, "Black Homes, White Homilies: Perceptions of the Slave Family and of Slave Women in Nineteenth-century Brazil," in David Barry Gaspar and Darlene Clark Hine, eds., *More Than Chattel: Black Women and Slavery in the Americas* (Bloomington: Indiana University Press, 1996), 126–46. Slenes says: "I define marriage, following [Melville J.] Herskovits, as 'socially sanctioned mating entered into with the assumption of permanency' (with permanency understood as a relative concept defined by each culture)" (141).

10. Mark D. Jordan, *Blessing Same-sex Unions: The Perils of Queer Romance and the Confusions of Christian Marriage* (Chicago: University of Chicago Press, 2005), 4.

Epilogue

1. Mende Nazer and Damien Lewis. *Slave: My True Story* (New York: Public Affairs, 2005).

2. Charles Johnson, et al *Africans in America: America's Journey through Slavery* (New York: Harcourt Brace, 1998), 89.

3. Ossie Davis and Ruby Dee. *With Ossie and Ruby: In This Life Together* (New York: Morrow, 1998), 5.

4. E. Ethelbert Miller. *Fathering Words: The Making of an African American Writer* (New York: St. Martin's Press, 2000).